Whitehead's Philosophy of Civilization

A. H. JOHNSON

DOVER PUBLICATIONS, INC. NEW YORK

CONTENTS

Contents   v

ACKNOWLEDGMENTS

The Macmillan Company of New York has kindly granted permission to quote from the following books by Alfred North Whitehead: *Adventures of Ideas, Modes of Thought, Process and Reality, Religion in the Making, Science and the Modern World, The Aims of Education.*

The *Atlantic* has kindly granted permission to quote from the following articles by Alfred North Whitehead: "An Appeal to Sanity," "Harvard: The Future," "Reconstruction."

I acknowledge, with thanks, permission from the Boston *Globe* to quote a letter signed by "Alfred N. Whitehead." Also, I wish to thank *The Journal of Philosophy* for permission to use several pages (with revisions) from my article, "The Social Philosophy of Alfred North Whitehead."

Other brief quotations have been acknowledged in the Notes.

Grateful acknowledgment is made to *The Beacon Press*, in particular to Mr. Melvin Arnold with whom initial discussions took place, and to Mr. Thomas Bledsoe, the present Director, under whose supervision the publication project has been undertaken. I greatly appreciate his assistance and the services rendered by his associates.

Tutorial sessions with Professor Whitehead at Harvard extended my range of interest from his metaphysics to include his philosophy of civilization. His approval of my initial publications dealing with this phase of his work, and the undimmed recollections of his unique embodiment of the ideals of civilization, have stimulated the undertaking of this study.

This book is dedicated to my wife, Helen Bolender Johnson. Her encouragement and assistance have been decisive factors in the production of this discussion of Whitehead's philosophy of civilization. For this, and "all else," I owe her a debt of gratitude which I can not, adequately, either express or repay.

A. H. Johnson

The University of Western Ontario
London, Canada

PREFACE to Dover Edition

The original edition of this book is now out of print. I am gratified that Dover Publications, Inc., has decided to reissue it in paperback format.

The only changes in the text are corrections of typographical errors, a few revisions in the Index, and the addition of a Supplementary Bibliography.

The extension of the Bibliography (bringing it up to date) calls attention to the fact that the discussion of Whitehead's approach to religion has continued. (There are a number of papers in the book edited by Leclerc and individual chapters in Geoghegan's volume and in the collection of essays edited by Stiernotte.)

It is to be noted that *Whitehead's American Essays in Social Philosophy* is a collection (with Introductory Essay and Index) of all the essays on this topic written by Whitehead during his life in America.

1962   *A.H.J.*

PREFACE

Alfred North Whitehead is justly famous for his outstanding work in the fields of mathematics and metaphysics. His contributions to other areas of knowledge are neither well known nor properly appreciated. Yet, his discussions of social philosophy, philosophy of history, education, and religion are part of his total scheme of thought. His characteristic sanity of judgment and his penetrating basic ideas are applied in these spheres of knowledge as effectively as in more abstract subject matters. The result is an impressive treatment of the meaning and values of civilization.

This neglected, though very important, phase of Whitehead's thought—his philosophy of civilization—is the topic under consideration in this book.

There are many modern discussions of civilization. Few men have had the wealth of experience necessary as background, and foundation, for this project. Whitehead is a notable exception. In addition to his professional training in mathematics, Alfred North Whitehead was at home and proficient in physics, astronomy, history, literature, religious thought, education, and philosophy. In the life of Whitehead civilization was an achieved ideal. This fact impressed itself on all who knew him. Here then was a cultured gentleman, a scientist of note, a man possessed of singular clarity of mind. His study of civilization, obviously, merits careful attention.*

It must be admitted that it is difficult to grasp all the details

---

* It does not fall within the scope of this book to provide even an outline, let alone details, of Whitehead's career as scholar and teacher at Cambridge, London, and Harvard. Nor is it necessary to discuss his activities as "amateur politician" and educational administrator in England. A consideration of these topics, and a delineation of his great personal charm and vast erudition in many fields of knowledge, would appropriately constitute a separate study. Such a biography of Alfred North Whitehead would constitute a highly desirable "companion volume" to an examination of his philosophy of civilization. However, it seems to this writer that it would be inadvisable to attempt to *fuse* the two projects.

of his "analysis," because Whitehead did not devote any treatise exclusively to this topic. However, the three major books of his mature years, *Science and the Modern World, Process and Reality, Adventures of Ideas,* are concerned with this subject, in varying degrees. Most of the articles he wrote after 1925 were focused chiefly on this area of interest. These discussions of civilization frequently occur, in an apparently chaotic fashion, in the midst of treatments of other topics. However, and this is highly significant, (a) Whitehead regards the "philosophy of civilization" as part of his total system, and (b) the apparent chaos, on closer examination, turns out to be systematic consideration of related elements. This book attempts to substantiate these two contentions.

As is well known, Whitehead makes extensive use of highly technical terminology. *Some* phases of his discussion of civilization are enshrouded in this veil. However, it is possible to translate these technical forms of expression into more familiar language. Hence, technicalities have been reduced to a minimum in this study. Those who wish a technical exposition will find it *outlined* in Chapter Seven. This final chapter also demonstrates that Whitehead's main ideas in his philosophy of civilization are in accordance with his metaphysics—i.e., his theory of reality.

It may be objected that a relegation of technical terminology to a final chapter is contrary to the spirit and practice of Whitehead's treatment of civilization. As a matter of fact, most of his discussion of civilization is couched in non-technical terms. In any case, Whitehead's technical terms (in whatever field of knowledge they may be used) are "descriptive generalizations." In order to recognize the data to which these technical terms apply, these data must be brought into focus of attention through the medium of more familiar, non-technical terms. This is exactly what Whitehead does. Hence the pattern of exposition followed in this book is approximately that used by Whitehead. (Sometimes, however, he employs a technical term before full identification of its "object" has taken place. In such situations Whitehead hopes that the reader will obtain adequate understanding of the term from later usage.) The final chapter is an integral part of the book for a person who wishes to make the technical approach to Whitehead's philosophy of civilization. The fact that the technical terminology is "held back" until the final chapter indicates that the data which make these terms fully understandable must first be discussed. It should be evident, further, that very considerable insight, though not by any means total insight, into Whitehead's philosophy of civilization can be obtained without recourse to the technical terminology.

This book is intended for the general reader. It may also serve to bring to the attention of students of philosophy certain phases of Whitehead's work which previously they had neglected. This is not intended to be an *intensive* study of civilization. Rather, it is an *introduction* to Whitehead's treatment of the subject.

In stating Whitehead's philosophy of civilization no attempt has been made, in the body of the text, to provide detailed references to the widely scattered source material. This would have entailed shattering the continuity of exposition by the interpolation of a very large number of references. The relevant material on which this exposition is based has been "identified" in the Bibliography.

Present tense verb forms are used in referring to Professor Whitehead because, despite his death in 1947, his life and work are still vital factors in the contemporary world. Moreover, the great philosophers of the past are usually referred to in this fashion.

It is customary to suggest that there is no substitute for first-hand experience. This is particularly true in the case of the writings of Alfred North Whitehead.

At a time when the applications of modern science seem to be dooming civilization to extinction, it is worth while to examine the attempt of a great twentieth-century mind— trained in science and steeped in the values of civilization—to develop a philosophy of civilization. Alfred North Whitehead (a) defines civilization, (b) states the conditions which make possible its existence, and (c) shows its worth. This "philosophy of civilization" is one of the most important contributions made by Whitehead to the life of his age.

To My Wife

Chapter 1 CIVILIZATION

Whitehead begins his discussion of civilization by emphasizing the great difficulty involved in defining this familiar term. Difficulty arises because its meaning is very complex, and the term has been used in a wide variety of ways. Frequently it has been defined by reference to an individual or a society; e.g., Pericles or Athens. This method may be useful as a first step, but it has serious dangers. As Whitehead points out, a particular example is likely to be a mixture of characteristics referred to by the term "civilization," and other qualities which are irrelevant.

GENERAL DEFINITION

Despite these acknowledged difficulties, Whitehead offers a simple, general definition. A man, or a society, is civilized if *truth, beauty, adventure, art, peace* are the *dominant* qualities, and if these five qualities are exhibited in all phases of experience. Whitehead does not regard civilization as an esoteric luxury to be enjoyed by a few "superior" people. Rather, it is "ultimate good sense," a necessary condition for a satisfactory life.[1]

It should be noted that although Whitehead proposes to discuss civilization in general, he tends to concentrate attention on Western society (and the *individuals* composing it). That is, he deals chiefly with the sociological behavior of the European races living in the area between the Ural Mountains on the east and the North American shores of the Pacific Ocean on the west.

The full meaning of the qualities listed in Whitehead's definition of civilization gradually will become apparent as the details of his philosophy of civilization are examined. However, a preliminary sketch is necessary at the start.

Adventure

Adventure is one of the most important ingredients in civilization. Speaking generally, it is the search for new perfections. It involves spontaneity and freshness of approach. It is heightened by an awareness of the contrast between what is and what might be. Creative imagination plays an essential part in producing this quality. Such imagination issues in novel and enriching activities, physical and mental. "Adventure" does not mean chiefly, or exclusively, the facing of physical dangers— hunting lions in Africa, for example. True, adventure may take a physical form as in the discovery of America by Columbus. But the basis of these activities was the creative imagination of the man. He first adventured in the realm of the mind. Then he set sail.

It follows that there is grave peril in regarding ancient Greece as *the* embodied ideal of civilization. Such a backward-looking, static state of mind is hardly the spirit of adventure. Worship of the excellences of the past will not produce civilization in the modern world. After all, in their day, the Greeks were examples of the ideal of adventure. The great dramatists and philosophers were not backward-looking copyists. Their greatness lies in their creative approach to their problems. Aeschylus, Sophocles, Euripides, Aristophanes expressed new insights concerning the religious, moral, and political problems of their day. Plato dreamed of an ideal state; Aristotle founded several sciences. Both developed new philosophies of life, complex and vital. If we imitate the Greeks we should follow their general example of creative thought, not try to reproduce, in detail, their particular thoughts, feelings, and institutions. Some of the theories and techniques which met the needs of their day and age may no longer be relevant to a truly creative life in the twentieth century.

For these reasons Whitehead objects to the familiar definition of culture (civilization) as knowledge of the best that has been said or done. The tense of the verb is wrong. It implies a completely backward-looking attitude.

Incidentally, the excellences of Greek and Roman life have

tended to encourage the notion that civilization and fine art are synonymous. Whitehead contends that there is much more involved in civilization than a concern for art. This, of course, is obvious from his list of the defining qualities of civilization.

In so far as civilization emphasizes adventure, peril is involved. The adventure may terminate in disaster. In turning one's back on the security of the familiar there is the uncertainty of the unknown. The dangers and uncertainties, however, frequently call forth skills to deal with them. Hence, there is no necessary ground for pessimism. In the last analysis, the price which must be paid for advance is heavy: loss, destruction, displacement. If something new and better is to be enjoyed, something old and less valuable must be discarded. In order to experience the relative independence of adulthood the safeties of childhood must be sacrificed.

Whitehead's stress on the importance of adventure stems from his conviction that there are only two possible alternatives: either adventurous advance or the deadly lethargy of decadence. One cannot cling to static perfection. The stream of life will not stand still.

New problems arise which cannot be solved by the old methods. Thus, adventure is not the only source of danger. The apparent safety of the old ways brings its own type of danger. Indeed, these dangers are greater because, without the spirit of adventure, there is no hope of escape. The history of the decadence of the culture of the Near East, and until recent date that of India and China, illustrates the danger implicit in the comfortable retention of traditional "fineness." The result is a brittle gloss on life which finally cracks, because the underlying structure has collapsed.

It must be understood that Whitehead is not a wild-eyed devotee of "change at any price." Nor does he find absolutely no value in the experience of the past. Few men excel Whitehead in his deep appreciation of the glories and stimulating efficacy of the past. The wisdom of those who have gone before is a priceless possession. But it must be appreciated in the proper fashion. The present is enfeebled either if the past is dominant or if the past is lost. As he once remarked: He who does not profit from the past is doomed to repeat the mistakes of his grandfathers. Adventure must be based on the firm foundation of past wisdom and skills. But, and this is Whitehead's main point, civilization must not be shackled by the past.

Peace

It will be obvious, from the preceding discussion of adventure, that Whitehead does not regard peace as an essentially static condition—anesthesia. Rather, it is a positive feeling, of rich complexity, of great efficacy in arousing and energizing human activity. He does not restrict the term to its political meaning; although, of course, the absence of war would occur if a sufficient number of men developed the state of mind which Whitehead calls peace. It is a state of mind characterized by the deep insight that "fineness" (beauty in the broad, Greek sense) is of supreme importance. It is based on a devotion to the *ideal* of a harmony in which moral rightness triumphs in a beautiful world. In this harmony truth must be given an honored place, since it is one of the supreme values. There is the further faith that "fineness" is an enduring element, preserved within "the nature of things." As will be seen in the subsequent discussion of religion, Whitehead's idea of peace involves a specific concept of the nature and function of God.

When peace is attained it engenders an unshakable calm. The fires of personal ambition, the petty irritations of everyday life, fade into their proper perspective. There is nothing crucial about them. They simply do not concern those who have glimpsed the vision of true excellence. Peace is thus characterized by a widening of perspective. Facts are placed against the background of value ideals. Peace produces a "selfless approach" to all phases of human life. That is to say, a man no longer concentrates on his own food, shelter, and intellectual development. The universe no longer "revolves about him." He is able to admire a job which is well done whether he has had anything to do with it or not. Fame, so cold and hard, no longer has any appeal. It is seen as a hollow sham. Purged of narrow selfishness, peace-filled men are able to attain a necessary prerequisite for civilization—love of humanity as such. The achievement of an unselfish self frees much vital energy which is ordinarily wasted in the pursuit of narrow goals. There is now more opportunity for really creative activity.

Incidentally, Whitehead is careful to warn against identification of love of parent for child and the "self-sacrifice" found in peace. In most cases, unfortunately, the parent has not escaped from narrow selfishness. He merely derives great personal pleasure from focusing his activities on an "object" outside himself with whom he identifies himself. In a few instances, however, the love of parent for child, or mate for mate, is an example of selfless devotion. A very close approximation to peace is thus attained. In such cases it is possible to catch a glimpse of how the ideal harmony of human activity, enshrining high ideals, actually may be achieved in a particular fashion.

Even the brutal, stinging facts of evil fail to shake the balance of the peace-filled mind of a civilized man. He does not deny the existence of evil. He admits the terrible tragedy of life. But, evil is not regarded merely as a brute fact. The tragedy of evil calls to his attention what might have been, is not now, but may be in the future. The spirit of adventure may be the agency whereby the ideal, now thwarted by tragic evil, in due time comes to final realization. No man will be aroused to overcome evil unless he has a vision of what "may be." In this sense, tragedy serves as a purifier of the emotions. The sting of evil is removed. Its value, contributary to a greater good, is seen and appreciated. The career of Albert Schweitzer, in Africa, is an excellent illustration of the "difficult doctrine" which Whitehead is endeavoring to express.

Whitehead's ripe wisdom does not blind him to the fact that *in youth* the lure of peace may be strong. In short, not only is there a peace which is the "issue of tragedy." There is also a peace which is the "crown of youth." He means that when a young person has succumbed to the lure of beauty, felt it intimately, immersed himself in the depths of aesthetic experience —then, unmindful of the narrow self, he will have a vision of peace, the harmonization of activities, directed toward ideal aims.

Like all great possessions, peace in a sense is a gift. It

comes to those who do not frantically pursue it for themselves, sacrificing all else. This truth was expressed long ago in the words: "He who seeks to save his life shall lose it."

Truth

A statement, or sensation, is true if it provides an accurate report of the data to which it refers. Without a resolute facing of "facts," and an accurate report on them, adventure and peace are unattainable. The fineness to which a civilized man is devoted requires honesty with oneself and others.

In stressing the importance of truth, Whitehead does not demand that every idea, and statement, be certain and be regarded as a literal truth. In the realm of scientific investigation, hypotheses are formulated which are deficient in these respects. But, the hypotheses of science are not a final resting place. This imaginative interlude is a creative phase of the total process whereby an increasingly accurate knowledge of persons and things is obtained.

Whitehead's advocacy of the spirit of adventure leads him to repudiate any statement which purports to be the final, and complete, truth. No set of statements can be the final truth because the world, in all its phases, is continually changing. New data emerge. The pursuit of truth in vital matters is long and arduous. There is no room for dogmatism and intolerance. Whitehead never tires of pointing out that the so-called "certainties" in mathematics and physics which he was taught at Cambridge in the 1880's became outmoded antiquities by the turn of the century. Frequently, conflicting views are neither completely true nor completely false. Thus a clash of opinions is not a calamity. It is an opportunity to profit from the work of others, and seek co-operatively a common good: wider knowledge.

Truth, however, is not always an unmixed blessing. An accurate knowledge of the facts may be put to vile uses. Also, an accurate report of the facts may be distorted by a fallacious interpretation.

It must be remembered that adventure, peace, and truth are not the only essential qualities of civilization. Beauty and art are also essential. In many instances beauty and art are not concerned with truth. Some great works of imagination—for example, the plays of Shakespeare—are not intended to be literal reports of facts. The glory of the setting sun does not settle, conveniently, into the simple intellectual pigeonholes of true or false. Nor can the value ideals—beauty, goodness—be given this treatment. *Statements* made about ideals, or their actualizations (a beautiful picture, a good action), may be true or false, accurate or inaccurate, reports. In the last analysis, the distinction between truth, beauty, and goodness (whether on the ideal or the actual level) is based on the fact that there are, for Whitehead, three distinguishable characteristics. They cannot be fused into one.

Beauty

Beauty is defined as the mutual adaptation of factors within experience, the absence of mutual interference. In the highest form of beauty, the harmonious arrangement is enriched by patterned contrast. Too much harmony reduces beauty to deadly triviality. The transparently simple rhythm which degenerates into a monotonous "hum," unmistakably devoid of distinguishable items of content, stands far down in the scale of excellence when compared with the more complex structure of verse in which individual ideas "break" from their verbal context. A comparison of the complexity of a great cathedral with the shallow simplicity of a prefabricated shack in the suburbs illustrates the same point. Other factors, in addition to patterned contrast, are instrumental in reaching higher forms of beauty.[2] For example color is an important ingredient. The enrichment of life, accruing from the experience of beauty, explains the inclusion of beauty as one of the essential factors in civilization. This becomes more evident in the course of an examination of another element in civilization—art.

Art

Art, Whitehead notes with cryptic insight, turns the abstract into the concrete and the concrete into the abstract. In other words, some idea, present in experience in a vague unimportant fashion, is given life and compelling vigor in a work of art. Human suffering, for example, may be transferred from the realm of "mere phrase" to the real world of unavoidable fact. On the other hand, some familiar fact of experience, so familiar that it is hardly noticed, is abstracted from its context and functions as a source of insight, or enrichment. The beauty of a city park may suddenly "break" upon one from the frame of a picture, revealing unsuspected fineness.

Works of art frequently express beauty. That is not their only function. Truth also may be conveyed through the medium of an art form. Indeed, Whitehead remarks that unless there is an element of truth in a work of art, it cannot produce a strong reaction in the beholder.

An art object may be the result of the basic human urge to express something that *has been* experienced. This, however, does not mean that art should be regarded as "backward looking." A work of art is an impressive demonstration of the creative powers of the artist. It has an emphatic freshness and novelty. It not only expresses, but also arouses, new ideas and "freshness" of emotion.

In stressing its stimulating aspect, Whitehead does not lose sight of the fact that art brings refreshment and relaxation. Men need periods of calm when the pressure of ordinary events fades into the distant background. A painting, poem, or musical composition which is "timeless" in its excellence provides an opportunity to lose oneself in a realm where life's most precious moments may be enjoyed, free from ordinary distractions. The stimulus, which is capable of arousing the joy of vivid feeling, is abstracted from the relentless flow of events. It is preserved as a continuing source of enjoyment. Thus, a man is free to enjoy the intense values which, in ordinary experience, flash into focus and quickly fade. For example, Whitehead suggests that if Odysseus could sit in "the other world," and listen to Homer reciting the *Odyssey*, he could relive and enjoy, to the full, those priceless moments which in ordinary life come and go too quickly for complete savoring.

Art is not to be regarded as synonymous with emotionalized chaos. In so far as it involves truth and beauty (harmony), art is obviously orderly. True, there is a strong emotional factor in both creation and enjoyment. Unless these emotions are subjected to discipline, however, the attempt to achieve excellence fails. No man can produce a work of art by merely random gyrations. Neither can a painting, for example, be understood unless a person exerts himself in a "directed" fashion. Further, as Plato said long ago, he who truly lives in the presence of beauty cannot bring himself to perform undisciplined actions.

Though the realm of art involves ideals never fully achieved by human effort, Whitehead reminds us that despite its imperfections a work of art is a tribute to the greatness of human beings. A man has taken a fragment of the universe and used it as a medium for the production of something of great worth. Perfection has not been reached, but an aproach to perfection has been attempted. The artist has demonstrated that *ideals can be expressed* (within the limits of human capabilities). In a sense, something of eternal value has been embodied in the midst of the transitory moments of human existence. The lives of men have been dignified, and glorified, thereby. This awareness should bring a sense of exaltation. Living in a vast universe, surrounded by overwhelming natural beauties, men need to be reminded of the impressive creative power of their own species. The beauty of a sunset overpowers by its magnificence. The sight, or sound, of a human work of art inspires men to further advances along the road to civilization. A work of art proves that "mere men" can focus their attention on something other than the necessities of brute toil for survival and bodily satisfaction. In this limited achievement, there is inspiration and the ground for hope.

More specifically, art should function to constitute civilization by stressing the principle of the *harmony of individuals*. Whitehead refers to the cathedral at Chartres as an example. The sculptures and tracings stand out with vivid detail, yet the excellence of these detailed facts makes possible the exalted beauty of the cathedral. The majesty and mystery of religion: this message is driven home by the harmonious impact of the many diverse individual elements which compose the structure, and adornment, of this great place of worship. In so far as a man appreciates the importance of individual fineness in harmonious interrelation, he rises toward civilized existence.

Within a work of art, all the qualities of civilization may be embodied: beauty, truth, the spirit of adventure, and the calm feeling of peace which comes to those who look beyond the obvious to the "fineness" of life.

Goodness

It will have been noticed that "goodness" is not included in the list of qualities constituting civilization. The explanation seems to be that beauty, in its broad sense, includes the usual, restricted, meaning of beauty—and goodness as well. Certainly, in stressing the civilized concern for fineness of all sorts, Whitehead did not intend to exclude moral excellence. In discussing the sense of criticism, which characterizes a civilized man, he states that one of the foundations of this critical faculty is an appreciation of the demands of moral duty. Further, he contends that all who profit from past civilization are confronted by a moral claim to transmit, and to add to, the benefits they have received.[3] In discussing ultimate ideals, Whitehead stresses goodness as well as truth and beauty.

The Status of Values

It should be emphasized that Whitehead regards truth, beauty, and goodness as ideals unchanging in their meaning. These ideals are eternal components of the universe. They are not to be treated as mere expressions of human wishes, summaries of majority opinion of some one social group. They are as inescapable as any ultimate physical fact.

Science

It may seem strange that Whitehead does not suggest that science (laws and particular factual knowledge, theory and application) is an essential ingredient in civilization. There is reason for this omission, however, as he clearly shows. Great progress toward civilization occurred in China; yet its achievements in science were negligible. The same is true of India and Persia. After all, the Greeks made little advance in the details of

accurate scientific knowledge. The Romans have less cause to
boast. Even our much-vaunted modern Western world has made
substantial progress in science only since the seventeenth century. Scientific knowledge is an important branch of knowledge,
necessary for the provision of a "machinery" which will serve as
the basis for civilization. Yet, science is only one aspect of truth.
In any case the fact remains that societies and individuals can
exhibit the qualities of beauty, art, adventure, peace, and truth
in many areas—without much concern for scientific activity. *In
this sense,* science is not an essential ingredient in civilization.

PREREQUISITES FOR CIVILIZATION

When all five qualities: truth, beauty, art, adventure, peace
—achieved or *closely approximated*—are the *dominant characteristics,* they constitute a civilized person, or society.[4]

Obviously, the creation and maintenance of civilization requires the creation and maintenance of these qualities. However,
it is important to realize that in addition to these basic or most
fundamental elements in civilization, there are other, closely
related, factors which may be regarded as prerequisites for
civilization. In short, these factors decisively facilitate the appearance of the five "defining" qualities. These factors are: the
recognition of the importance of each individual, freedom of
thought and action, tolerance, the use of persuasion rather than
force, wisdom.

Importance of Individuals

The individual is important because civilization depends
upon the fullest possible development of the powers of individual
human beings. Adventure, peace, art, truth, and beauty are
present in the world only as phases of the experience of individual men and women. Any institution, political, legal, educational, cultural, or religious, which *unnecessarily* restricts the
development of individuals, stands in the way of civilization.
Further, there are potentialities in some persons which cannot
be brought to fruition in any ordinary social context. The highest

values of civilized living are enjoyed in solitude, or at best within a very small circle of kindred spirits. When a man is subordinated to the standards of a group, when his thoughts, feelings, and deeds are "dictated" down to the last detail, the richness of life evaporates in the heat of oppression. So, let us "render unto Caesar the things which are Caesar's" but remember that there are realms of moral and spiritual experience over which the control of the recognized rulers of a society should not extend.

This is not to say that Whitehead recommends completely uncontrolled behavior, even for a few superior people. We must remember that *no* individual "lives to himself alone." We owe much to our environment. It has nourished the various phases of our being. It provides an opportunity for the development of potentialities within the individual. The great playwright needs a theater, a staff, a group of actors, an appreciative audience, if his message is to be fully expressed and entirely efficacious. We should discharge our debt to others by participation, in the best fashion, in the common life of man. There are limits, then, to the freedom which is implied in the claim that the individual should be respected—respected, that is, in the sense that he be given full opportunity to develop the qualities of civilized existence. Those who, in developing themselves, thoughtlessly or knowingly interfere with the self-development of others, must be restrained.

Freedom

The preceding comments raise the problem of the freedom of the individual within a social unit. The details of Whitehead's discussion of this phase of the problem of freedom will be found in Chapter 4, entitled "Social Philosophy." It is important to observe in passing that, in his judgment, the problem of freedom has several other aspects. Freedom of thought, press, speech, and religion (as these are usually interpreted) are important matters. Without them civilization cannot be achieved. Yet, other freedoms are also important. The forces of physical nature restrict our freedom, our freedom of action. Heat, cold, disease, hunger, death, distance all drag man down, distracting his attention from the higher values. Unless the "animal needs" are, in a measure, satisfied there is no opportunity to walk the "higher" ways of life. The wisdom of the Prometheus myth is relevant here. Prometheus did not bring mankind the freedom of the press. He brought fire, which made possible warmth and better food.

As is the case in so many discussions, the Greeks call attention to the *highest type* of freedom. This is the freedom which does not depend on the manipulation of intransigent matter, or on soothing the base passions of men in social situations. These are temporary victories at best. In any case, only some phases of personality are liberated. Rather, one should give priority to the freedom which comes from the contemplation of the "ultimate meanings" and values enshrined in the universe. This insight brings the peace which is freedom from distracting concern with things of lesser importance that do not endure. Here also, as in other types of freedom, there is compulsion, a restriction on freedom. It is the compulsion exercised by devotion to "fineness." Some alternatives are ruled out. Such is the price of freedom. This is an important phase of the messages of Plato, the Stoics, and the leaders of Christianity. There is no easy way to civilization. Its freedom is not that of uncontrolled excess, unrestricted experimentation in living. Rather, it is the discipline of those free men who love the best and deny themselves what is appealing but inferior.

Tolerance

Tolerance is implicit in Whitehead's emphasis on the value of the individual, and the importance of freedom. More specifically, it is sanctioned by good sense and demanded by intellectual honesty. Ultimately, it is a condition necessary for the development of civilization. Without toleration much valuable human experience would be lost.

The history of science has shown that conflicting theories are not a calamity. Rather, if given a fair hearing, they are the first step toward new discovery. Two distinguished physicists obtained different results for the atomic weight of nitrogen. One did not denounce the other. The field of science did not divide into "x" men and "y" men. New discoveries took place: the element argon and the concept of isotope. Thus, the apparent differences in the atomic weight of nitrogen were explained. In one process of measurement the results had been distorted by the presence of a previously unknown factor. The unknown became known. The difficulty was cleared up. Scientific knowledge was advanced.

Among the Greeks, Pericles' famous "funeral oration" was a vigorous and impressive illustration of the spirit of tolerance. The Platonic dialogues, in showing the plausibility of various alternative positions, demonstrate the kindly tolerance of their author, a man who in many instances is typical of the best of Greek civilization. The Sophists "live" in Plato's dialogues though he heartily disagrees with them. In the *Parmenides* he states the basic objections to his own metaphysical position. He admits that he may be wrong. At crucial points in his argument he offers what he terms only a "likely story." Thus, a recognition of human limitations, the possibility of some truth in many quarters, issues in the tolerance which is the fruit of honest humility.

This spirit should be manifest on the international level, as well. It becomes possible when men travel in space around the world, and also voyage in time, familiarizing themselves with the life of the past. Having developed this tolerant perspective, it is possible to view appreciatively other races and ways of life, and come to recognize that other nations, of different habits, are not enemies. They are "godsends." The stimulus of "the other which may be better" is an essential source of the adventure which is civilization. Tolerance is a duty which a wise man recognizes because of the rich complexity of present achievement, and the possibilities of even further development the future may hold.

With characteristic insight Whitehead remarks that tolerance is not frequently found in "advanced," or creative, thinkers. They are too busy destroying the old and building the new, to develop the maturity, depth, and sanity of judgment which are basic to tolerance. They are in too great a hurry. As he aptly remarks, "Intolerance is the besetting sin of moral fervor." [5]

History is studded with the names of men who sought freedom of thought and action for themselves, yet denied it to others. Such men did not understand the general implications of freedom and tolerance. For example, in Egypt, Akhnaton was a reformer who broke, courageously, with his religious past. Nevertheless, he tried to impose his will on others. Some of the Hebrew prophets fell into the same unfortunate pattern of behavior. Some Christian thinkers have paid little attention to the profound insight of the parable of the wheat and the tares. After Christianity's establishment under Constantine, intolerance flourished in the Church. The great Protestant reformers, Luther and Calvin, were as intolerant, in their day of pre-eminence, as those against whom they originally rebelled. The pages of the present offer little cause for congratulation.

On the other hand a genial orthodoxy, secure in its ripe wisdom, kindly desposed toward all men, frequently feels that it can "afford" to be tolerant of the mistakes and foibles of others. John Locke, the Quakers, and Erasmus, are examples of the tolerance which can be generated by a "genial orthodoxy." This, in its highest form, issues in the amused appreciation of divergences which would irritate less liberal men. Such "amusement" is neither "superior" nor "sourly cynical." Incidentally, here is a criterion of civilization: the point at which a man becomes angry (or controls himself) when confronted by an opposing point of view.

Persuasion

Whitehead contends that a civilized social order is maintained because of the persuasive attraction of the ideal qualities involved.

There are a number of factors which make people susceptible to rational persuasion. The experience of a successful family life develops the requisite habits and attitudes. The enjoyment of ideas and value experiences involved in scientific, moral, and aesthetic activities are also important conditions. Indeed, in this common concern for value (ideals and specific experiences), there is a profound religious basis. Men are open to persuasion because they are bound together by sympathy, one for the other. This arises from a common devotion to the divine element in the universe which is the source of the value ideals exemplified in specific achievements of value. The affairs of commercial life also are effective. After all, success in business involves persuasion (in some instances rational persuasion) among those who direct the affairs of the industry. This is also true with reference to the relations between managers and the labor force, as well as those between the industry and the consumers of its products (See Chapter 4).

Modern efficiency experts are stressing, increasingly, the importance of rational persuasion, rather than the blind pressures of irrational forces. Even on the international scene, where force seems so necessary and rational persuasion so silly, there are examples of the power of persuasion based on common appreciation of value ideals and experience. The relations between Britain and India (and Pakistan) illustrate this principle. Formerly subject peoples have attained independence. They now co-operate with their former conquerors who once used force rather than persuasion. The fruitful associations between British peoples and the United States, over the past century and a half, is further substantiation of Whitehead's point of view concerning the feasibility of the civilized approach to the problem of human interrelations.

In a trenchant utterance, Whitehead remarks that "the recourse to force, however unavoidable, is a disclosure of the failure of civilization." [6] This springs from his basic conviction that a reliance on force kills the values of civilization. Those who use force as the *primary* instrument in human affairs descend from the level of humanity to that of the brute. As a result, they tend to find their satisfactions in the obvious pleasures of the senses rather than in the rich complexity of truth, beauty, goodness. Peace is flouted. Their adventures are on a low level, and frequently are disastrous. The careers of Hitler and Mussolini are cases in point.

This is not to say that Whitehead is a pacifist. He recognizes that war must be used as a last resort, the lesser of two evils. "War can protect; it cannot create. Indeed, war adds to the brutality that frustrates creation. The protection of war should be the last resort in the slow progress of mankind towards its far-off ideals." [7] In general, as will become evident from an examination of Whitehead's *social philosophy* (Chapter 4), he is well aware that there must be a mixture of freedom and compulsion. Some men are not open, at least on occasion, to persuasion. They must be compelled to do and to refrain, for their good and the common good. Nevertheless, Whitehead's basic point remains unchanged. When compulsion is used, in the place of rational persuasion, there is a decline from the ideals of civilization.

Wisdom

Civilization is characterized by an awareness that the universe is vast and complex. The obvious, and familiar, facts are not enough. In so far as it is possible, all data must be brought into the focus of attention. The civilized mind then attempts to discover the basic elements and laws which are involved in these data. Also an awareness of the meaning and values of life is of particular importance in elevating a creature from the level of the brute to that of civilization.

Philosophy is essential in civilization for two reasons. First, it is the attempt to organize, in terms of general ideas, all available data—facts *and* values.[8] Second, civilized wisdom involves not only the ability to grasp, in unified fashion, a vast range of facts and values; above all the civilized mind is vitalized by a "noble discontent," the philosophic attitude of "criticism." Having surveyed the "fineness"—intellectual, moral, and aesthetic—which "might be," a wise man cannot be satisfied with the shoddy inadequacies of "what is." The lure of the ideal is a gadfly ever energizing the civilized man.

The best example of a wisdom competent to apprehend values and meanings as well as facts, and capable of exercising critical insight, is found in the dialogues of Plato. In *The Republic*, for example, there is a masterly outline of the weaknesses and strengths of human personality, the dangers and possibilities in social action. All these data are fused into one coherent picture expressing a guiding ideal—the ideal person in the ideal state. Here is one of the high points in intellectual achievement:

a profound but critical discontent, not sour and vindictive but sane and unceasing in its search for the ultimate good. Thus, it should be obvious that criticism, in Whitehead's sense, is not mere witless denunciation. It is a process of careful, balanced evaluation, firmly based on exalted standards.

Whitehead realizes that there is peril in vigorous criticism, if it does not adhere to the high standards which he sets. What is valuable may be destroyed as well as what is worthless. For example, criticism of religion may destroy, on rational grounds, symbols and forms of worship which may have great aesthetic and spiritual value. Thus, in singing the praises of the reflective intellect, Whitehead is careful to warn against the dangers implicit in a *narrow intellectualism*.

It is an all too common human tendency to demand clarity in intellectual formulations. A neat formula is produced. The thinker relaxes in smug self-satisfaction. The difficulty is that life is actually very complex. A simple, clear-cut formula won't do. "Insistence on hard-headed clarity issues from sentimental feeling, as it were a mist cloaking the complexities of fact." [9] This point is part of Whitehead's general contention that one should seek clarity but distrust it; i.e., be as clear as possible but not make impossible demands on the limited powers of the human mind. Whitehead has done yeoman service in warning against exclusive reliance on those elements in our experience which are clear and obvious. Science has paid too much deference to clear-cut sense data and neat systems of logical deduction—for example, in mathematics. Such data are, of course, important but Whitehead's stress is *also* on the vague, on the complex, on the obscure phases of experience. Frequently, vital and decisive factors are revealed in such experiences. Profound moral, aesthetic, and religious data, for example, do not appear in the guise of clear-cut sense data; nor do they fit adequately into some neat mathematical formula. In any case, a comprehensive and accurate view of a situation must take into consideration as many factors as possible.

Wisdom, of course, requires width, depth, and accuracy of thought. Yet, this is not the complete basis of wisdom. Man is a complex creature. He reasons, but he also feels. There is an emotional aspect of wisdom. The sense of critical insight, so important in civilization, does not depend only on the awareness of values and the ability to make accurate deductions. In addition, there is a sense, a feeling, of duty. More specifically, Whitehead makes it clear that wisdom is not obtained, nor civilization achieved, unless intellectual excellence is interfused with feelings or attitudes of respect, sympathy, kindliness toward all those with whom we find ourselves in social relations.

THE HERITAGE OF WESTERN CULTURE

Whitehead is well aware of the fact that modern cultural life has a complex heritage. The chief sources of influence have been "Greece," "Palestine," and "Egypt." These centers of "progress toward" civilization have served as channels of transmission for other sources farther afield in space and time. China and India, bound by trade routes to the Near East, have made contributions. However, the chief sources of influence have been Greek (including the Hellenic), Egyptian, and Semitic (including the contributions of Mesopotamia and the Arabian Desert). From Greece we have obtained the gifts of the trained intellect, capable of logical and metaphysical thought—indeed, capable of generalities in all fields of thought. From Greece, also, has come the appreciation of beauty in the broadest sense: fineness in thought and action. The Hebrew genius has provided a moral and spiritual emphasis, and a view of the world centered in a divine being. The Egyptian contribution was chiefly in the realm of practical techniques. In tracing the impact of the past on Western civilization one cannot safely overlook the function of Rome. Rome not only transmitted but also imposed order and unity on the diverse elements which it received.

These "sources" are not an unmixed blessing. In Greece, even the best of men never really felt respect for the individual human being. Slavery was permitted to exist. In the later Hellenic period, men developed the comfortable feeling that there was nothing new to discover. Scholarship, in the worst sense, replaced the search for new truth. The spirit of adventure died. The so-called civilizations of the Near East—Constantinople, Mesopotamia, the delta of the Nile, Arabia, and Asia Minor—also had grave defects. That is to say, they did not fully merit the honorific title: "civilization." There was a shocking disregard of the "souls of men"; disregarded of the possibilities of an inner life of real value experiences. Men who developed the techniques of commerce, in particular navigation, sacrificed their children to Moloch. A correlation of their inner slackness was their reliance on brute force and its resultant social implications. Men were regarded as superior to women. Society had an aristocracy of power and a large servile population of weaker men. Finally all initiative failed. The population of the Near East accepted the dictum that "there is nothing new under the sun," and so turned to obvious, gross, sensual gratification.

The Renaissance, for all its vitality, was deficient in that it concentrated on one phase of its cultural heritage, the Greek. It tended to overlook the rest. Indeed, in a real sense, it was backward looking, and paid the penalty in lack of full achievement. Further, although the Italian Renaissance, paradoxically, made progress in the realms of truth, beauty, art, and adventure, it was lacking in an essential ingredient of civilization—namely, peace. It was ruthless, hard, and cruel.

In eighteenth-century Europe wisdom faded. Men were satisfied with a small intellectual horizon. The backgrounds and complexities of experience were disregarded. The nineteenth century carried on this emphasis. The ruthless individualism of competitive business made the appreciation of the values of civilization increasingly difficult. The sympathy and reverence, which characterize wisdom, were restricted to a small segment of the population. No unifying philosophy of life was available. Western civilization suffered from the schizophrenia of two opposing intellectual emphases: (a) values, (b) facts devoid of values.

Our so-called civilization is the heir of these ancestors. Our way of life shows the strengths and weaknesses of those from whom we have descended. This Whitehead states with penetrating clarity and honesty. These weaknesses are delineated in the subsequent chapters of this study. The means by which the ideals of civilization may be more fully realized, and the ways by which present weaknesses may be overcome, are also discussed in subsequent chapters.

It is appropriate to note, at this point, that Whitehead's definition of civilization is so "idealized" that perhaps no social group (and certainly few individuals) can "fully measure up" to this lofty, and difficult, complex ideal. The so-called civilizations and civilized human beings have, at best, "come close" to a realization of the ideal. Yet, some of them merit the designation because of the *degree* of their achievement and their continuing efforts toward further realization of the ideals of civilization.

It should be clear, from the preceding discussion, that though many social groups and individuals may, in varying degrees, manifest *some* of the defining qualities of civilization, they do not *merit* the laudatory title: "civilized." This is so because the *dominant* qualities are not those of civilization; or become some of the defining qualities are lacking, or are not sufficiently developed.

Chapter 2   PHILOSOPHY
OF HISTORY

BASIC FACTORS

The attainment, retention, or destruction of civilization depends on a number of basic factors in addition to those discussed in the previous chapter. These additional factors vary in importance. However, *none* can be disregarded. *Ideas, great men, economic activities, technological devices, the facts of "geography," God*—all influence the behavior of human beings. Whitehead's discussion of these factors and related "questions" constitutes his philosophy of history.

Ideas

"As we think, we live." [1] The ideas we accept, as guiding principles, determine what we experience and what is barred from experience. Indeed, there are a few general ideas which contribute greatly to the establishment of a pattern of behavior in an entire social group during vast periods of time. For instance, in the ancient world, slavery was an idea accepted by Greco-Roman society. Its application was the foundation on which that society was based. In the modern democratic world, two other ideas are fundamental: freedom and equality of opportunity. Each point of view, the ancient and the modern, with its differing ideational foundation, issued in different approaches to each important phase of human life: industry, education, politics, recreation, religion.

Many of the most influential ideas in Western civilization were formulated by Plato. In his dialogues we find discussions of: laws and ideals, matter, soul or mind, the striving to achieve excellence, harmony as a condition of excellence, mathematics, organic interaction. [2] The following pages will indicate the aptness of Whitehead's contention that these Platonic conceptions are fundamental in the development of Western civilization.

Other very important ideas, which were efficacious in shaping Western civilization, are those of original sin and divine grace. Further, the political behavior of the people of North America, at least in the early days, was an expression of theories derived from John Locke and the French democratic thinkers who followed his lead. The doctrines of human rights, majority rule, tolerance—all exerted a decisive influence.

It must be noted that some ideas function merely as records of past experience. Others are explanations, or justifications, of the status quo. Such ideas, of course, effect human behavior and cannot be disregarded. Incidentally, as Whitehead points out, ideas do not retain their meaning unchanged. What is significant to one generation may be almost meaningless to another. Antiquated political speeches, religious services, learned lectures weary old and young alike. It is wise to realize that ideas lose their dynamic just as food loses its nutritive value.

The most vital ideas are those which look beyond, and above, the familiar levels of experience. Whitehead illustrates this sort of idea—the speculative, contemplative type—by referring to the Hellenic and the contrasting Hellenistic civilizations. The Greeks (who lived in Athens and her colonies) were speculative. They pushed out intellectual boundaries in all directions. On the other hand, the typical Hellenistic man (living in Alexandria) regarded himself as the heir of Greek culture, but his approach was different. Instead of wide-raging speculation, his attitude was that of scholarly clarification, arranging, and thus conserving, the wisdom of the past. Both types of men have their place. The two types of ideas should be complementary. One without the other is a menace to civilization. Of the two, the "Alexandrian" is the greater danger.

Whitehead deals with this important topic in considerable detail. He refers to the tremendous value of abstract speculative thought in science. In mathematics, for example, complicated intellectual systems were constructed which had no practical use for centuries. Yet, there came a day when they were found to be of great value both in theory and in practice. Kepler, Descartes, Newton opened the door of the modern scientific world. They used the instruments forged by the Greek geometricians 2,000 years before. Thus, as Whitehead aptly remarks, "To set limits to speculation is treason to the future."[3] Yet, Whitehead is equally aware of the dangers of abstract speculative thought. With great care he calls attention to the disastrous effects of undue emphasis on mathematical abstractions in religious thought in particular and in philosophy in general. Since mathematics is concerned with timeless entities and relations, misguided men have contended that all reality is timeless, that change is an illusion. Thus, the ordinary affairs of life are regarded as unimportant. God is portrayed as a static being unconcerned with the world. Knowledge is focused on the eternal. Therefore, there can be no relation between thought and action. These then are some of the unfortunate results of the uncritical use of the Aladdin's lamp of mathematics. The danger implicit in undue reliance on ancestral ideas is illustrated by the fate of some of the Asiatic nations. China and India, centuries ago, developed an impressive set of guiding principles. However, these became the objects of uncritical devotion. No new ideas were developed. As a result, these nations relapsed, for centuries, into the slough of decadence. On the other hand, Western civilization has retained its vitality because of its ability to replenish and enlarge its capital of fundamental ideas.

It is very important to note the very slow formulation, and rise to efficacy, of new and decisive ideas. Consider, for example, the transition from the primacy of the idea of slavery to those of freedom and equality. Even at the height of Greco-Roman culture, the critical sense of a few men was at work. Plato's dialogues reflect dissatisfaction with the institution of slavery. The Stoics advocated the brotherhood of man. The Gospels stressed the grandeur of *any* human soul. Some men treated their slaves gently, even freed them in due time. Nevertheless, the institution of slavery remained. The idea was subject to criticism. It was not seriously shaken. However, other ideas were at work. Came the seventeenth century and the competing ideas became increasingly prominent. The humanitarian teachings of John Locke exerted a profound influence. The "common law" of England added its weight. Religious leaders (Quakers, Catholics, Methodists) contributed to the rising tide of constructive protest. Early in the nineteenth century, slavery was abolished in the British Empire. Later, it was given its death knell in the United States. The stretch of time from Plato to Abraham Lincoln was long indeed; but one form of society finally was replaced by another. For centuries the ideas of human freedom and equality were vaguely apprehended, their implications only partially formulated. Yet, like the waves of the relentless ocean, they kept pressing against the sluggish consciences of man. Like a gadfly stinging to disturbing awareness, like a beacon beckoning to a better place, great creative ideas do their work slowly but with tremendous efficacy.

One of the great perils confronting any society is the danger of conflict between ideas of apparently equal efficacy and appeal. In the modern world, the related ideas of mechanism and matter are supreme in one area of thought. The universe is considered to be composed only of material elements. The laws of natural science are applicable everywhere and serve as an adequate basis for prediction. On the other hand, the human mind and soul are regarded as being more than matter. Men claim to have initiative, responsibility, and the power to rise superior to environmental forces. It is contended that beyond facts of physics, chemistry, and biology is the realm of values such as truth, beauty, and goodness. This basic conflict between these two patterns of thought is a serious weakness in our society. Either men are divided within themselves, uncertain how to combine these conflicting opinions; or else society is split into two opposing camps, each espousing one of the opposing positions. For example, during the nineteenth century, Jeremy Bentham and Auguste Comte advocated the value ideas: "the supreme worth of man" and "the supreme value of majority happiness." They made the assumption that there is "love of mankind as such." This position was opposed by men who like David Hume could find no love of mankind as such. Developments in zoology, summarized in the evolutionary theory, indicated a lack of love. The elimination of many members of *all* species implied a lack of importance assigned to human beings as such. Thus, the disputants were left with ideas about facts and ideas about values, and no apparent possible unification of the two points of view.

Whitehead has provided a classic discussion of this general theme (and several other phases of his treatment of ideas) in the justly famous Chapter Five of *Science and the Modern World*: "The Romantic Reaction." Here he portrays, with great brilliance and insight, the gradual entry of the idea of mechanistic determinism onto the stage of English literature. He sketches the transition *from* Milton's attempt to "justify the ways of God to man" *to* the frantic cry of Tennyson ("the stars . . . blindly run") and the despair of Arnold. Both nineteenth century poets regarded the mechanistic implications of science as being totally destructive of belief in God and human initiative and values.

The origin of ideas has been explained in many ways: the mere summary of habitual experience; a rationalization, or explanation, of social patterns of action; the creative genius of gifted men; the revelation of the Wisdom of God; eternal principles, part of the structure of the universe. Be that as it may, the fact remains that ideas exercise an important function in arousing and controlling human behavior.

It must be noted, however, that unless there is adequate food, clothing, shelter, and the related articles of commerce, intellectual activity cannot take place. It will be a complete luxury until other needs are met in at least a minimum fashion. Further, lacking the stimulus of commerce (in the broadest sense), ideas will be deficient in content and vitality.

In stressing the importance of ideas Whitehead is careful to emphasize that ideas, without knowledge of techniques necessary to apply them, are of no use in the active world of human living. For example, it is not enough to have the idea that all men should be freed from slavery. One must know how to persuade owners to give up their slaves: how much it will cost; and where the money is coming from. Further, it is necessary to know how to effect the transition from slave mentality to that of a free man.

In discussing ideas, Whitehead does not lose sight of the

fact that an idea will not be effective unless it is emotionalized and hence becomes a focus of attention. A merely inert idea, contemplated with absolute calm, will never serve as a stimulus, or lure, to action. In other words, men are not only creatures of reason. They have also impulses, emotions, and complex unconscious habits. After all, we frequently act without thinking. Unfortunately, our thoughts are sometimes swamped by our impulses and emotions. Even the initiation of thinking is somewhat of a mystery. As Whitehead remarks: "We find ourselves thinking, just as we find ourselves breathing and enjoying the sunset." [4] With characteristic irony, and balanced judgment, he states that during the first half of the nineteenth century, gin did more harm to the English people than all the noble thoughts of the Royal Society did good.

The final judgment is that, though man is an animal and his mental activities are strongly influenced by his body, yet he is capable of creative thought. Thus, he can look above and beyond the characteristics which he shares with the brutes.

Great Men

The preceding discussion of ideas involves a reference to great men. They serve as agents in developing these ideas, implementing them, and bringing them to the attention of their fellows. This is one of the important factors in human affairs.

The efficacy of great men can be understood best by an examination of outstanding samples of human greatness. Plato, the Stoics, the Hebrew prophets, Jesus of Nazareth, Galileo, Newton, Locke, Lord Shaftesbury, Dewey—many names come to mind. Not only did these men formulate and spread ideas. What is more important, they translated ideas into action. By demonstrating the excellence of the civilized way of life (or at least some of its aspects), they have served as symbols, examples of the powers of achievement of human beings. Round them have clustered lesser men who caught the inspiration of their genius and, within the limits of their ability, followed the example of their leaders. John Dewey, to mention a contemporary figure, outlined a way of life centered on the basic assumptions of New England democracy and modern science. The skills and techniques derived from these sources have been applied to most of the detailed problems of life. American education has been transformed. In politics, ethics, and religious thought, the mark of Dewey is on many minds and hearts. Indeed, Whitehead is of the opinion that John Dewey is the "chief intellectual force providing [the North American continent] . . . with coherent purpose." [5]

And yet, paradoxically enough, the great importance of Dewey's work is a source of genuine danger. There is the possibility that Dewey's followers will be content to rest on his foundations, forgetting that Dewey himself was above all an adventurer. This is the calamity which haunts the work of any great leader. Little men forget that the master's formulae do not, necessarily, give the final answer. Rather, they beckon men to unexplored areas of future knowledge.

Turning back to the beginnings of our attempts to become civilized, Whitehead suggests that the Hebrew prophets are among the few men who decisively altered the course of history. In his opinion, we owe more to them than we can express, because of their pioneer emphasis on moral emotions. In this prophetic tradition stands Jesus of Nazareth, a person of supreme significance. There were many great leaders in the realm of thought in the ancient world. Chief among the Greeks were the Pythagoreans, Plato, and Aristotle. These men were pre-eminently curious. They sought to examine and understand everything. Their approach to knowledge was careful and systematic. They tried to obtain a comprehensive view of the vast complexity of persons and things. Yet, they were practical men wrestling with fundamental human problems. Pythagoras sought to understand everything. Nevertheless, he endeavored to found a religious brotherhood and to engage in the affairs of power politics. Plato took all knowledge for his province, and dreamed of an ideal state. But he trained some of the rulers of the ancient world and went to Syracuse to help set up his ideal state in actuality. Aristotle tried to systematize knowledge. He too conducted a training school for princes. He undertook extensive field trips to study biological and political phenomena.

There are grave gaps in the knowledge provided by these men. Some of their methods were very faulty. They were not impressively successful in the complex affairs of practical life. Yet, undeniably they helped to lay the foundations of the civilized world.

In the sixth century A.D., Justinian's influence was a decisive factor. His generals cleared Italy of barbarians and made possible the development of civilized societies. His lawyers promulgated civil and canon law, a fundamental condition for civilization. His capital, Constantinople, was the home of art and learning, a source of inspiration and a focal point from which men of proved excellence could move about to other less civilized cities.

St. Bernard, in his monastery, maintained an interest in practical affairs such as agriculture and language as well as in religious matters. He helped preserve, through the Dark Ages, those phases of life which are the roots from which civilization flowers. In England, as well as on the continent, through the centuries great churchmen kept civilization alive: Augustine of Canterbury, Anselm, Becket, Cranmer, Laud, and (in Whitehead's day) Tait. These men regarded the Church as the conserver and creative source of civilization. They considered themselves leaders in establishing the highest values of human life. They believed that the Church was the *only* valid agency in promoting civilization. These men, and this point of view, are out of place in the modern world. When this approach is imposed, as in contemporary Spain, the results are completely unsatisfactory. Yet, such men (and such an approach) at one time were highly beneficial.

The cultural development of Europe cannot be understood unless the influence of Galileo and Newton is fully appreciated. These men were the chief architects of the scientific world-view which, until recently, was the foundation of modern life and action. Galileo died the year Newton was born. Thus, there was a continuity which made possible a fusion of effort. Their interests, and abilities, had elements in common as well as diversities. Both had great ability in understanding physical facts. Both had remarkable powers of generalization. Galileo was an experimenter, with sufficient mathematical knowledge for his purposes. Newton was primarily a mathematician, with enough appreciation of experimentation to enable him to appreciate Galileo's work and carry it on to the joint pinnacle of achievement. It is Whitehead's judgment that if this intellectual foundation had not been laid in the seventeenth century, other developments would not have taken place. For example, Locke would not have formulated his influential analysis of human understanding, nor his treatises on civil government. The ideas of democracy would not have come, chiefly from this source, to France. Hence the dwellers on the North American continent would not have derived the vision which beckoned them on to their great experiment in applied democracy. In a real sense, then, Galileo and Newton are men who have shaped the civilization of the modern world.

Whitehead has a very high opinion of Bentham and Comte, as instigators of reforms. They outlined practical techniques which were such that "most of what has been practically effective, in morals, in religion, or in political theory, from their day to this has derived strength from one or other of these men." [6] They expounded the challenging principles of democracy and undermined the claims of special privilege. They showed how these democratic principles could be translated into the details of action.

Among the moderns, William James shares the spotlight with Dewey. The greatness of James lies in the width and depth of his personal experience, and in his willingness to pay attention even to the "lunatic fringe" experiences of others. His great personal charm attracted many eager minds. His example of unceasing search for new knowledge, his kindly iconoclasm, his intellectual honesty, make him an outstanding example of "civilization at work" in the twentieth century.

Great ideas and great men are mutually dependent. Without great men great ideas will not be formulated, made available to others, and translated into action. But, conversely, unless a man is vitalized by the lure of a great idea, he will be blind to the complexity, richness, and adventure of life. Whitehead notes that all great men do not necessarily formulate entirely *new* ideas. In particular, some of our great literary men merely deal with the familiar. But they make it new in the sense that new insight is now obtained, new vitality provided.

It must be remembered, further, that greatness is found not only on the intellectual level. Courage and hope are frequently essential ingredients in the lives of great men. Indeed, moral and spiritual greatness can be attained even without impressive intellectual gifts. Whitehead refers to the clergy of East Kent (of the nineteenth century) who, in their kindly commonsense fashion, ministered to the moral and spiritual needs of their parishioners. They gave practical advice concerning personal problems. They ensured that children were educated. In a relatively simple way, they exemplified and encouraged devotion to truth and beauty. In their quiet way they adventured, and achieved peace. Their lives, on a small scale, were works of art. They were great in the sense that their moral and spiritual soundness exemplified the "glory of the commonplace."

In discussing the efficacy of men of intellectual, or moral and spiritual power, we must not forget the "men of iron." There is no denying the impact of military leaders on the lives of men. Alexander, Caesar, Napoleon have altered the history of the world. But, in the last analysis, the leaders of the mind and spirit are stronger than those who make the body march. Their influence is stronger because most human beings resent the brutal impact of physical force, even when it is disguised or made palatable by skillful propaganda. On the other hand, most men are impressed by the lure of an excellent moral and spiritual life. In any case, Whitehead argues that the reliance on force is self-destructive. A person who employs this technique exclusively becomes opaque to those experiences which enrich and refresh life. There is a relapse into concentration on the obvious gratifications of sensory experience. The careers of Alexander, Mussolini, and Hitler illustrate Whitehead's theme, particularly when they are compared with Socrates and Jesus.

It is important, however, to regard great men in their proper perspective. The past lives in the present. Great intellectual leaders are, after all, "heirs of the ages." Their intellects have been nourished by their intellectual environments. Any great achievement is the culmination of a long sequence of development. Further, the time must be ripe. Men must be in a mood to listen, or be led. The preceding discussion of the final abolition of slavery is relevant here. This is not to deny the outstanding contributions of great men. It is, rather, a balanced evaluation of the total situation.

A great man's debt to the past is genuine. Yet, it should not be overemphasized to the neglect of the genius of the man himself. The message of a great thinker is couched in some recognized symbolism. It is made meaningful by reference to some specific context of life. Shakespeare wrote in English. The plots of his plays were set mostly in England and Italy. His message is, in a sense, universal; but its roots are in England of the early seventeenth century, and before. Nevertheless, the insights of a genius cannot be compressed within the limits of some specific vehicle. There is always an unexpressed halo of enlightening suggestion which points beyond to new worlds of experience. The techniques used by great men of action are likewise dated and redolent with local color. These factors, also, do not confine his spirit. When properly appreciated, these techniques are seen to be novel approximations to an ideal of social efficiency which has not yet been reached. The preceding discussion must be borne in mind. Otherwise one may misunderstand Whitehead's somewhat cryptic remark that "the problem is not how to produce great men, but how to produce great societies. The great society will put up the great men for the occasions." [7]

While he respects the great men of the past for their contributions to the present, Whitehead warns against uncritical respect for "ancestral voices." In some areas of human experience their insights are sound and merit careful consideration. With reference to other problems, the ancestral voices simply "don't know what they are talking about." This is no fault of theirs. Our world is vastly different, in some respects, from theirs. For example, we do well to listen to Aristotle when he discusses the basic principles of ethics and politics. However, some of his detailed suggestions concerning ethics and politics are worthless today. The same is true of much of his natural science.

Geography

In dealing with factors that influence human history Whitehead recognizes the significance of geography. Centers of population grow up where the soil is rich, water is available, and there are facilities for transportation. In particular, rivers and oceans are important factors in shaping human life.

This point is considered in detail with specific reference to England. The city of London rose to a position of prominence because at the mouth of the Thames there is a fine anchorage at Deal, on the English Channel. The channel is the gateway to the world. The treacherous tides and currents of its territorial waters saved England from invasion by the Spaniards. The ships of Spain were designed to sail the broad ocean. They were almost helpless within the narrow seas of the English Channel. The fire ships of England, the greater maneuverability of the English fleet provided the final touches to the Spanish defeat. Thus, English liberties were preserved and made available for future generations. Similarly, the North American continent has become the center of Western life today because of its location on the shores of the Atlantic Ocean and because of the ample resources of all sorts which can be found within its land mass.

Those who live by the shores of the English Channel are characterized by obstinacy and lonely thought. The rigors of the environment (washed by Arctic currents) produce a different type of person from that found in the warmer climate of the southwest coast. Here semitropical currents provide a more temperate environment. There is greater relaxation and friendliness among the people. Whitehead remarks in passing that it was the men of obstinacy and lonely thought who developed the ideas and institutions of free government on the shores of the channel (in England on one side, and in Holland on the other). This was the "land" from which the Pilgrim Fathers sailed to the "new world."

The south of England is rich in historical remains going

back to Roman times and earlier. The mere existence of such physical objects, rich in memories, exerted a profound influence on Whitehead in his formative years. He was typical of many Englishmen. A people, surrounded on every hand by the records of its history, unconsciously feels the hand of the past heavy upon it. In the case of England it is a reminder of past greatness and an inspiration to future achievement. Also, the beautiful countryside enhanced by works of art, cathedrals with their deep-toned bells, tends to keep ever before consciousness the existence of ultimate ideal values that can have a decisive place in the lives of men.

In dealing with geography, attention focuses on such phenomena as rain, floods, trees, coal, iron. These so-called "senseless" factors cannot be neglected. Ideas and men are not enough to bring about changes in human life. "The great transitions are due to a coincidence of forces derived from both sides of the world, its physical and its spiritual natures." [8] In discussing the inanimate objects of geography, Whitehead notes that these apparently non-rational factors—e.g., rainfall and trees—are actually elements which come within the *order* of nature. As such they are understandable and can be used for human purposes. In this "context," they are not "senseless." However, for practical purposes, they may be termed "senseless" since there is no obvious, internal, clear, conscious formulation of a definite purpose. There are, of course, other important senseless factors which must be taken into consideration. In the physical world there are, for example, steam and electricity; among men, barbarians.

Technological Developments

Whitehead is well aware of the importance of technological developments. Thus he states: "The life of man is founded on Technology, Science, Art and Religion." [9] As far as modern society is concerned, he suggests (in somewhat extreme fashion) that changes have occurred primarily because of steam, internal combustion engines, and machine tools used in factories. Such factors are more influential than all the political theories since the world began.

This same emphasis on the importance of technology is seen in his remarks that Mesopotamia was made possible by irrigation, and that the Roman Empire existed because of its technological equipment—roads, bridges, aqueducts, sewers, agriculture, merchant marine—and its army (the result of applied military science). One of the main causes which aided the decline and fall of slavery was the development of alternative sources of power such as coal, oil, steam, and electricity. Machines were invented which, making use of these new sources of energy, could perform the work formerly done by hundreds of slaves. The invention of printing facilitated the freeing of men's minds. This provided an instrument for social advance. New methods of transportation and communication opened up vast areas of land and made possible the enrichment of life for more men. For example, the invention of the method of oceanic navigation led to the discovery of America. Changes in transportation and communication have effected a drastic alteration in the pattern of life for modern men. People need no longer live beside the industries in which they work. Cultural activities may be enjoyed through the medium of radio, films, television regardless of where one lives. It is no longer necessary to be crowded into large groups in order to make possible the enjoyment of cultural pursuits.

It will be recalled that, in discussing the nature of civilization, Whitehead contends that civilized life is characterized by persuasion and that commerce is one factor promoting the practice of persuasion. For example, in most commercial contexts, a producer can not *force* a consumer to buy his wares. It is, of course, obvious that commerce (in the widest sense of the term, implying exchange of all types of goods, material and ideal) is essential to a vigorous civilization because commerce encourages adventure. When commerce lags there is a correlative decline in civilization. Yet, commerce is not an isolated phenomenon. It depends on many other factors. For example, in the past, commerce depended on Roman power and Roman roads, the improvement in the art of navigation, and the foundations of unity provided by the Christian Church with its set of common ideas and its support of a definite ethical code.

Whitehead recognizes that technology, since it is applied scientific knowledge, cannot flourish unless exact knowledge is available. This presupposes a system of laws of nature. Unless nature is dependable and understandable, no (relatively) exact knowledge is possible. It is suggested that speculative vision, formulating exploratory hypotheses which are tested in the crucible of experience, is a necessary condition for exact knowlledge and hence for technological developments. Indeed if, as Whitehead says, one of the great inventions of the modern world is the invention of the method of invention, then the controlled imagination of speculative reason is obviously a necessary factor. However, this indebtedness is not all one way. Unless there is a secure basis for life (involving an adequate technology), unless there is leisure to think, men cannot afford to engage in speculative thought. Further, he notes that the technologies of agriculture lead men to find general ideas in an attempt to understand the processes of nature. This is one of the first and basic stages in the development of civilization.

There are technological devices in realms other than the physical. Social techniques, expressed in institutions, cannot be overlooked. The systems of law, canon and civil (formulated by Justinian's lawyers), served as the basis of social life for centuries. These laws helped produce a society in which activities were regulated in an impersonal fashion. The patterns of government became well established. Restraints were thereby placed on the wielders of power. The Church is another example of the efficacy of social institutions in shaping the lives of men. Particularly during some parts of the Middle Ages, its influence permeated all phases of life. The importance of the Church as a factor in history has been noted previously, as well as implied in the references to the efficacy of great religious leaders, members of this institution. Further reference will be made to this topic in Chapter 3, on Whitehead's *philosophy of religion.*

Among the institutions which, on occasion, have served the cause of civilization well is the British Parliament. It translated into action the ideal of the freedom of every man. In two separate acts of legislation, involving two different administrations, it passed the laws which freed the slaves and voted the money to reimburse slave owners. This, of course, was only one factor in the situation. Another powerful agency at this time was the Methodist Church. Behind these two institutions was a long line of men, known and unknown, who felt the impact of a great ideal and did their part in bringing about its realization. Whitehead suggests that in the modern world universities are, or should be, the chief agencies in conserving and extending civilization. Indeed, he goes further and specifies universities in the north and central United States.

Perhaps the greatest technological achievement of man is symbolic expression. Symbols (words, gestures, designated objects, men) serve to unite societies into smooth-running, integrated groups. This function is performed most effectively when the symbol carries a strong emotional flavor and embodies a meaning which, while not clearly defined, conveys a value judgment concerning the importance of the institution or group it represents. For example, the flag or a national hero unites the people in emotionalized loyalty to their country which they feel is superior to any other. The flag brings to memory the nation's honored past. It implies that the future will be equally glorious. The meanings hovering around such a symbol are vague, but extremely powerful. There are some symbols that facilitate social activity for the opposite reason. They have no richness of meaning. They serve merely as stimuli that touch off a conditioned response; for example, a green light in a traffic situation.

Some symbols (i.e., words) have a clearly defined meaning that is much more complex than that of the conditioned response type, and yet not usually so emotional as symbols like the flag. Words are of value in aiding the march of reason through experience. The wisdom of the past is recorded. Plans for the future are formulated. Clarity of thought is facilitated. Communication of ideas, and hence social co-operation, is made possible. If a society has at its disposal an adequate set of symbols, with clear meanings, its members can think and act together. Each will know what the other means. The ideas they share bring unity of purpose. The ideas, having become clear by co-operative checking, will be effective guides to individuals in theoretical and practical activities. Thus, Whitehead states that civilization is the outcome of language, since freedom of thought is made possible by language. Incidentally, one indication of the advance of civilization is an increase in the complexity and clarity of its symbols.

Whitehead is very anxious to emphasize the point that *no one factor*, technological or otherwise, can be given complete credit for any social change. For instance, war is an institution or technique that produces a great shift in the patterns of life of millions of men and women. But other factors are also at work. The waves of dissatisfaction and disillusion which follow a war depend not only on the destruction and misery of war but also on industrial developments, enlightenment from increased education, scientific developments, new labor-saving inventions, and the demand for better living conditions for more people.

Economic Forces

Whitehead states that the fusion of ideal ends and economic processes makes the stuff of history. More specifically, he contends that decisive changes take place in human affairs when strong economic urges (the desire for food, clothing, and shelter) among the lower classes of society are linked with a remedial ideal formulated by some of the more fortunate, but sympathetic, members of the upper class. These economic urges provide at least some of the dynamic which the ideals direct into fruitful consequences. Further, of course, unless a man has attained at least a minimum satisfaction of his basic needs, he will be unable to formulate or implement high or effective ideas.

The apparently flippant remark that the Egyptians wanted bricks so they captured the Hebrews, is an oversimplification. However, it indicates Whitehead's recognition of the importance of economic needs in shaping national policy. Yet, in the last analysis, he regards an exclusive emphasis on the economic motive as an example of abstract mythology. There are many motives and causal factors that produce human behavior. For example, it is ridiculous to attempt to explain religious behavior entirely in economic terms without some reference to religious beliefs and emotions and the impact of religious institutions.

In general, he contends that economic activities (the provision of food, clothing, and shelter) are important up to a point, i.e., the adequate satisfaction of these needs. After that, however, economic activities become "the mere background for these activities which form the distinction between mankind and the animal world." [10]

The impact of the techniques of production and distribution, on all concerned, is clearly stated by Whitehead. He notes, for example, that our present capitalistic system in North America places grave restrictions on the activities of both labor and management. There is too much concentration on efficiency in producing goods. Moral, aesthetic, and spiritual values are disregarded. For many men, work is available only if the majority of their interests are surrendered. Many men find that expression of their special, or creative, abilities is impossible. The factory worker has to perform a routine task which he regards as drudgery. The employer also is caught in the tangled web of the requirements of his position in the industry which he manages. The rigors of competition make it difficult for him to cultivate any interests not directly related to the pressures of business. Industrial plants and transportation systems are, for the most part, designed by men who have no concern for beauty. Further, the present economic system does not give the majority of the people economic security. Job tenure is brief and uncertain.

Yet, on the credit side, it must be emphasized that commercial activities do, on occasion, support the development of civilized life. Enlightened men, in both labor and management, encourage new experiments (i.e., adventure) in production, distribution, and human relations. Some factories are beautiful. Peace also is experienced by at least a few fortunate members of modern economic society.

Evolutionary Philosophy of History

The evolutionary philosophy of history has received considerable support from concentration on the more ruthless aspects of business life. Whitehead's refusal to accept this as the *only* interpretation of economic activity is part of his general refutation of the evolutionary theory as it is usually formulated.

There is, of course, struggle in the universe. As a result of strife, many living organisms are eliminated. It is impossible to disregard this fact. However, this is not the whole story. There is also co-operation. It is evident on all levels of existence. Trees continue to flourish because certain insects kill organisms which would otherwise destroy the trees. In their turn, the trees constitute the environment which makes possible the existence of the insects. Within any animal species there is mutual support based not only on family relationship, but also on membership in a species. The behavior of members of a flock of birds, when danger approaches, is an example of a phenomenon common in nature—mutual aid.

A traditional doctrine of evolution stresses "passive" adjustment to the environment. It is true that some phases of the environment are (at least for the time being) fixed, and to them an organism must adjust itself or die. However, there are many phases of the environment which can be changed in accordance with the needs of organisms. Insects and birds modify the environment in order to find homes for themselves and to find, or provide, food. Human beings demonstrate these same principles on innumerable occasions.

In any case, the theory that maladjustment to the environment is the cause of the elimination of an organism, turns out to be so general that it is practically useless as an explanatory principle. It seems to be employed as a convenient formula, applicable to everything that happens. It is used to avoid the necessity of more detailed and thorough examination of the actual causes for the elimination of a particular organism. As Whitehead ironically remarks: The principle is like "the liturgical refrain of a litany, chanted over the fossils of vanished species." [11]

The theory that the fit survive, merits critical examination. Mere survival is not necessarily a criterion of excellence. A stone is capable of enduring for centuries. A man has a much shorter survival expectancy. Further, adjustment to the environment is not necessarily a condition for survival. On occasion the environment changes. Then the organism that is too closely adjusted will perish. Flexibility of adjustment, the possibility of novelty of behavior, is an essential element in survival. The heavily armored creatures of the past, confined to a restricted diet, perished when the climate changed. Men and insects have survived. Thus we return to the vital point. Mere survival, in any case, does not constitute the criterion of excellence. The higher forms of life have sometimes shown a very cavalier attitude towards the demands of mere "continued existence." Some men cultivate the civilized virtues of truth, beauty, art, adventure, peace—and survive. On the other hand, because of their devotion to civilization, they may sacrifice their lives for their friends. It is difficult to find, in the traditional evolutionary hypothesis, any real explanation as to how this can happen. Specifically, there is no explanation as to how development occurs if the basic principle is survival in a static environment. There is no challenge, or lure, to higher levels of achievement which involve risk of destruction.

Whitehead provides a refutation of the Malthusian version of "elimination by struggle" theory. He begins by admitting that in certain countries, China and India for example, the Malthusian law does apply. Here, apart from checks to child-bearing and survival, the population increases more rapidly (geometrical progression) than does food supply (arithmetical progression). The result is misery for most, comfort for a few. The conclusion seems to be that such a state of affairs is inescapable. Whitehead's criticism consists in pointing out that this theory simply does not apply in every part of the world. This "application" has not taken place in Europe because of the rapid expansion in commerce, technology, and the discovery of vast empty continents. More specifically, it is simply not true that density of population and misery are equated (vary directly). For example, in the sixteenth century, the Low Countries were heavily populated, but the standard of life was high. In Germany population was sparce, but misery was rampant. As in the case of all "too simple" theories, the Malthusian theory disregards some relevant facts. It assumes that checks will not work until population becomes excessive. It also assumes that changes in commerce, technology, and geographical expansion will not play any significant parts. Hence, the facts have made the theory untenable for a large part of the earth's surface.

Whitehead deplores the tendency, present in some evolutionary thinkers, to explain the later, and more complex, in terms of the earlier and less complex. Here again, as in the case of the economic motive, we have an abstract mythology, a neglect of some of the facts in the situation, an undue simplification of life.

In one sense of the term, Whitehead advocates a philosophy of evolution. He agrees that it is possible for an organism to develop. More specifically, he contends that men can develop the characteristics of civilization to a higher degree than at present. The spirit of adventure can give rise to the achievement of more truth, beauty, goodness, and peace, and also to the creation of more works of art.

God

The ultimate basis of Whitehead's rejection of traditional theories of evolution, and the foundation for his own positive position, is found in his theory of God. *The efficacy of God in the process of history,* and the related questions of purpose, order, and value in the universe, will be discussed in the next chapter, dealing with Whitehead's *philosophy of religion.*

THE GOLDEN AGE—DOOM

The Golden Age

Reflective men, from time to time, have toyed with the tantalizing question of the "golden age." Was it in the past, or will it be in the future? (At least in this era of the twentieth century, few men will claim it is now.) Whitehead seems to be of two minds in this matter. Writing *Science and the Modern World* (1925), he envisages a possible golden age in the future. Increasing intellectual skills, plus great material and technological resources, makes possible vast social improvement. "If mankind can rise to the occasion, there lies in front a golden age of beneficent creativeness." [12] The same approach is implicit in *Adventures of Ideas* (1933). However, in *Modes of Thought* (1938) the view is *apparently* different. He states that in the 1200 years preceding and including the beginning of Christianity, "human genius reached its culmination." [13] The main concepts of all major areas of human experience were formulated: aesthetic, moral, religious, political, deductive mathematics, even "observational science." These ideas not only were formulated; they were focused on the specific problems of human existence. Also, fundamental techniques were brought to a high degree of excellence—road-building, navigation, the use of metals. This was the age of Confucius, Virgil, Jesus, the Gospel of John, the Roman Empire. Any progress in theoretical knowledge, or in practical techniques, has been "along the path laid down by the activities of that golden age." [14]

On closer examination, however, it becomes evident that these two *apparently* different approaches are not as diverse as they first seem. In the passage in *Modes of Thought* Whitehead is *not* saying that there can be no progress beyond the achievements of the past. What he does say is that *progress has been along the lines laid down by a golden age* occurring in the past. In the few articles which he wrote after the publication of *Modes of Thought,* he expresses hope for the future. This is the dominant characteristic of his system of thought.[15]

Doom

The widely prevalent doctrine of the "doom of civilization" is subjected to careful evaluation by Whitehead. If a person approaches the universe in terms of some phase of physical science he may be convinced that, as a result of an inevitable decline (more accurately, "transformation") in energy, the world is headed for ultimate destruction. A more comprehensive survey will reveal tendencies opposing this apparent general relapse or collapse. In Whitehead's judgment, these gloomy scientific views of the universe are woefully inaccurate. They are partial, and hence neglect other and more important factors.

He is convinced that there is a strong creative process at work. Further, in human experience we find reason and speculative imagination, the enjoyment of beauty, the continuing development toward civilization. He admits that in the process of creative development there is transition, loss, and decay; but there is also the replacement of inferior by superior. Thus, there is no cause for gloom. If new harmonies of fresh experience are to be achieved, the old and drab must be replaced by the new and vivid.

There are those who shake their heads, long for the good old days. They point to the decline in faith, gross materiality, the worship and practice of brute force, an unbalanced birth rate (the inferior overbreeding, the superior not reproducing themselves), the loss of aesthetic appreciation. To all these "prophets of doom" Whitehead replies that complaints about such evils are as old as the human race, and yet man has progressed. Somewhat impishly, he suggests that the present pessimism, among members of the middle class, about the state of human society may be the result of an identification of their own security with civilization. There is likely to be less security and stability than in the past. Whitehead does not regard this as necessarily an evil.

In short, a "civilization" is capable of revival. This happened in Europe at the end of the Middle Ages, during the Reformation, during the later part of the eighteenth century. Placed in a sufficiently broad perspective, the prophets of doom lose much of their awesome appeal and claim on public attention. It is true that they perform an important service in pointing to evils which need to be corrected. But if their theme of doom produces social paralysis, then they are expendable. In the last analysis, whatever the fate of civilization may be, Whitehead does not regard a civilization (or a culture) as an entity like a biological organism which, having come into existence, *must* inevitably perish.

Incidentally, he calls attention to a social phenomenon which is symptomatic of decline. It is satire. As Rome declined, Lucian plied his art. As France and Britain wandered toward the age of revolution (one at home, the other on the North

American continent), Voltaire and Gibbon reflected the spirit of the age. After World War I came Lytton Strachey and Sinclair Lewis.[16]

SUMMARY

In summary, Whitehead states that there are four factors which decisively govern the fate of social groups: (1) "apart from some transcendent aim the civilized life either wallows in pleasure or relapses"; (2) "the iron compulsion of nature that the bodily necessities of food, clothing, and shelter be provided"; (3) "the compulsory dominion of men over men"; (4) persuasion.[17]

Chapter 3 RELIGION

There can be no doubt of the importance which Whitehead assigns to religion, as an ingredient in civilized life. He states that apart from religious vision, "human life is a flash of occasional enjoyments lighting up a mass of pain and misery, a bagatelle of transient experience."[1]

DEFINITIONS OF RELIGION

Whitehead offers several definitions of religion which are statements of what he thinks religion *should be*. He is willing to admit that many religions fall far short of the ideal religion set forth in these definitions. According to Whitehead, religion (ideally) is "the art and theory of the internal life of man, so far as it depends on the man himself, and on what is permanent in the nature of things."[2] As the result of these beliefs and the resultant actions there is a perfection of the inner life of the devotee.

In attempting to emphasize the deficiencies of a common type of (inferior) religion, Whitehead offers his most famous definition: "Religion is what the individual does with his own solitariness."[3] By this statement he is expressing his conviction that religion, at its best, is *not essentially* a social concern—mass behavior taking place within the confines of a distinctive building, making use of approved impedimenta such as books and forms of service. These factors are of great importance in some religions, but they should not be regarded as of primary importance. The truly religious man is he who faces the mysteries of life "alone with God" and achieves, or receives, salvation without *dependence* on other men or man-made instruments. As Whitehead expresses it: "If you are never solitary, you are never religious."[4] We are reminded that the great religious leaders experienced their supreme moments of exaltation and insight

46

when alone: Mahomet in the desert, Buddha secluded beneath the branches of his tree, Job deserted by family and friends, Jesus in the wilderness or on his cross.

Most assuredly, Whitehead is *not* suggesting that religion requires a man to cut himself off from his fellowmen and live like a hermit in a cave or a bramble bush. There can be no such thing as absolute solitariness. We depend on our environment. One of his definitions of religion is that "religion is world-loyalty" [5] and world consciousness. After all, the "great solitary ones" came back to the world of men. They engaged in acts of public worship. Jesus preached to crowds. He participated in marriage feasts. So did Mahomet and Buddha. However, the basic fact remains: if a person is never solitary, he can never have the highest forms of religious experience.

Whitehead states that religion is characterized by a concern for value, "the value of an individual for itself . . . the value of the . . . individuals . . . for each other." [6] There is recognition of the fact that the world in general contains elements of value which are essential to the existence of each of these individuals. No individual can achieve its fullest possible development until it adjusts its claims to those of the other individuals in the universe. This is an expression of Whitehead's basic conviction that the individual's experience is the focal point for the achievement of value.

In contrasting solitary (rational) religion with communal (social) religion, Whitehead provides a useful analysis of the latter (inferior) type. Here the emphasis is on *ritual* and its accompanying *emotion*. Beliefs (*myths*) are formulated to explain and justify these rituals and emotions.

In passing, Whitehead makes the interesting comment that the semicivilized level of communal religion meets the pragmatic test. Its devotees are "satisfied" with these rituals, emotions, and supporting myths. It works for them. Hence, truth is claimed for this type of religion. But in communal religion there is lacking the rational, critical insight which comes from solitary meditation. There is a narrowness and lack of depth in an essentially social religion. Not only is the individual lost in the excitement of mob action and emotion; further, the outcome of such a religious life *may* be evil. For example, there have been wars of national expansion with the halo of religion superimposed. The supreme being is regarded as restricted in his interests to the welfare of a small group of worshipers. He is regarded as emotional and ritualistic in his procedures.[7] He must be bargained with, his favors bought. He likes praise and requires it of his worshipers.

On the other hand, those who have achieved the highest level of religion, based on solitary communion, realizes that God is not the God of one nation or class, that God is not a petulant tyrant. Rather, the way to worship God is to live a life excellent within the limits of human ability. In communal religion, God is an enemy to be conciliated. In rational, individualized religion, God is a companion to be imitated. In the very earliest stages of religion, God is a mysterious unknown force—a void. Thus we have Whitehead's formula that in religion there is transition from God the void to God the enemy to God the companion.

In this discussion of religion, four factors or aspects of religion have been under consideration. First, there is *rational religion* with its emphasis on individuality, solitariness, the pursuit of high values, the fruitful blending of reason and emotion. This, in Whitehead's judgment, is religion at its best. There are other elements which are most prominent in religions of a more social, external, inferior type. These other factors are irrational *emotion, ritual,* and *belief* (with accompanying myths). Whitehead is prepared to admit that all four factors may well be present in any particular religion, ancient or modern, excellent or inferior. Yet, in general, and for practical purposes, one may say that as religion develops it passes through four stages involving vigorous emphasis on each of these factors in turn. In the most primitive stage (first in time), ritual is most prominent, and the other factors, particularly reason, are very much in the background. Then emotion becomes most prominent; next, beliefs; and finally, rational religion, the most excellent type.

In the final stage, as has been noted, the individual escapes from the *inhibitions* of his social environment and penetrates to the depths of life, relying on his own intuitions—valid immediate experience, moral and spiritual. This break with the "customary" frequently is both mental and physical. For example, Abraham traveled; the Jews were uprooted and taken to Babylon; Paul voyaged far; Augustine and Aquinas were incessant travelers. However, these spatial travels were not the decisive factors in their lives. Whitehead does not contend that a man can escape entirely from the influence of his environment or that he should disregard the experiences of other men. He is continually stressing the necessity of appreciating the historic roots of our religious tradition. Yet, in the last analysis, the truly religious man is "alone" in his creative use of the past and continuing insights.

Whitehead offers the prophet Hosea (incidentally, in the physical sense, he "stayed at home") as an example of the emergence of rational religion. This great man broke with his ecclesiastical tradition and stressed moral excellence rather than "proper" ritualistic observances. "I desire mercy and not sacrifice; and the knowledge of God rather than burnt offerings." Thus Hosea focuses attention on two main aspects of individualized, rational religion: (a) the ethical element, (b) the attempt to understand the universe in religious terms.

In stressing the development of the idea of God from void to enemy to companion, Whitehead is well aware of the fact that in the contemporary world all three "approaches" are illustrated. Further, he points out that once the level of rational religion has been reached, decay may set in. That is, the rational religion may degenerate into a social type of religion.

Whitehead states briefly the relations between (communal) religion on the one hand, and play and magic on the other. In so far as ritual involves the use of energy not required for the preservation of the body, there is kinship with play. The difference between play and religion, according to Whitehead, is in the type, or quality, of emotion linked with the ritual. If a man bows before an object with the emotion of reverence, this is religion. If one bows with the motion of joy, that is play. The distinction between religion and magic is based on the nature of the object involved. Men seek blessings and try to avoid disasters. Certain ritualistic procedures take place. If the source of the "response" is regarded as a person, religion is present. If the source is non-personal, this is magic.

This chapter begins with laudatory comments concerning religion. This is a recurrent theme. For example: "Religion can be, and has been, the main instrument for progress" [8] (in civilization). Yet, there is another side to the coin. Whitehead delineates, with relentless clarity, the shortcomings of religion. There have been human sacrifices, wild orgies, abject superstition, bigotry, brutal torture—all these and more of the same—in the name of religion: "A melancholy record of the horrors which can attend religion." [9] Thus Whitehead, with characteristic sanity and balance of judgment, is not saying that religion is completely good, or that religion is completely bad. Rather his point is that religion has been and can be good, has been and can be bad. When all the evidence is considered, however, he reaches the conclusion that religion at its best "is the one element in human experience which persistently shows an upward trend. . . . The fact of the religious vision, and its history of persistent expansion, is our one ground for optimism." [10]

THE DEVELOPMENT OF CHRISTIANITY

General Sketch

One of the main phases of Whitehead's discussion of religion is his penetrating outline of the development of Christianity. He shows the many strands of thought and action which have constituted it. Interspaced with the outline of its development is a recurring series of evaluations, delineating the strengths and weaknesses of traditional Christianity.

Stated in the most simple terms: the development of Christianity involved a few protesting prophets, irritating and inspiring the Jews, then a solitary man, with twelve feeble disciples, suffering rejection and death. There followed a man (Paul) who never knew "the master" in the flesh. In spreading the message of Jesus, he deleted some elements and added others. However, the Gospels survived as a corrective. This is the story of the crucial beginnings of Christianity. But, of course, this is too simple and restricted in scope and depth.

More specifically, Christianity is the result of a series of historic occurrences starting with the Hebrew prophets and culminating in the synthesizing work of Augustine. In this period of 1200 years, the focal points of Christianity were Galilee, Jerusalem, Athens, Antioch, Ephesus, Egypt, Rome, Constantinople, Africa. From this rich storehouse, men living in other centers of life drew their characteristic doctrines. Here is the heritage of the Papal Church, the Eastern Church, Wycliffe, Huss, Luther, Cranmer, Jonathan Edwards, John Wesley, Ignatius Loyola, George Fox. In Whitehead's opinion, they added nothing essentially new.

Turning from "men" and "places," Whitehead provides a developmental sketch of Christianity dealing with "ideas" and "attitudes." He notes three phases. First, there is Plato's great insight that "the divine element in the world is to be conceived as a persuasive agency and not as a coercive agency." [11] The approach is intellectual, but there is an underlying foundation of moral seriousness. Second, the life of Jesus demonstrates the validity of Plato's principle. Here the emphasis is on moral dynamic, the fineness of supreme excellence of life, and simple directness of thought. Third, the theologians of Alexandria and Antioch provided a metaphysical systematization of the preceding two phases. Once again the emphasis is primarily, indeed almost excessively, intellectual. Having provided this general analysis, Whitehead proceeds to a more specific discussion of the various periods and men who chiefly have contributed to the development of Christian religion.

Hebrew Prophets

Reference already has been made to Job and Hosea as solitary men illustrating the pattern of rational religion with its criticism of the inhibiting tendencies of communal religion. Such men were the religious ancestors of the founder of Christianity, Jesus of Nazareth. These men demanded freedom of expression for moral insights. They attributed to

Jehovah the moral qualities which they themselves valued. They risked their lives for their doctrine. But, unfortunately, they who demanded freedom of expression for themselves did not escape a certain ruthless intolerance with reference to others. Freedom and tolerance were not attributed to Jehovah by some of his prophets. There was a further unfortunate element in Hebrew thought concerning God. He was regarded as a person who transcends the world he has made and controls. Because he transcends the world, very little can be known about him. Because he is different, familiar terms lose their meaning when applied to him. This concept of God is useful in the sense that he can be referred to as the explanation of anything that cannot otherwise be explained.

Jesus

The exalted stature, and supreme efficacy in the realm of religion, of Jesus of Nazareth is clearly implied in the reverent words in which Whitehead refers to "the lowly man, homeless and self-forgetful, with his message of peace, love, and sympathy: the suffering, the agony, the tender words as life ebbed, the final despair: and the whole with the authority of supreme victory." [12] "The life of Christ is not an exhibition of over-ruling power. Its glory is for those who can discern it, and not for the world. Its power lies in its absence of force. It has the decisiveness of a supreme ideal, and that is why the history of the world divides at this point of time." [13]

The message of Jesus, when expressed in words, is direct and simple, even pictorial in its clarity. There is no complicated process of reasoning; rather, fundamental facts and values are stated with inescapable clarity so that even the "ignorant" can understand. This effective expression of fundamentals is one of the great heritages of Jesus.

In accordance with his rejection of *barbaric* elements in his religious tradition, Jesus refers to God as father rather than as king of kings. The transcendence of the Semitic God is overcome by the doctrine that "the kingdom of heaven is within you," thus implying the presence of God within the hearts of men.[14]

Early Christianity

The Gospels preserve for us one the greatest achievements of the human spirit, the impracticable interim ethic of early Christianity. It is impracticable in the sense that if these principles were really practiced one would not long survive. It is interim in the sense that these teachings were formulated by people who confidently expected the end of the familiar world, and hence were inclined to dream dreams and formulate lofty ideals. There was another causal factor. The early Christians were, for the most part, peasants of Galilee. They lived a simple, kindly life, protected by the vast machinery and power of the Roman government. They did not have to face complex political problems. They were God-fearing, generous, sympathetic. In such a situation it was almost plausible to recommend forgiveness "seventy times seven." Thus, among the simple peasants of Galilee, the Christian emphasis on high moral standards was clearly expressed.

These impractical ideas should not be the object of derision just because there seems little likelihood of their realization in the immediate future. It is of the essence of ideals that they should exceed one's grasp. Nor should the so-called simplicity of these men of Galilee be overemphasized. They were well versed in the historical and religious lore of their people. Also, great trade routes, linking east and west, passed nearby. Further, many of them possessed keen intellects. The inner meaning of Hebrew culture could be discerned more readily among the quiet hills of Galilee than in the sophisticated and degenerate environment of Jerusalem.

During the early years of Christianity, the criticisms of the transcendent Hebrew God continued. The "logos" doctrine, of the Gospel of John, shattered the unity of the Semitic God. The presence of the "logos" in the world is obviously a denial of God's total transcendence. Soon, however, there occurred what, in Whitehead's opinion, is one of the great calamities in human history. The emphasis on the tender and persuasive elements in the divine nature, as stressed by Jesus, was pushed into the background of Christian thought. This was replaced by the barbaric emphasis on compulsive power, found in some phases of the earlier Hebrew religion. Here the influence of Paul was decisive.[15] "God is love" was replaced by such statements as these: "In flaming fire taking vengeance on them that know not God. Who shall be punished with everlasting destruction from the presence of the Lord, and from the glory of his power" (II Thes. 1:8, 9). Thus, "the Church gave unto God the attributes which belonged exclusively to Caesar."[16]

Christianity travelled from the back country of Galilee into the complex life of the Greco-Roman world. Inevitably, it was modified by the forces at work in this new environment. During this period the influence of *Platonic thought* was very important. Implicit in Platonism was an "other worldliness" which issued in emphasis on mystical experiences and withdrawal from the world. This attitude was fully developed in early Christianity. If the world was soon to come to an end, why bother with it? Later, when the world seemed more enduring than at first assumed, the attitude was "The world is not our home, Heaven is. Let us leave the world behind and concentrate on Heaven." The mystic tradition, offering an immediate approach to God through the medium of a program of training which could be mastered by a devotee, had vast appeal. The mystic "way," practiced by Paul, Augustine, and a host of others down to modern times, is an important factor in the development of Christianity.

Whitehead contends that, despite the excellence of Plato's emphasis on the persuasive elements in the divine nature, and his stress on eternal ideals, his influence on early Christianity was, in general, unfortunate. Plato believed that God was not directly present in the world. The world, at best, was only an imitation of eternal elements present to God. Between God and the world were intermediaries. This view, to the Christian theologians at Alexandria, was heresy. They believed that God was present in, indeed *was*, Jesus the man who lived in Galilee and died near Jerusalem. They, further, claimed the direct presence of God, as Holy Spirit, down to the present. However, in a sense, the influence of Plato remained. Having contended that God is immanent, the theologians proceed to state that he could not be thought of in terms applicable to data in the temporal world. Thus the Platonic doctrine, of a perfect world over against an imperfect one, reappeared. God was regarded as absolute, omnipotent, omniscient, the source of all being, independent of all his creations. His moral characteristics were different from the moral characteristics of men. God is a Being, high and lifted up, like an Egyptian or Babylonian king supreme over a servile population. This issued in the Augustinian notion of a transcendent God bestowing his predestined grace on an undeserving people.

Whitehead is convinced that the Hellenistic civilization of Alexandria was a sad decline from that of Athens. The men of Alexandria—Greeks, Egyptians, Semites—were men of restricted vision, though proficient technicians in the realm of ideas. They strove for accuracy and classification within strict limits. In the opinion of these men, the chief sin of Satan was his curiosity. He tried to understand God. These men conventionalized and restricted religious thought. They tended to kill the spirit of religion. Yet, they did "save" some of the heritage of the past, since they preserved its intellectual monuments. This theological system was accepted by West European barbarians when, in due time, they turned toward civilization. Living at the end of this period, Augustine performed a very great service for Christianity and the civilization that sprang from it. He provided accurate definitions of important topics, just before the barbarians came. Thus he saved Christianity from the danger of degenerating into an irrational, emotionalized superstition. Like the men of Alexandria, he may have conventionalized learning, but at least he saved it.

Medieval Christianity

As Christianity proceeded to the end of the medieval period, another great Greek made his contribution to the now venerable religion. Through the medium of men like Aquinas, Aristotle— with his sweeping speculative system buttressed by his appeal to facts, his neat classifications and rigorous system of presentation—provided "the physical background for the Christian scheme of salvation." [17] Unfortunately, the high regard for

Aristotle on the part of many thirteenth-century thinkers tended to produce a lack of critical insight. Aristotle did not fully appreciate the importance of mathematics as emphasized by Plato. His stress on the classification of qualities illustrates this.

A religion that disregards essential factors in the universe cannot serve a man with complete efficacy. A man's search for the highest form of life in the universe will fail if he is prevented from understanding it by the inadequacies of his guiding philosophy. Yet, no one can deny that the scholastics had great ability in synthesizing thought. Like the theologians of Alexandria, they clarified and organized a vast store of traditional ideas and linked them with a new wealth of information recently made available.

The medieval proofs for the existence of the supreme being are, in Whitehead's judgment, inadequate for two reasons. The ontological proof is too flimsy since it moves from concept to existence. The causal and the teleological proofs are inadequate because they argue from facts, in *this* world, to reputed facts in *another* world. You can prove the existence of an immanent God from observations of the world. You cannot prove the existence of a transcendent God.

Aristotle emphasized the importance of the "unmoved mover" and called it God, a being completely perfect and yet utterly unconcerned with the affairs of men. This view of God was combined with the theory that God is the ultimate and only reality. From these sources the theologians of the Middle Ages summarized, developed, and stated with impressive clarity, a very influential view of God which had been in process of development for centuries. God was regarded as a transcendent creator, first in every respect, who created the universe without any assistance and controls it absolutely. Here, then, was a view of God as "the ultimate metaphysical principle." This, however, was not the only strand in Christian theology of this period. Present also, and likewise clearly summarized, were two other major emphases: God as imperial ruler and God as ruthless moralist. Both of these reflect phases of thought which already have been noted.

The monasteries of the Middle Ages made their contribution

to the development of Christianity. At their best they demonstrated the possibility of an effective social organization devoid of reliance on physical force. Whitehead mentions the Cluny foundation. He also shows enthusiasm 'for the Benedictines.[18] Here the Middle Ages demonstrated a fruitful fusion of spiritual exaltation and practical vigor in dealing with the problems of food, shelter, and the understanding of nature.

Protestantism

Whitehead's comments concerning Christianity from the Middle Ages to the end of the eighteenth century have to do chiefly with Protestant religion in general and with the impact of modern science in particular. (Certain similarities between Roman Catholicism and Protestantism are mentioned.) As in the case of his treatment of other periods, there is no detailed systematic presentation. Rather, what is expressed is a series of insights. The Reformation is set in the context of world history. It is thus seen as a "domestic affair of the European races," not a turning point in the history of the world. Even the Eastern Church regarded it as unworthy of particular concern. Yet, in focusing attention on the destiny of the individual soul, the Reformation was a great step forward in the development of rational religion. Here is the ideal of solitariness. Further, because men were interested in individuals, slavery became increasingly impossible.

In later days, Methodism, by concentrating on saving the souls of individuals, became one of the great agencies of reform in eighteenth-century England. It provided the emotional dynamic necessary to translate current noble ideals into effective action. Whitehead, in the midst of his appreciation of the practical efficacy of Methodism, remarks that it was "singularly devoid of new ideas." [19] As such, it was in striking contrast to other important movements in Christianity whose leaders were "intellectuals"; for example, the Hellenistic theologians, Augustine, Aquinas, Luther, and Calvin.

Protestant theology, in some aspects, was no improvement over Catholic theology. Whitehead points out that Protestant Calvinism and Catholic Jansenism both regarded man as a helpless element in the universe. Divine power is irresistible. There is striking similarity between these religious views of human efficacy and that provided by eighteenth-century science. For practical purposes, there is little difference between the irresistible mechanism of nature and the irresistible power of God. In either case, man is helpless. This kinship between the religious and the scientific points of view is not surprising when it is recalled that God imposes the laws of nature (according to the Newtonian view which was authoritative for several centuries).

Whitehead is well aware of the defects of the Newtonian world view. According to it, matter and values are set in different realms. There is no essential relation between them. Values are localized in the private experiences of men. Matter exists publicly, valueless and lifeless. This view strongly influenced Protestantism. In Whitehead's opinion it accounts, in part, for the lack of interest in external beauty which characterizes Protestant Christianity. With customary penetrating irony, Whitehead remarks that the intellectual austerity of science influenced religion. It is reflected in the austerity of places of worship. In the eighteenth century those who regarded God as "first cause" worshiped in whitewashed churches. When Whitehead thinks of an example of the supreme embodiment of beauty his mind recalls the cathedral at Chartres, or Canterbury, or the little Saxon-Roman church at Minster (Kent, England)—not a whitewashed chapel. Intellect is very important in religion, but man is also a creature of emotion as well. The solitary man thinks deep thoughts, but he *feels* profoundly as well. As the great mystics have demonstrated, there are insights which cannot be intellectualized by the finite mind of man.

ASPECTS OF CHRISTIANITY

The Bible

Whitehead regards the Bible as the record of the speculative thoughts, and the moral and spiritual attainments of gifted men. The record is fragmentary. It was written, for the most part, by

men whose mentality was different from those whom they were
describing and interpreting. After all, the educated mind of
Paul was very different from the "picture-thinking" mentality
of the Galilean peasants who were the first followers of Jesus.
When he was converted, Paul retired to Arabia and adjusted
himself to this great experience. He did not at once proceed
to consult with those who knew Jesus in the days of his flesh.
In a somewhat exaggerated reference to the difficulties involved,
Whitehead suggests that in interpreting the Bible, one is in the
same position as a person who tries to understand the histories
of Denmark and Scotland by reading *Hamlet* and *Macbeth*.
Further, in the Bible there are conflicting reports of the same
event; there are passages of doubtful authenticity; there is the
final great difficulty of translation from one language to another.
All this makes it necessary to approach the Bible with caution
as well as with deep appreciation of the record it provides of
basic moral and spiritual insights.

Whitehead's approach to the Bible is further clarified by
noting his comments on some of its contents. In the books of
Proverbs and Ecclesiastes is found a reflective, witty, detached,
"homely," middle-class wisdom. This serves to add "balance"
in the midst of speculative flights and emotional intensity. There
is, for example (Eccles. 9:11): "The race is not to the swift, nor
the battle to the strong, neither yet bread to the wise, nor yet
riches to men of understanding, nor yet favor to men of skill;
but time and chance happeneth to them all." When Whitehead
turns to the Revelation of St. John, his attitude changes. The
Revelation is an interesting historic document; but as a source of
higher religious principles it is shocking. He suggests that it
might well have been replaced by Pericles' "funeral oration"
to the citizens of Athens, as reported by Thucydides. The Bib-
lical emphasis on obvious physical force has no place in a genuinely rational and spiritual religion. Thus, Whitehead objects to
the glorification of power found in some of the more exuberant of
the Psalms; for example, "The Lord of Hosts, He is the King of
Glory" (Ps. 24).

The Bible is a record of the religious thought and experiences of some of the men who contributed to the development

of Christianity. It deals with Hebrew prophets, Jesus of Nazareth, Paul, and the origin of new churches. It is a very valuable
document, but it must be used with discretion. Most assuredly,
the worship of the Bible should not replace some other form
of idolatry.

Dogma

The place of dogmas in religion is dealt with by Whitehead
in his usual balanced fashion. By dogma is meant a precise
general statement. There is no question as to the need of
dogmas. They control and guide the impulses of men in religion
as in all other areas of life. But a religion that derives its inspiration from its dogmas is committing suicide. The true basis
of religion is (valid) immediate experience.

The dangers in dogmas are well known. They may be accepted dogmatically, i.e., uncritically. A dogma is, at best, only
part of the truth. Concentration on one dogma, or even on a
group of dogmas, will blind the devotee to other important
factors in the universe. Further, satisfaction with one's first set
of dogmas neglects the fact of development in religious experience. A creed or dogma is an instrument to be used. It is like
a vehicle in which one can travel in safety. But in the interests
of a normal life, it is necessary, in due time, to leave the vehicle
behind. It should not be a permanent habitation. In stressing
the instrumentality of dogmas and creeds Whitehead notes that
they are frequently lethal weapons used to dispose of enemies.
"Wherever there is a creed, there is a heretic around the corner
or in his grave." [20] Like any instrument, a dogma must be used
frequently; otherwise it is useless junk inhibiting efficient action.

This discussion of the dangers of dogmas is directly relevant
to the problem of religious education. Whitehead's comments
are brief and general. His position is expressed thus: "Whatever
be the right way to formulate religious truths, it is death to
religion to insist on a premature stage of precision." [21] In other
words, if religious education is to be effective, the natural
rhythm of education must be taken seriously. Religious truths
must be presented in such a fashion that they are vital, relevant

to the basic interests of the student. Precision is this area of knowledge must be lightened by the lure of the significant rather than darkened by the pressure of meaningless compulsion. (See the general discussion of *education*, in Chapter 5.)

Dogmas are an attempt to state some general idea precisely. This fact focuses attention on one of the great difficulties involved. Words are woefully inadequate instruments for the expression of general ideas. The words we have available are those which refer to common occurrences that attract our attention to objects which are immediately useful. We simply do not have completely adequate verbal equipment to deal with general ideas or particular facts which fall outside the frequent, striking, or useful. The greatest moral and spiritual experiences are, unfortunately, very rare. Hence an adequate vocabulary for their expression has not been developed. An excessive devotion, therefore, to the verbal formulation of a dogma or creed is simply naive. In any case, even familiar words change their meaning. The word "father," within the context of Roman society, has a much different meaning from the same term in the context of modern American society. These difficulties in the use of words haunt the first steps of any attempt at religious communication.

CHRISTIANITY AND BUDDHISM

While Whitehead's main discussion of religion focuses on Christianity, his recognition of the impact of other religions on Christianity is evident. In general, he believes it is very important to compare various forms of religious experience. Each can learn from the others. When each understands the other, it is possible that hatred based on suspicion can be replaced by love arising from appreciation (if not agreement). Whitehead asks a penetrating question: "Must 'religion' always remain as a synonym for 'hatred'?" [22]

His attitude toward religions other than Christianity is illustrated by his discussion of Buddhism. He suggests that the decay of practical efficacy in both Christianity and Buddhism, in the modern world, is partly due to the fact that they have practiced solitary exclusiveness because of "self-sufficient pedantry of learning and the confidence of ignorant zealots." [23]

Each religion begins at some inspired moment in history. The life of Buddha and the life of Christ are striking examples. There are similarities between the two religions. Both have a personal Saviour; both teach that the souls of the blessed return to God. However, there are crucial differences. As Whitehead expresses it, Jesus gave his life, Buddha gave his doctrine. More specifically, Buddhism starts with a theory about the universe and man's place in it. Christianity starts with a divine man, and is still in the process of developing an explanatory, speculative theory. Basically, the patterns of life are different. Buddhism is passive; Christianity is active. Buddhism regards evil as something inescapable in human existence, and recommends the blotting out of personal identity. Jesus, on the other hand, preached and practiced the theory that individuals are of supreme worth. Further, he tried to show how evil can be overcome by good.

MODERN CHRISTIANITY
(From the Eighteenth Century to the Present)

Whitehead's reaction to modern Christianity is a mixture of strong denunciation and vigorous hope. Few men have equaled the vitrolic pungency of his remark that "Religion is tending to degenerate into a decent formula wherewith to embellish a comfortable life." [24] Yet, on the other hand, he sees the beginning of a "new reformation" led by a few members of the Protestant clergy.

Deficiencies

Whitehead sketches the deficiencies of modern Christianity in some detail. For several centuries it has been on the defensive, *a weak defensive,* unprepared for the new developments in human knowledge in general, and in natural science in particular. It has offered violent criticisms of new ideas in astronomy and biology because they were not in accordance with a discredited science "preserved" with a halo of ecclesiastical respectability. When the new scientific ideas become firmly established, then the leaders of Christianity execute a face-saving maneuver, reinterpret the new scientific facts, and point to them as approved revelations of divine truth. For example, in traditional theology, heaven and hell were definitely located in space. It took Christianity a long time to accept an expanded universe in which the earth was removed from its place of importance. The battle over the theory of evolution has scarcely yet died down in the uneasy truce: "This is how God works."

Another source of weakness is that modern Christianity relies on *ineffective motives* in presenting the claims and values of this type of religion. In many instances the appeal is to fear. "Be good or God will punish you." The portrayal of God as a wrathy tyrant, burning sinners in everlasting fire, has little appeal to modern man. Such a deity commands no respect or genuine devotion.

Some so-called "liberal theologians" who criticize the crude motivational techniques of the "rank conservative" are not much better in the long run.[25] Christianity is propagandized in terms of "social orderliness," "the pleasant life," or some such superficial appeal. Both extreme liberals and extreme conservatives forget the insights of the founder of Christianity. Jesus of Nazareth could be fierce when necessary. He most certainly was a happy social being on occasion. But, he taught unmistakably that the basic religious motive is the persuasive force of high ideals, moral and spiritual, love, and the lure of an intimate relationship with the supreme being. This relationship could be stated best in terms of father and son, not of a servile wretch cowering before a spiteful despot or membership in a service club.

A third source of weakness lies in the fact that many liberal theologians cut themselves off from the wisdom embodied in history. Also, they avoid the rigors of systematic theology as they would the plague. It is true that some of the past is dead and does not merit resurrection. Yet, there are insights of enduring value to be found in the records of the past. Some of the greatest religious experiences occurred long ago. If such experiences are to be repeated, the past must serve as example and stimulus. The liberal theologian, striving desperately to be an "enlightened modern" who tries to deal with the vast complexity of religious experience in terms of a very few, very simple contemporary ideas, is attempting the impossible. Religious life is too complex to be fitted into these frail formulae. As Whitehead points out, there is no simple psychological formula, such as "mal-adjustment," which may be used to explain away the facts of evil and sin. In short, he aptly remarks: "An attack upon systematic thought is treason to civilization." [26] Unless the continuing revelations of Christianity are expressed as accurately and as systematically as possible, there cannot be even the beginnings of an understanding of what is taking place. It is true that the dogmas of the past have, in some cases, inhibited true religious experience; true also that words cannot express the depths of religious experience. Yet, the fact remains that unless a man thinks as clearly as possible, in religious matters, his so-called religion will degenerate into unguided emotion and random activity. Worse still, it may sink to the status of a depraved emotion, a narrow ritual based on uncriticized concepts inherited from a dead past which should be left in its tomb.

Evil

The preceding reference to evil makes necessary a brief examination of Whitehead's discussion of this topic. He regards evil as a definite and positive factor in the universe, something which cannot be explained away by any simple "word magic" involved in new psychological or sociological terms. He contends that these liberal theologians who disregard the fact of evil are demonstrating woeful incompetence. No one can solve a problem if he refuses to admit that it exists.

Evil is essentially loss due to obstruction, loss and obstruction which need not have occurred. For example, evil may arise as the result of the impact of brute force when persuasion was "called for," or as the result of missing an opportunity to reach "excellence." Whitehead recognizes that what, in a limited context, may be good (because it is an achievement of positive value) may be evil in the end, because of its interference with the attainment of a greater good.

Whitehead argues, rather optimistically, that *specific* evils are self-destructive in the long run. For instance, the evil of disease may, in due time, kill the organism which is diseased. Thus, disease (evil) is self-eliminating. Or, the evil may be so obnoxious that steps are taken to remove it. Yet, despite this optimism concerning the *ultimate* fate of a particular evil, Whitehead claims that any particular fact of evil must be faced honestly as just that—i.e., a fact which cannot be disregarded. That *good and evil are ever-present "qualities" of the universe* is one of the basic insights on which Whitehead's philosophy is founded.[27]

THE NEW REFORMATION

Whitehead suggests that the decay of modern Christianity can be stopped by the emergence of a "new reformation." This will occur if theologians face squarely the problems before them, profiting from the past, formulating concepts accurate and adequate for the present. These ideas must then be used for advance into an uncertain future. If the *eternal truths* of religion are provided with a better method of exposition, one of the chief pitfalls will have been avoided. But always it must be borne in mind that man is a creature with aspirations. The most effective appeal is not to the emotions which he shares with the animals; rather, to those higher aspirations which make him akin to the divine. Those who claim to adhere to the unchanging faith of their fathers frequently cling to the eternal husk, a formula which once expressed a basic insight but is no longer adequate. Indeed, such people lack the faith to restate the heart of their message in more effective terms. After all, Jesus of Nazareth did not rest content with "the faith of his fathers" (Hebrew religion). Further, he predicted the acquisition of new truth, through the Holy Spirit, after his departure from the earth.

Surveying the long history of religions, Whitehead hazards

the prophecy: "That religion will conquer which can render clear to popular understanding some eternal greatness incarnate in the passage of temporal fact." [28]

Religion and Science

The newly reformed religion, which Whitehead proposes, will obviously have a positive relation with science: that of co-operation. Science is concerned with the study of generalities applicable to facts. Religion is primarily concerned with values. A modern natural scientist, for example, would take the blood pressure of a saintly man and view him as a complicated physical organism complete with heart, lungs, nervous system, and other essential apparatus. From the point of view of religion, a man like Schweitzer is the embodiment of lofty moral values and spiritual achievement. Thus, science and religion, if they stick to their legitimate business, are not in conflict but rather they are co-operating in the search for as complete knowledge as possible. This does not mean that conflict is avoided by "dividing the field." The ideal of wisdom is that of a *harmony* of truths. The factual field of science and the value data of religious experience must be fitted together in one coherent scheme. If philosophy is able to produce this desirable result, then there will be a fruitful interchange between the two areas of human experience.

A reformed religion will learn from science the importance of accepting, rapidly and willingly, the need for change in theory and practice. Conflicting theories in science are an opportunity, not a calamity. The scientist who retains the ideas and techniques of his youth is not worthy of the name. By adopting a favorable attitude toward creative change, religion will not be doing anything completely new. Rather, there will be an increase in tempo, and a more gracious attitude toward what is taking place anyway. The doctrines of Christian religion have undergone considerable change, as has been noted earlier. Whitehead reports the researches of Father Petavius who showed that many ideas held by Christians in the first three centuries were considered as heresy after the fifth century.

Whitehead also suggests that if a modern Calvinist were transported to sixteenth-century Geneva and there expounded his beliefs, historical and doctrinal, another stake would be required, another fire. The same might well be true of a modern Roman Catholic appearing in sixteenth-century Spain.

Whitehead remarks that the lessons which religion may learn from science, in a sense, constitute the repayment of an old debt. Medieval Christianity provided for the newly arising science the habit of rigorous care in systematic thought. There was also the religious conviction that nature was orderly. Without that belief, modern science could not have begun.

Interestingly enough, both science and traditional theology suffer from a common malady. There is a tendency to have a high regard for concepts and method, and insufficient respect for some kinds of data. Certain facts are approved as worthy of study, others are relegated to outer darkness. The danger here is great. The scientist may well reply that Whitehead has been praising him for his treatment of new ideas, the rapidity of his advance. Yet, Whitehead's criticism remains. There are basic assumptions as to method and types of data which are suitable for study. These assumptions frequently are accepted uncritically. The scientist demands clarity and distinctness of sense data and intellectual concepts. But there are data that do not fit into these neat pigeonholes. To that extent the scientist is left holding the bag of abstraction and is in no position to scoff genially, or irritably, at the theologian for hugging his private delusions. For example, the behavioristic psychologist concentrates on objective data and the methods of exact science. Thus he misses the data of private life revealed by the method of intuition.

This discussion of the relations of science and religion is typical of Whitehead's penetrating awareness of the complexity of any important human problem.

Religion and Philosophy

The relations between philosophy and reformed religion may be briefly stated. Philosophy provides the general ideas that

make possible a fruitful fusion of the insights of religion with the
factual knowledge and techniques of science, providing thus one
harmonious scheme of thought. Further, philosophy is of service
to religion in that it clarifies, and thus tries to save from am-
biguity, the terms used by religion. When religious experience
is aided by rational formulation and criticism, it can escape from
the *excesses* of emotional fervor. In short, the balanced Judgment of the philosopher may save the religious devotee from
extravagant forms of experience which render him unmindful of
the lofty insights and achievements constituting true religion.

Religion, in its turn, should clothe the general ideas of
philosophy with vigorous, though rationally controlled, emotions.
Religion thus is a source of dynamic. Also it is an agency for the
application of general principles to the particular situation of the
society in which the philosophy and religion are ingredients.
However, the ultimate purpose of religion is to free the individual from "self-defeating" particularity. In this sense religion
not only is concerned with the particular. It also focuses attention on generality of outlook. Religious experience provides,
of course, one type of datum which no adequate philosophy can
afford to overlook. Further, in some instances, the language of
religious devotion affords better statements of some of the main
elements in experience than other, more intellectualized, forms of
expression. "One of the reasons of the thinness of so much
modern metaphysics is its neglect of this wealth of expression of
ultimate feeling." [29] The mutually important concepts of flux
and permanence, frequently sundered in the thought of philosophers, are correctly and effectively linked in the devotional lines
of the familiar hymn:

> Abide with me;
> Fast falls the eventide.

The contributions of the Greek philosophers to religious
thought have been noted in the preceding historical sketch. The
contributions of a great contemporary philosopher, Whitehead
himself, will be discussed when we turn, shortly, to a consideration of Whitehead's theory of God, a theory formulated by a
philosopher who was a man of deep religious insight.

WHITEHEAD'S VIEW OF GOD

Sources

Whitehead has done yeoman service in laying the foundations of the "new reformation" which he advocates. He has made a serious attempt to outline a view of God based on the most penetrating and accurate insights concerning the divine nature. Whitehead contends that any valid view of God must take seriously these profound religious insights: that "redemption comes through suffering"; that "values found in the temporal world must be preserved"; that "God's power is persuasive love, not the outpouring of brute force." There is the further insight that "the order, reality, and value of the world depend ultimately on God," and also the related insight that "life is zestful, evil is conquered, peace of mind is attained as the result of the activity of the divine being." These insights[30] have been expressed by many great-souled men: Plato, the later Hebrew prophets, Jesus of Nazareth. Chief among them is Jesus.

Whitehead's detailed discussion of God is based on these and similar insights. *In general, the qualities which Whitehead attributes to God are those illustrated in the life of Jesus of Nazareth, as reported in the Gospels.*[31]

Whitehead remarks that his suggestions concerning the nature of God may be regarded as the addition of another speaker to Hume's famous *Dialogues Concerning Natural Religion.* In the *Dialogues,* as written by Hume, three views of God are presented. God is portrayed (a) as imperial ruler; (b) as a personification of merciless moral energy (formalistic in emphasis, lacking in "spirit"); and (c) as an ultimate philosophical principle. But Hume neglects another view of God which, in the judgment of Whitehead, is the correct view. Whitehead, therefore, proceeds to provide the necessary "fourth speaker" in the sense that he states the theory of God which Hume neglected. As Whitehead himself expresses it: "There is, however, in the Galilean origin of Christianity yet another suggestion. . . . It does not emphasize the ruling Caesar, or the ruthless moralist,

or the unmoved mover. It dwells upon the tender elements in
the world, which slowly and in quietness operate by love. . . .
Love neither rules, nor is it unmoved." [32]

In working out the details of his theory of God, Whitehead
does not often refer specifically to the teachings and example of
Jesus of Nazareth. Yet Whitehead unmistakably is carrying out
the project which he set for himself. He is implementing the
imperative implied in his statement that "Christ gave his life.
It is for Christians to discern the doctrine." [33]

The Gospel record is clear that Jesus stressed the efficacy of
persuasive love rather than overwhelming brute force. Hence,
he was patient and tender in his dealings with others. He was
concerned with high ideals and with their realization in the
ordinary affairs of life. He had great respect for individual human beings, recognizing qualities which others overlooked. He
shared the good and evil experiences of his fellow men. He was
an ideal companion. He faced the evils of life, and used them
as steppingstones to good. He "grew," using in his self-development the wisdom of the past as well as the data presented by the
present. In this activity he preserved what was of value and
discarded what was unsuitable. These, then, are some of the
major characteristics of Jesus of Nazareth as portrayed by the
earliest Christian writers. These characteristics are attributed to
God by Alfred North Whitehead. An examination of his discussion of God will substantiate this statement.

The Philosophic Context of Whitehead's Discussion of God

Whitehead's discussion of God is expressed, for the most
part, in highly technical language and concepts used in his
general metaphysical deliberations. However, it is possible to
state his main ideas in relatively non-technical terms without loss
of accuracy, except perhaps in some matters of detail. More
specifically, it is possible to translate Whitehead's technical terminology into familiar terms such as *individuality, process, creative interaction, permanence, value.* In order to understand
what Whitehead has to say about the nature and function of
God, it is necessary to consider briefly his view of the universe in

general, since *God is one individual among others in the universe.*

According to Whitehead, the individuals, or basic elements, composing the universe are centers of energy. Each individual develops by creative interaction with other individuals, taking in data which they provide. Thus there is a process of change or development taking place. But, in addition, there are permanent factors in the universe, namely, patterns of change and value ideals. Further, everything that happens is important, i.e., cannot be disregarded. In that sense, a general type of value is achieved in the universe (as well as the realization of the specific value ideals: truth, beauty, and goodness).

Some of this is familiar enough to those who have a nodding acquaintance with modern physics. We have been told by the physicists that the familiar objects of the everyday world are composed of centers of energy, radiating this energy all over the universe and receiving energy in return from other centers. These changes, however, exemplify laws or patterns. Certainly the "pattern" aspect of change is important.

It should be noted that human beings and all other objects in the familiar world of common-sense perception are, by Whitehead, regarded as being composed of a large group (society) of actual entities (individual moments of experience). This of course is analogous to the procedure of the physicist who regards all macroscopic objects as composed of a large number of atoms.

In his theory of reality, Whitehead is trying to describe the most fundamental factors in the universe. How then should these basic individual centers of energy be conceived? Rather than think of them in the simplest possible fashion, he believes they should be considered in terms of a more complex type of individual; not the atom or some such "element" of the physical scientist, but rather the complex "richness" of mental experience. Thus, Whitehead proceeds to concentrate on an individual "moment" of human mental activity. What he finds here he attributes to every individual, that is, every fundamental center of energy in the universe. (He terms these centers of energy: *actual entities.*)

In an *individual* moment of experience there are ideals, possibilities, principles, patterns (these words are synonyms) in terms of which we shape our experiences, as stimuli come to us from outside ourselves. We select some factors for inclusion in our experience; others we reject. Thus, we make ourselves. For example, at any moment a person may be confronted by a number of possibilities. He can read a book, watch television, sit, or sit and think. These possibilities are contemplated. In due time he makes a selection. As a result of this choice his subsequent thoughts, feelings, and actions are directed in a definite way. He is what he is as a result of this selection. Sometimes the possibilities before him are not the relatively simple ones of the type indicated. Sometimes they are general ideals which will direct other, less inclusive patterns of life. After a brief duration, a moment of experience fades, and is followed by another. Thus a person's mental life is really a series of "moments of experience" in sequence. This analysis of a moment of experience reveals the nature of the ultimate components of the universe. All "actual entities" have these characteristics.

GOD'S CHARACTERISTICS (In General)

Whitehead proposes to think of God in this fashion also. God, like any other actual entity, is an individual. He grows, like any other actual entity, by creative interaction with other centers of energy. God selects, from available possibilities, his characteristic pattern of behavior. There is, however, a fundamental difference between God and other—i.e., *ordinary*, actual entities. God endures; every ordinary entity "dies." What then are the specific characteristics of God? What are his relations to the rest of the world?

God as "Source of Order"

One of the most basic insights concerning the divine is that God is a source of order in the universe.[34] In developing the implications of this insight, Whitehead points out that we find possibilities of all sorts available for consideration: possibilities of action, possible ways of organizing the elements of experience, possible values. He contends that these possibilities must be present in the experience of some enduring entity when they are not being contemplated by any transcient—i.e., ordinary— entity. After all, there is a definiteness about these possibilities. We are confronted by them. We select from them but do not make them. Thus, Whitehead suggests that these possibilities of all sorts must exist eternally in the experience of an enduring being, God. Further, it has been observed that if one plan is selected, if one possibility is carried out, certain possibilities follow. Others are rendered impossible. In short, there seems to be a vast system of relationships between possibilities. This complex relationship of possibilities must be explained. Whitehead refers to God as the organizer of these possibilities. In brief, God provides, for other individuals, a complex organized pattern of possibilities from which selection can be made. Some possibilities are familiar patterns of action. For example, if you wish to be an effective runner you must possess "x" characteristics, follow training pattern "y," for "z" period of time. By this choice other possible kinds of behavior are "ruled out." It should be re-emphasized that among the available possibilities are the value ideals: i.e., truth, beauty, goodness, adventure, peace.

By making possible organized patterns of behavior, God is acting as a *principle of concretion.* That is to say, God provides the patterns which are used to guide the selective process of appropriating data whereby an individual becomes a definite—i.e., concrete—being. Since this process is selective, and many available data are rejected as unsuitable—to this extent, God may be termed a *principle of limitation.* The term is also applicable because God arranges the realm of possibility in a definite fashion. Certain patterns are excluded; hence there is limitation in this sense.

The possible patterns of action are available to any individual which cares to use them. Since these possibilities are made available to all, God is not concerned whether an actual entity is old or new. In other words, God does not focus his attention *exclusively* on any one actual entity. God's general purpose is that *all* actual entities will achieve the highest possible

type of individuality. However, as a particular individual begins
to develop, God is deeply concerned with it. "His tenderness is
directed towards each actual occasion, as it arises." [35]

In so far as God organizes possible patterns of action and
makes them available for the use of men in their process of
self-development, God is concerned with *novelty*. Because these
possibilities are presented in patterned arrangement, God obviously is concerned with *order* in the universe. This foundation
of order in the actual world, this pattern of possibilities which
God establishes and makes available, is order of an aesthetic
sort. That is to say, it is a type of order which makes possible the
development of experience rich in depth and complexity, its intensity heightened by patterned contrast.

In stating that God sets up a pattern which makes possible
aesthetic experience, and in remarking that moral value is
"merely certain aspects of aesthetic order," [36] Whitehead may
seem to be assigning undue priority to aesthetic experience and
relegating morals to a secondary position. However, it should
be realized that he tends to use the term *aesthetic* as a synonym
for value in general. He is saying that value experience depends
on the expression of a complex order of possibilities. In suggesting that morality is merely an aspect of aesthetic order, he
is only stating that goodness is one type of value.

In so far as God provides an orderly pattern of possibilities,
in logical interrelation, he *establishes reason*. That is to say,
he lays the foundations for rational deliberation. Since God is
concerned with higher value ideals (as well as other types of
possibility), he can be said to *distinguish good from evil*. Thus,
God wishes to focus attention on values as well as facts. In so
far as any individual has some value, and any individual follows
a pattern provided by God, in that sense God is concerned not
only with ideals, values (such as truth, beauty, and goodness),
but also with the values of individual self-development.

God confronts the individual with the vast realm of ideals
beyond the range of narrowly selfish interests. He attempts to
convey the idea that by "going beyond oneself" and being
interested in a wider good (including the welfare of others), a
person may develop a higher type of self. In so far as an indi-

vidual responds to this idea, or to any other possibility provided by God, God becomes an object of desire, a lure for feeling.

God's Purpose and Power

Whitehead suggests that God is interested in the development of individuals as an intermediate step "towards the fulfilment of his own [God's] being." [37] As has been noted, Whitehead regards God as one individual among many interacting individuals, each deriving from the others much of benefit. It is, therefore, obvious that God should be interested in the development of other individuals who will be of assistance to him in carrying out his purposes. After all, the purposes of God are of the highest.

It will be clear from the foregoing paragraphs that God may be said to have a purpose. He is concerned with order and novelty, the rise of individuals who will express the value ideals which God envisages. God also aims at the achievement of the full development of his own (divine) possibilities.

The question naturally arises: Does God force any human mind to accept a specific possibility? Does God force any individual to translate into action any specific possibility? Whitehead's answer is in the negative. God ensures that possibilities are available for use by others. In this fashion he persuades. But he does not *force* these ideals on any other individual. This is a supreme insight of Jesus of Nazareth. God makes available the complete complex realm of possibilities. He is thus interested in the self-development of the other individuals in the universe. But, to repeat, he does not impose his will. Every individual selects his own path. God is not a transcendent power creating, and then controlling, everything in the universe. God can only lead men to higher values by confronting them with the lure of these higher value ideals. Thus God is "the poet of the world, with tender patience leading it by his vision of truth, beauty, and goodness." [38] However, the fact remains that he cannot lead if men will not follow.

It is only in this context that one can, legitimately, speak of the *"power"* of God. "The power of God is the worship He inspires." [39] Incidentally, this devotion to God, this vision of ideals to be realized, is not a "rule of safety." It is a challenge to adventure in the realm of the spirit.

God's *love* is expressed by his action in making possible our envisagement of infinite possibilities, his tenderness in leading, not forcing. However, his love is not a sedative. It is a stimulus. Whitehead's remark that divine love is "a little oblivious as to morals" [40] should not be interpreted to mean that God is indifferent to morality. Rather, the implication is that love will temper justice with mercy. The strict letter of a moral law, the rigorous applications of a "provincial" moral code, may well be set aside in the interests of the ultimate well-being of an individual. After all, Jesus disregarded many of the petty details of the moral codes of his day, thus furthering the true spirit of moral goodness. In this connection, it is well to remember Whitehead's suggestion that the "reformed" way to think of God is in terms of goodness rather than (arbitrary and all-powerful) will.

In the midst of this emphasis on tenderness and love, it must be noted that Whitehead finds a certain inexorableness in God. God has arranged the patterns of possible behavior. If one pattern is selected, its specific implications follow inevitably. There is no escape. Yet, to return to the main theme, God does not exercise overruling force—even for constructive purposes. The only power that God can exert is the "worship he inspires." Thus, when Whitehead refers to "the overpowering rationality" of God's vision of the realm of possibilities, he is not deserting his main position. The individual is not influenced by the *inexorable implications* of the divine order of possibilities (overwhelmed in this sense) unless the individual so wishes. In other words, unless an individual accepts on his own volition a specific pattern of possibilities, the implications of that pattern of possibilities will have no effect on him.

Whitehead refers to God as an "ultimate irrationality." This is so because God is an ultimate factor in the universe. Other factors must be explained in terms of God. He is one major basis of rational explanation. Thus no reason can be given for God. In this sense God is an ultimate irrationality. The basic axioms and definitions of Euclid's geometry could likewise be termed "irrational."

Toward the end of his discussion of "Religion and Science" in *Science and the Modern World* (Chapter 12), Whitehead provides a profound statement of the nature of ideal religion. Within this brief paragraph is compressed the theory of God's envisagement of "possibilities" (particularly of those of value) which has been under discussion here in the preceding pages. The statement is as follows: "Religion is the vision of something which stands behind and within the passing flux of immediate things; something which is real, and yet waiting to be realized; something which is a remote possibility and yet the greatest of present facts; something that gives meaning to all that passes, and yet eludes apprehension; something whose possession is the final good and yet is beyond all reach; something which is the ultimate ideal, and the hopeless quest."

God's Growth

So far only one phase of Whitehead's theory of God has been discussed, that which Whitehead terms God's primordial nature. It is now necessary to proceed to an examination of what are termed the consequent and superject natures of God. God does not only provide possibilities to be contemplated by individuals. He also receives, from other individuals, *some* data which they provide. God's contemplation of the infinite realm of eternal possibility is complete and unchanging. Those possibilities are there, once and for all. Yet, God, like other individuals, is subject to change. He grows as the result of creative interaction with others. Jesus increased in wisdom and "stature" as the years passed. The increase in stature was not merely physical. If one takes seriously Jesus' humanity, his life right up to the moments on the cross was a development in moral and spiritual grandeur. This development took place because of his reactions to the other individuals with whom he came in contact.

God's "Tender Care"

Whitehead contends that one of the most important activities of God is that, in his associations with other individuals, he preserves what otherwise would be neglected and lost. Moments of human experience are brief, their contents finite. Human memory is incomplete and not always wise in its selections. If human experience were all there is, much of great value would be lost forever. One of the basic insights of religion is that some positive values are not lost. They are preserved by the divine being. Thus Whitehead suggests that as the individual's experience fades, values are preserved in God's experience. Within God's rich complexity of experience, guided by his characteristic pattern of behavior, harmonization of achieved value is obtained. Yet, it must be noted that *God does not save everything which is valuable.* He exercises a tender care which loses nothing that *"can be saved."* [41] With the passage of time some elimination takes place. Jesus of Nazareth lost one of his chief disciples. Many who offered themselves, as disciples, were not accepted.

By his reaction to other actual entities—more specifically, by the use which he makes of the data which they provide, either accepting or rejecting—God *passes judgment* on the world of other individuals. In this sense, the day of judgment is ever with us. It is not a far-off event. Each present moment is important since God's evaluation takes place at each moment.

The question of *personal immortality* naturally arises at this point. In *Religion in the Making* Whitehead states that he is entirely neutral on the question of personal immortality. He sees no reason why the question could not be settled, providing adequate evidence could be found. With this brief and inconclusive remark he leaves the topic. Later developments in his system of thought seem to indicate that personal immortality is specifically ruled out. The human mind or soul is composed, according to Whitehead, of a large number of parallel and successive "moments of experience." Each moment of experience has a brief duration and then passes out of existence, its inner life "spent." Some part of its experiences *may* be preserved in God's experience, but there is not a complete immortality. As Whitehead states it: "Each actuality in the temporal world has its reception into God's nature. The corresponding element in God's nature is not temporal actuality." [42] Since the human mind or soul is composed of these moments of experience, it must suffer their fate. *Part* of "what has been" may be preserved in God's experience. *All* cannot be. God, like any other actuality, reacts in a selective fashion. In the selective process some available data are rejected. In any case, when a moment of experience is past, its inner life cannot be recreated—try as we may. To return to the source of many basic insights, Jesus of Nazareth did not include everything available for experience in the rich texture of his life.

The selective process that characterizes God and all other actual entities should not be misunderstood. Particularly in the case of God, it is *not* a technique by which evil, pain, suffering—in short, all types of negative value—are disregarded. In the process of life some data are lost, data of all sorts, factual and value data. God is chiefly concerned with positive value, but he does not disregard negative value. In other words, God experiences the world *as it is*. His perception is true.

God as "Fellow Sufferer

Thus Whitehead refers to God as "the fellow sufferer who understands." By this he means that when God receives data from other individuals he takes what is of importance, be it good or evil, pain or pleasure. Evil is there at full face value. God feels evil *tragically*. But, in the light of his understanding, in the wisdom of his life, evil is seen and used, *ultimately*, as a means to the good. God does not deny the brute reality of evil. He faces it and uses it for a final good. In so far as God has achieved in his own nature the conquest of evil, even at the cost of intense suffering, he has experienced an exalted type of happiness which is evoked by heroic effort successfully completed. This, of course, is not a shallow pleasure. Rather it is a state of supreme spiritual well-being—peace. It thus becomes very evident that God's goodness is not to be conceived as a static perfection. It is the result of divine effort.

The Patience of God

The patience of God [43] and the nature of his influence are shown by his approach to evil. He wishes to banish it from the world. However, he does not do so by overwhelming decree.

Good is achieved in the world, evil is "put in its place," only when the individuals in the world follow the example of God—that is to say, only in so far as other persons deal with evil as God does (within the limits of their ability).

God the Great Companion

God's experience is made available to other individuals. The benefits of God's experience are felt by mortal men: Jesus walked the hills of Galilee and the streets of Jerusalem, and the glory of divinity shone through. Thus, the "kingdom of heaven" was in the midst of men. Thus, God's love is demonstrated. This is the basis of the claim that God is "the great companion," one among many other individuals participating in the affairs of life, helping others (and being helped).

Whitehead suggests that without such a being as God, the crowning quality of civilization, peace, would not be achieved. Peace is the state of mind which flows from the conviction that what is "fine" is preserved in the nature of things, preserved as only God can preserve it. In general, God not only envisages the ideals of civilization but shows supremely how they can be expressed in the life of an individual.

WHITEHEAD'S ANSWERS TO SOME "TRADITIONAL" QUESTIONS

There are the old theological questions: Is God one or many; immanent or transcendent; temporal or eternal? Is God infinite in wisdom, goodness, and power? Whitehead's answers are at first sight confused or conflicting, even evasive. He suggests that God is one individual but has many functions. For this reason he may be called either one or many, depending upon the approach. Similarly, God is immanent, in that he provides data for other individuals and receives data from other individuals. Yet, he is transcendent since he contemplates possibilities, many of which are not yet actualized in experience; some of them may never be realized. Further, he is different from others and hence transcendent. God is eternal in the sense that he contemplates these eternal possibilities, and also because his life never fades. But God changes, develops. Thus he is temporal. God is free because his envisagement of the realm of possibilities is not restricted by anything outside him. But God is limited since he depends for his being, in part, on the activities of other individuals. God is infinite and complete in the sense that he contemplates all possibilities. He is finite and incomplete since he is not everything. He is good but not evil. Yet, he experiences evil as real—i.e., tragically. Also, as has been noted, his goodness is not that of static perfection. God is limited in power because he cannot force anything on any individual. Further, though he is omniscient with reference to the realm of possibility, he is limited in his knowledge of actual individuals. He does not have fore-knowledge of what an individual will do.

God is not the only reality. All other individuals are real, though none reaches the level of God in richness and complexity of value experience. God is not the creator of the world in any absolute fashion. He and every other individual make data available for the use of others. In a sense God creates the world (of other individuals) since he provides data for them. However, it is equally correct to say the world (of other individuals) creates God since they provide data for him. There was no first day of creation. God did not create the world out of nothing. God was "not *before* all creation, but *with* all creation" (i.e., the process by which all individuals develop).[44]

Thus, in Whitehead's theory, God is not the first cause either in the sense of temporal priority, or in that of being *the* ultimate causal factor to the exclusion of everything else. He is *one* causal factor among others. He is, however, superior in excellence of experience to all other actual entities. He sets an example and, in this sense, may be termed "final cause." God is also "efficient cause" since he is self-energizing. However, other actual entities are efficient causes for the same reason. Within each individual there is an urge toward self-development. This purpose is a final cause. All individuals, ordinary ones and God, provide data ("material") for the use of others. The ideal possibilities (eternal objects) envisaged by God serve as "formal" patterns which all actual entities (including God) use in their process of self-development.

Incidentally, Whitehead's frequent contention that God, and ordinary individuals, are engaged in a process of self-development has given rise to the mistaken notion that there is a reality —"creativity"—more ultimate than God or any other individual. It is true that Whitehead sometimes uses this term in a confusing fashion. Actually, however, when he refers to creativity, he is referring to the self-development (creative activity) of God and other individuals.

DOES WHITEHEAD'S METAPHYSICS "DICTATE" HIS VIEW OF GOD?

Whitehead, in discussing God, sometimes refers to "what the metaphysical principles, here developed, requires . . . as to the nature of God." [45] He is not suggesting that his metaphysical system is *dictating* to him a specific view of God. Rather, it is his way of saying that if God is to be regarded as one individual among other individuals, as envisaged by his philosophical system, then God will be thought of as being in creative interaction with other individuals, concerned with values, influenced by data presented. God's special function, in the system, is to be an orderer of possibilities and a saver of what otherwise would be lost. However, these functions, as well as God's other characteristics, *are not arbitrarily imputed.* These qualities are *found,* in moments of supreme insight. It is discovery, not arbitrary invention.

THE "RELIGIOUS AVAILABILITY" OF WHITEHEAD'S GOD

In view of the preceding discussion, it is difficult to accept at face value the apparently different approach in Chapter 11 of *Science and the Modern World.* In that chapter he states that a view of God which is adequate in a metaphysical sense cannot go "very far towards the production of a God available for religious purposes." [46] He is referring, however, to the metaphysical God of Aristotle. He then "slides" into a sweeping generalization. There is the qualifying admission that a metaphysical basis is required for a more specialized experience of a religious sort. In any case, this *earlier* statement was followed by the exposition of a view of God which has been outlined here in the preceding pages. It is assumed that the later, more detailed position should be regarded as a theory of God which Whitehead wished to be attributed to him.

As should be evident from the preceding discussion, White-head stated a view of God (in *Process and Reality* and subsequent books) which is expressed in terms applicable to all the basic factors in the universe, in so far as they are open to human knowledge. Here is a view of God which is metaphysically "respectable." Further, this theory of God is in accordance with basic religious insights. Whitehead reports that God is an individual, sufficiently like other individuals to be described in the same terms. The only basic differences are that God (a) makes available organized possibilities, (b) is vastly superior to others in the level of his attainments, (c) and endures. This being may legitimately be characterized by the terms "love" and "patience." There is justification for referring to him as "a great companion," "a fellow sufferer who understands." Surely such a God, metaphysically satisfactory, is also "available for religious purposes."

In *Religion in the Making*, Whitehead argues that it is unnecessary to consider God as a person. He refers to the fact that in Confucian and Hindu thought God is not so regarded. Those who claim to have a direct experience of a personal God are, in Whitehead's opinion (as expressed in *Religion in the Making*), open to the objection that they are without rational justification, relying on an unverified personal opinion. On the other hand, he contends that there is a universal concurrence of experience concerning the presence of a "permanent rightness" in the nature of things. The word "rightness" is used in a broad sense, apparently as a synonym for orderliness. However, included also is the more obvious and usual meaning of value.

The earlier statements in *Religion in the Making*, that God should *not* be considered a person, must be re-examined in the light of the preceding discussion of the "religious availability" of Whitehead's God. In the early treatment, Whitehead argues that there is no universal agreement about the personality of God; but that there is agreement concerning a permanent rightness in the universe. The later books, *Science and the Modern World, Process and Reality*, go far beyond the minimum "permanent rightness." Indeed, even in *Religion in the Making* Whitehead refers to the "ideal companion" who saves what otherwise might be lost. This theory is greatly amplified in *Process and Reality*, as has been noted. What Whitehead seems to be chiefly opposing is the ascription of *a certain type of personality* to God—that of a transcendent creator, a brutal tyrant, or a petty moralist.

True Christianity tends to bow before the ultimate mystery of the divine being and use what is admitted to be incomplete knowledge. Certainly, Whitehead does not offer what purports to be a dogmatically certain creed. He outlines a tentative, possible interpretation of available facts of religious experience. In dealing with the "profound things" of life, he advocates (in his more mature philosophical deliberations) the avoidance of too simple symbolism (e.g., "permanent rightness"). The symbolism of "personality" (purged of theological corruptions) seems entirely appropriate to Whitehead, in his later writings.

Whitehead offers only suggestions, "images." We cannot achieve an exact or complete conceptual formulation of the divine nature. To that extent he agrees with practically all theologians. (Incidentally, the same difficulty confronts us in dealing with *any* complex datum, be it human personality or basic physical elements.) Nevertheless, he believes that our insights are sufficiently accurate to enable us to avoid some of the most serious errors of past theological speculation. What is more important, these insights can provide the basis for a more adequate and accurate *positive* system of thought concerning God.

Thus, he contends that the weight of available evidence—the intuitions of recognized leaders in religious and philosophical thought (Jesus, the later Hebrew prophets, Plato)—justifies the rejection of ideas of God stressing imperial power, unbending petty morality, barren metaphysical ultimacy. These insights justify the use of concepts emphasizing aspects of ideal personality: love, patience, companionship, a concern for the higher values both as ideal and as actualized.

GOD "IN HISTORY"

At the end of Chapter 2, on the *philosophy of history*, it was stated that God is an important factor. Whitehead's theory concerning the function of God in history should now be clear. God does not impose any particular pattern on the course of historical events. What happens in history is the result of the selective process going on in the experience of the individuals who exist during the historical period under discussion. God exercises a purely persuasive function. He confronts other individuals with ideal possibilities. He demonstrates the excellence of these ideals when realized. Thus, he persuades but he cannot coerce.

It has been noted that Whitehead refuses to account for the course of history by reference to *one* factor. Such is the importance of individual powers of selection that he consistently suggests that no law can be regarded as a permanent factor in history—not even a physical or chemical law. The basic physical and chemical elements illustrate the same selective process. The patterns of behavior stated in the so-called scientific laws of this age may be replaced by other patterns of behavior. Thus, there may be new laws.

There is, then, no inevitable process of history to be explained by fatalistically inflexible Divine Providence, or by eternal laws of nature or history. It may be said that the future is "open." We are not predetermined to Utopia, or its opposite, or to the "recurrences" of the cyclical view. The future will be what individuals of all types—God of course included—make of the data of the past and present, and the ideal possibilities which confront us.

Chapter 4 SOCIAL PHILOSOPHY

THE ECONOMIC PROBLEM

"In the immediate present, economic organization constitutes the most massive problem in human relationships." [1] Whitehead contends that the economic system which developed in the Western world after the Middle Ages was one of the major causes of human misery. He believes that its baleful influence is still felt, though some improvement has taken place.

Origins

This economic system at its beginning was characterized by free competition among individuals. It was later assumed that if this form of strife were allowed to take place, the result would be the achievement of an ideal, beneficial, social system. Thus, in theory, it was possible to give allegiance to high ideals, such as the brotherhood of man, while engaging in ruthless economic strife with individual men.

This economic theory received powerful support from developments in natural science. The public world of material objects was considered to be outside the range of moral, aesthetic, and other "high values." Such value could be found only in the private experiences of men. The evolutionary theory in biology was thought to prove the naturalness of strife and destruction in the relations of biological organisms, including men. A specific form of this general approach to life, the so-called Malthusian law, threw the halo of "science" over a situation in which a few are comfortable, and the majority are "semi" or completely destitute. It was assumed to be a fact of nature that there never could be enough food, and other goods, for all; therefore, no permanent reform of existing social evils could be achieved. Misery must be accepted by the majority as their destined lot.

This view of life implied that the successful members of society were those who engage effectively in competition with their fellow men, for financial return. These successful men frequently achieved a high level of *private* and personal excellence. But in their relations with other men, truth, beauty, and goodness were regarded as irrelevant. They tried to be deeply religious on Sunday. They were vigorously acquisitive the other days of the week. When questioned as to their responsibilities for the welfare of their fellow men they, for the most part, gave the answer of Cain: "Am I my brother's keeper?" True, there were some legal restrictions placed on the ruthless competition among individuals. But before this was done, in the middle of the nineteenth century, many men were reduced almost to the level of slavery, while a few lived like feudal barons. Even with the implementation of reforms, the evils involved in this system were only partially removed. They remain to the present day.

Present Deficiencies

Briefly expressed, the chief social evils at the present time are (a) the loss of freedom, and (b) the loss of opportunity to enjoy the higher values of life. Whitehead contends that, in a very real sense, there is less freedom in England in the twentieth century than there was under the tyrant Charles I. The level of subsistence may be higher, and political restrictions are less obvious. But there are massive restrictions in many areas of experience. These restrictions are extremely serious. In all parts of the Western world, modern man is immersed in some vast commercial enterprise. He is required to carry out some relatively simple routine task. In many cases it is meaningless drudgery. There is no opportunity for creative initiative. He does as he is told or loses his job. Generally speaking, his amusements are also restricted non-creative and reflect, either directly or indirectly, the profit motive. He is amused only when others are amused. He is amused only when someone else provides the stimulus. His aesthetic *appreciation*, for example, is also inhibited. He works in surroundings which are not likely to be beautiful. When he is offered goods that are supposed to be beautiful, even these are standardized and bear the stamp of mass-produced shoddiness and pseudo glitter. There is a restricted choice of goods, none of which a person with a remaining glimmer of individuality may wish. Whitehead, with characteristic chivalry, points to the fact that on one occasion the stores of Boston offered only a few shades of a certain color of cloth for ladies' dresses. The result was that a lady, with highly developed aesthetic tastes, would not buy dress material even though it happened to be in fashion. In brief, the modern man is profoundly inhibited by his environment. As a cog in a massive economic system he has lost his initiative. His horizon is limited by the bare brutal necessities of his job. His higher sensibilities are thwarted. Even his leisure activities are imposed upon him.

This blight, the result of the modern economic system, falls on all classes of society. The research scientist is told what to find in his laboratory, so that his employer may flourish by providing a new commodity. Even the executives of an industry are not immune to the corroding influences of the economic system in which they live. They too must play their assigned parts. An executive cannot afford to experiment in the realms beyond the strict requirements of competitive business. If he loses himself in aesthetic contemplation he is lost indeed. What Whitehead has said about business enterprises is applicable as well to other modern institutions. Here also there is a tendency to overemphasize competition and a narrowing of interests, with the resultant loss of many of the higher values of life. These dangers are found even in churches and educational institutions.

Always there hangs above the heads of those employed in business, on whatever level, the possibility of unemployment. Perhaps it will be due to overproduction or to a shrinkage of the market. Perhaps a more efficient person will come along and be given one's job. Even to top executives the rule applies: if the firm cannot use you, you are through. The business world has no place for the unsuccessful competitor.

One of the great weaknesses in the modern economic system, according to Whitehead, is that its guiding ideas are too simple. It tries to explain economic life in terms of a small, simple environment inhabited by a few people who will behave in a very simple, absolutely predictable fashion. It is as though you tried to interpret the complex life of the North American continent on the analogy of two men and a boy on a desert island, the men being illustrations of the ideal "economic man." The trouble with this conception is that it is much too naive. There are millions of people in North America. We are not free to produce in accordance with demand. Supply and demand are controlled by a few very skillful men. Supplies are artificially restricted or increased. Demands are not permanent mental factors. They also can be artificially manipulated. The myth of free competition is just that, a myth. A man in the modern business community is not a free agent. Thus, Whitehead argues that the traditional economic concepts are inadequate to guide modern thought and action.

Further, many of the traditional terms have changed their meaning in a very drastic fashion. Originally, "individual" or "person" meant *one* man, or woman, or child. Now the term applies as well to a vast corporation which may continue for generations, and control the lives and destinies of thousands of men and women. How can an individual, in the old sense of "John Doe," compete with an individual in the new sense, "——— Co., Inc."? The term "property" has also undergone a change in meaning. There was a time when most men had some private property, a house, a few acres of land. Now many man have the "title" but not the "substance." The house, or car, is mortgaged. Much "private" property is now owned by that new type of person, the business corporation.

Favorable Aspects

Whitehead is prepared to admit that there is considerable truth in the traditional economic theory, *if* it is used with qualifications. For example, a certain amount of competition undoubtedly is of value in calling forth the full creative powers of the individual. But the competition should be "fair," and directed along lines conducive to the welfare of all concerned. There can be no objection to a struggle to provide the best possible type of car at a low price, if all concerned receive a fair return for their labor and if no artificial restrictions are placed on sales and price.

In general, Whitehead recognizes that he is presenting a somewhat extreme critical picture of modern business practice. Many corrective tendencies are at work. In the realm of theory, economists for the past thirty or forty years have been working to overcome the undue abstractions, and simplifications, of these theories. Thus, there has been a more thorough study of the actual state of affairs in the complex modern world. In the realm of actual business procedure, much-needed reforms are being initiated. These are providing better conditions for civilized life. Factories are more beautiful within and without. Music has been provided as a background for work. Employer-employee councils have been established. Attempts have been made to make work meaningful. A good man is given an opportunity to express himself in a creative fashion. However, only an encouraging beginning has been made.

Whitehead is strongly of the opinion that these tendencies should be encouraged and the scope of their application extended. There are still many faults in our society because of its present economic foundations. Even today, the man who is immersed in the complex life of modern society does not have maximum opportunity to practice truth, enjoy beauty and art, adventure in the world of ideals, or achieve peace. For example, telling the truth is not always a sound practical procedure in modern society. Beauty and art are still sacrificed to business efficiency, when ugliness means a few extra dollars. Thus, in developing natural resources, in placing industries, in selling goods, beauty and art are frequently forgotten. Further, some forms of beauty and art are prostituted to the purposes of business. A great painting may be reproduced in close proximity to a "better mousetrap."

SUGGESTED ECONOMIC REFORMS

General Statement

The reformed economic system Whitehead proposes involves an emphasis on certain *minor* tendencies which are now apparent in modern business procedure, plus the addition of new elements. This approach stresses the principle of organic interdependence instead of exclusive individualism, co-operation instead of ruthless competition. It re-emphasizes an ancient ideal in Western thought, that of the dignity and worth of the individual human being. It thus embodies the democratic ideal of the potential greatness of man, of even the average, or the common, man. That is to say, there are powers of intellect, also moral and aesthetic appreciation and development, which have hitherto been thwarted. This new economic system must take into consideration the basic rights of men to develop their potentialities of value experience. The approach to economic activities must be that of the Benedictine insight: a man's work should be a source of joy and embody devotion to the "finest," and to God. Work should challenge the intellect, have moral and aesthetic worth, and, of course, produce useful consequences which further the welfare of mankind. How can this ideal be realized in modern society?

Whitehead suggests that the worker in the factory be allowed more individual initiative. There should be a combination of the efficiency of mass production and the creativity of the craftsman's approach to production. He does not advocate a return to the laborious hand techniques of the Middle Ages. Mass production machinery must be used to do the heavy and routine work. But the distinctive "finishing touches" should be carried out by individual workmen who are interested in, and understand, what they are doing and who are given scope for creative imagination. Whitehead suggests that in France, for centuries, this principle has been applied with great success in the dressmaking industry. He feels that a person in the production room of a "salon" should be encouraged to experiment with style possibilities and the use of a wide range of materials. This obviously will make the worker's life meaningful and enjoyable. Incidentally, business will benefit. (Whitehead notes, with approval, the studies of problems of industrial morale being made at Dartmouth and Harvard by Professors Ames and Mayo.) Whitehead admits that the public will have to undergo considerable re-education so as to accept slower production schedules, and even somewhat higher costs. However, the product will be better made and more attractive.

The Enlightened Executive

Many heads of business organizations must change their habits of thought, and attitudes, if these and other reforms are to take place. The business executive must expand the horizon of his understanding by enlightened imagination. He must learn to appreciate the problems that confront the people who are engaged in producing and transporting the raw materials used in his factory. He should have insight into the strength and weakness of human nature, the causes of illness and fatigue, the factors that produce reliable employees. He should know "the deep aspirations which are buried in the hearts of men." He must be flexible, in order to adapt himself to new situations—perceiving general principles not previously apprehended and applying them to relevant facts. He must realize that the affairs of men are undergoing rapid changes, that old-time "certitudes" may no longer be adequate. Social customs, habits of thought, institutions, methods of transportation and production literally change overnight. New raw materials become available; old raw materials become exhausted. In short, width of understanding and a highly adaptable attitude of mind are essential, if economic activities are to provide the conditions for the higher levels of human living.

This emphasis on flexibility and forsight concerning trends which necessitate changes in business operations, however, does not mean that a business executive should be a devotee to St. Vitus. Without routine any activity degenerates into chaos. Every new technique involves a set sequence of events which must be followed if the technique is to be successful. Thus, the flexibility and awareness of *novelty* should not be allowed to rule out stability and *routine*. Rather, imaginative intelligence (foresight) must be used to determine the strengths and weaknesses of a specified routine: when to set it up, when to replace it by another.

In addition to the qualities noted above, the ideal business executive must be able to judge, on sound grounds, what is the best policy for his industry and for all concerned. Thus, to repeat, the sympathetic understanding of men must be linked with a calm appreciation of the values of civilization. A well-trained mind, flexible in face of the changing flux of facts, will stand in the way of civilization, unless there is a concentrated search for truth, beauty, art, adventure, and peace.

The "traditional" exclusive devotion to a narrow view of success, namely, profit, must be replaced if leaders of business are to be agents furthering the development of civilization. After all, as Whitehead points out, if the only reason people (factory hands, or executives) work is in order to make money, they will not be primarily interested in their jobs. The quality of their work will be inferior. Further, there is a self-defeating narrowing of interests and a long-range loss of efficiency. The old Benedictine ideal, once again, comes into focus. The civilized approach to work is to regard it as a source of intellectual and moral development, a source of genuine happiness. The intelligent and adaptable executive, in association with workers with similar characteristics, can make modern industry measure up to these ideals. Such men will not be the victims of the economic process; rather, they will master the frankenstein and turn it into a useful robot. Incidentally, Whitehead realizes that, in portraying his ideal business executive, he is demanding characteristics all of which are not likely to be found in any *one* man. However, he reiterates that such knowledge and attitudes should be at the disposal of the man who makes ultimate decisions.

Possible Misunderstandings Corrected

At this point it might be wise to clear up several possible misunderstandings.

It is important to realize that Whitehead is not recommending the abandonment of large corporations. He regards them as necessary ingredients in modern life. His contention is that these agencies should be used in order to reach higher levels of civilization than at present exist.

Whitehead, of course, does not suggest that all the pleasures one needs can be derived from his work. He also opposes the theory of vigorous spurts of work and long periods of relaxation. Rather, he favors a smooth rhythm of work *and* relaxation. (In this context he notes the fatiguing nature of some types of so-called play.) Particular reference is made to the relaxation afforded by many forms of art.

Whitehead's general approach to social problems is optimistic. He envisages the possibility of extensive improvement, and indicates how these improvements may be effected. However, it must be admitted that in one of his earlier discussions of this topic, he adopts a darkly pessimistic view. "You may, perhaps, by some great reforms, obviate the worse kind of sweated labor and the insecurity of employment. But you can never greatly increase average incomes. On that side all hope of Utopia is closed to you." [2] It should, however, be stressed that this is an isolated remark quite different from *later*, more extensive discussions. Further, it is set in the context of a consideration of education, and is an incidental comment rising out of a plea for a greater emphasis on art in education. The point is being made that enjoyment of art is something that can be made readily available to the majority of men, whereas escape from uncertainty of employment and unsatisfactory working conditions is not as easy to arrange.

POLITICAL THOUGHT

Democracy

Whitehead's own political philosophy, obviously, is democratic in the sense that he regards the welfare of the individual as of fundamental importance. "The worth of any social system depends on the value experiences it promotes among individual human beings." [3] He takes issue with Plato who envisaged an ideal society ruled by philosopher kings. "To-day, in an age of democracy, the kings are the plain citizens pursuing their various avocations. There can be no successful democratic society till general education conveys a philosophic outlook." [4]

Whitehead's support of the democratic point of view is clearly implicit in his comments concerning a "totalitarianism" which localizes value in one exclusive social group, in a pseudo-mystic unity, or in a superperson. When any individual is subordinated to the state, the individual is thereby dwarfed and deformed. This is so because of the fact that some of the most fundamental phases of human experience are private, not social. The profoundest moments of experience are deeply individual and cannot be reduced to some shared experience, in accordance with a rigorously simple formula, imposed by a "god-man" functioning on behalf of a "divine state." Further, a narrow totalitarian nationalism drags human experience into the shallows of life by its obnoxious restrictions. Since there are bound to be several such competing national groups, each demanding complete allegiance, there arises a barbaric pantheism. This condition of affairs prevents fruitful interaction between men of different nations and different "times." In this sense, totalitarianism is contrary to the tolerance and persuasiveness which are so important in civilized life. It is the tendency of totalitarian governments to rely chiefly on force. The result is a blight of civilization.

The linkage of nationalism and totalitarianism, in Whitehead's writings, should not blind one to the fact that he is in favor of an *enlightened nationalism*, provided its leaders and people are internationally minded and use the national organization as an instrument for the development of civilization at home and abroad to its fullest possible extent. Writing at the end of World War II, Whitehead states that he can see no hope for civilized life unless the nations of the world are willing to direct themselves to the well-being of all citizens and accept a compromise of "narrowly national" interests. Such a compromise must have a moral basis, and involve a profound emotional *rapprochement*, a firm foundation of genuine sympathy and understanding. The machinery for this type of compromise has been provided by the United Nations organization.

Freedom and Compulsion

Whitehead is not an advocate of unqualified individualism. He contends that it is nonsense to speak of absolute individuals with absolute rights. In his opinion, this is evident because each individual depends on his environment for his existence and well-being. Further, Whitehead agrees with those who claim that rights are relative to the total situation, and also involve reference to correlative duties. He summarizes his position by suggesting that there must be a mingling of individual liberty and environmental compulsion. The fact of the matter is that if a satisfactory environment, suitable for the development of the value experience of individuals, is to be maintained some compulsion is necessary. Certain kinds of destructive activities must be prevented. A few people, in any social group, are a constant menace to life. Most people at some time are a mild disease in the body politic. Despite the admitted loss of freedom, some compulsion is necessary. It is the lesser of two evils. In attempting to make his point as specific as possible, Whitehead refers to Athens in the days of Pericles (as described by Thucydides). In other words, he suggests that the freedom one can expect within a social group is a limited freedom, limited so as to avoid the destruction of the general purpose of the society. This purpose, in a civilized society, is the harmonious development of the positive value potentialities of each individual.

Whitehead makes the interesting suggestion that one way to deal with the problem of freedom and compulsion, in certain spheres of human activity, is to vest the "control" of the individual not in the officials of the state but in the professional group to which he belongs.[5]

The control which these professional groups should exercise involves an examination of the skills and general competence possessed by members of the group. This does not mean complete control of all phases of life. There is room for wide differences of opinion in non-professional matters, and also concerning some of the details of professional practice. But, to repeat, with regard to the *fundamentals* in a man's professional field—his training and judgment, and his resultant ability—these are most carefully evaluated. For example, a medical doctor will be examined by other doctors as to his professional competence. No restriction will be placed upon his recreations or his religious or political beliefs unless they undermine his efficiency as a practitioner.

It should be noted, also, that a professional group can exercise a certain amount of control over non-members of the group by evaluating, for the information of the general public, ideas and actions which fall within the scope of a professional field. This makes it possible to allow a greater amount of freedom to those outside the profession, since the profession acts as a "judge" of the amateur's activities. For example, if a man wishes to experiment with a cure for cancer, let him proceed. Some good may come of it. There is little danger because there will be an ultimate evaluation provided by professional medical judgment. Whitehead contends that one of the greatest virtues of this general scheme is that it will make possible an increase of freedom. Without freedom a society is in grave danger of relapsing into a state of inertia.

This approach to freedom, in terms of the authority of professional groups, is relatively new in the modern world. The ultimate center of liberty is essentially the profession, not the individual. The profession is free and authoritative in its field. For example, no individual should be allowed to teach as he wishes. The authority in such matters is vested in the considered opinion of competent educators. In saying that the profession (not the individual) is the center of liberty, Whitehead is not setting up a "mythical monster." The profession is composed of *competent individuals.* They will say, for example, to any individual who wishes to instruct in a school or college: "You are not free to do so until you prove to us your competence. We, on the basis of our proved ability, are *free* to offer instruction and to determine the validity of your claim to carry on this activity." The medieval guild, at its best, is an example of what Whitehead means by his approach to the problem of freedom and compulsion.

The State

The role of the state in regulating human affairs should be drastically restricted. Thus, as will be obvious from the preceding discussion, it loses any claim to exercise authority when it presumes to settle technical questions which lie within the scope of professional judgment. For example, the state of Tennessee had no justification for interfering with the teaching program with reference to the topic of evolution. Here it was in opposition to the "considered opinion" of most members of the teaching profession in the civilized world.

Yet, in the midst of this somewhat destructive criticism of the nature and function of the state, an essential fact must not be forgotten. The state embodies the general wisdom of the community and, therefore, can pass "a general judgment on the activity of the various organizations." [6] For example, the officials of the government would be justified in objecting to a profession which did not encourage initiative and ability and did not command the respect of similar professions in other free countries.

It is obvious that, in Whitehead's opinion, loyalty to the state should not depend on the motive of fear engendered by force. Rather, loyalty must have a moral basis. In so far as a state acts in accordance with enlightened wisdom concerning the highest possibilities of value experience of its citizens, to that extent it merits loyalty.

Social Unity

The preceding discussion of freedom, with its necessary protective compulsion, impinges on the problem of social unity. Compulsion, in its various forms, brings about a degree of unity of behavior in a social or national group. There are, of course, sources of unity other than the compulsion consciously exercised by individuals or social groups. There are: blind prejudices and hatreds directed toward enemies; flashes of good sense leading to the recognition of the importance of uniting oneself with others, for the common good; rational persuasion, by self or others, of the value of a properly organized social or national group; the requirements of commerce. All these are important factors. Religions also function as creators of unity. Rome used a state religion as social cement. The foundation of Jewish solidarity is the common faith and ritual.

Whitehead casts a critical eye on the theory of the "original contract," whereby, supposedly, a political unity is established by agreement among free individuals. He remarks that this theory helped "to dismiss the Stuarts into romance." It was an important intellectual instrument in facilitating the French and American revolutions. However, it grossly overestimates the efficacy of "reason" in political affairs.

The fact that there are many non-rational factors productive of social unity leads Whitehead to remark that an increase in civilization does not necessarily enhance social unity. Indeed, by introducing a critical discontent, it may have the opposite result.

Whitehead provides a very useful discussion of the efficacy of symbols in promoting social unity. Symbols focus attention on techniques and objects. With such factors brought into clear perspective, a common and understood world is made available for unified experience. Symbols record and convey information. Without this medium of communication there can be little unity of thought and action. Some symbols are chiefly useful in touching off immediate reactions. For example, traffic lights or military commands are this type of symbol. Such symbols also are very useful in bringing about co-ordinated social activity. Effective symbols have a definite emotional flavor which provides their chief dynamic factor. Among the most effective symbols, productive of national unity, are the flag or some national hero. They, like other symbols, arouse people to perform certain definite actions. But they include a richer core of meaning in the realm of values. In this sense, the symbol points to excellences of behavior; and, in a vague, yet profound, fashion provides reasons why the action in question should be performed.

The "father of our country" symbolizes the highest ideals of the nation. In some fashion, difficult to explain, he guarantees the excellence of these ideals.

Whitehead points out that national unity can be maintained, even in the midst of a revolution, if the basic symbols are retained with little change. The American colonists repudiated George III and the British Parliament, but they retained a relatively unchanged symbolism: George Washington and the United States Congress. The nation remained.

The Problem of Leadership

One of the great weaknesses in modern society is the inadequacy of those who offer themselves as leaders. These men frequently are highly specialized in some restricted field of knowledge. Herein lies their inadequacy. The doctor or engineer who is given executive power may be well trained in his field, both theoretically and practically. But he is ignorant of other important areas of knowledge. He has had no experience in moving across a broad intellectual territory and making sound judgments as to paths to be followed and materials to be used. There also arises another grave difficulty which Whitehead aptly stresses. Since the most able men stay in their fields of specialization, the *co-ordination* of the activities of these professional men frequently is left to some second-rate person who has not been able to meet the rigorous requirements of a profession.

The solution, in Whitehead's opinion, is not "less professionalism." Progress depends on an increasing depth of knowledge. Further, he believes that the dogmatism which plagues some who have achieved eminence in a profession can be overcome and is being overcome. Whitehead is chiefly interested in broadening the scope of training without sacrificing depth. Thus, for example, the medical doctor should carry on research in some special field. But at the same time he should be capable of high-grade amateur performance in many other areas of human experience. Only thus will there be a healthy and progressive society.

Social Well-Being

Social well-being depends on the use made of the various factors discussed in Whitehead's philosophy of history. More specifically, technology, science, art, morality, and religion must be recognized as important ingredients in a flourishing community. True religion and morality are basic to the health of a society. Rome, at its best, illustrates this principle with reference to morality. Regulus returned to Carthage to die. He placed national and personal honor before the obvious comforts of life. The dangers implicit in too rigorous and uncritical use of a specific moral code should not blind us to the stability which a high ideal provides, if it is expressed through the medium of a flexible code adjusted to changing conditions. Unless scientists, technicians, and artists, as well as those engaged in industry, are able to combine sensitivity to the ideals of civilization with the energy to implement these ideals, their society will collapse into decadence. In this context, Whitehead stresses the value of a university in providing for social health and progress. Scholars must be closely linked with practical men. Indeed, the average citizen must also develop a fusion of theory and practice. Thus, the physical necessities of life (food, clothing, and shelter) and the impact of the physical environment will be met successfully. The "decks" will then be cleared for experiences of truth, beauty, art, adventure, and peace.

The preceding *comprehensive* approach to social welfare and progress must be kept in mind when one reads Whitehead's statement that "the plain economic facts of life must be the governing force in social development." [7] Here he is emphasizing the *particular* point that although a fortunate minority may provide the intellectual leadership which results in social change, and these leaders are in a sense free from the immediate pressure of economic factors; yet, unless a measure of economic satisfaction has been obtained by the "masses," there will be no social progress. Indeed, all classes of society must co-operate if there is to be well-being and progress.

Among the basic lessons which must be learned is the fact that social life requires stability, routine. No one can live ef-

fectively as a person, or as a member of society, in a state of
chaos. However, the routine must be kept within limits. If it
interferes with the spirit of adventure, rather than serves as a
useful instrument, then disaster comes to a society. The ideal
situation, then, is an enlightened balance of routine and creative
development. This principle must be linked with the related
one that: "the achievement which is excellent to-day may be
grossly inadequate to-morrow." A society cannot stand still or
live on inherited capital. "Advance or Decadence are the only
choices offered to mankind. The pure conservative is fighting
against the essence of the Universe." [8]

Incidentally, one area in which progress is needed is the
place of women in society. All his life Whitehead was an advocate of equal rights for women. The inferior position of
women in society is a thinly veiled expression of the old appeal
to force, which is not characteristic of a highly civilized society.

Social Reform

In discussing social progress, Whitehead notes that, on occasion, violent methods have been used which have resulted in
revolutions. He suggests that some of these revolutions were
both beneficial and necessary. The revolution in England in
the seventeenth century, the French and American revolutions
in the eighteenth century, have resulted in great social good.
Yet, he issues a warning against too rapid change. Revolution
may destroy great values and provide little, or nothing, in their
place.

He considers, for example, as an extreme case, the institution
of slavery in the Roman Empire. It was unquestionably an evil.
Yet, what would have happened if it had been removed, say at
the time of Cicero? There is a strong possibility that it would
have brought about the destruction of Rome, its laws, its stand
against the barbarians, its activity as preserver of Greek and
Latin culture. Would not this have been a greater evil than the
continued existence of slavery? Whitehead seems willing to con-
clude that "the slaves were the martyrs whose toil made progress
possible." [9] This is not to say that he approves slavery as such.
He is stating that in some instances reforms, if they are to be

successful, must come slowly. The values of Greco-Roman life were preserved at the price of slavery. But these values were saved, and in the end the problem of slavery was solved without destroying the possibility of civilized life. Thus, Whitehead is convinced that "successful progress creeps from point to point." [10] His advice to the hot and hasty devotee of immediate reform, the blazing impractical idealist, is "We cannot be social reformers all the time."

National Standards and the Ruling Class

Whitehead's insight concerning the realities of political life is shown in his recognition that the ruling class of a nation tends to set up standards in accordance with its own interests. This is so in all fields of experience. For example, when an aristocratic group is in power the emphasis is on social control, the subordination of the individual to *authority*, not only political but also religious and cultural. On the other hand, when the middle-class businessman is in control of the state, *freedom* is emphasized. "A Free Church in a Free State" is a slogan implying not only political and religious freedom, for the individual of the ruling class, but also freedom in all phases of life. Nineteenth-century English life was predominantly controlled by middle-class businessmen. Since they did not feel the immediate pressure of the need for food, clothing, and shelter, they did not see any point in initiating social reforms designed to alleviate the misery of starving fellow men. "Let the Buyer Beware" was given an honored place among "moral" stipulations. The sale of adulterated food was sanctioned on this basis. In one of his apparently flippant, yet actually penetrating, comments Whitehead remarks that the doctrine of the "sole sovereignty of the state" is both shocking and unworkable. It was "a mere stick with which to beat the Papists" in the 16th and 17th centuries and "to provide policemen for the counting houses of merchants." [11] In short, it was an invention of Protestant businessmen, used to further their interests. They were so immersed in commerce that they were not interested in the new ideas developed by natural science. They were satisfied. Hence, they opposed, in the name of freedom, any alteration of the *status quo*. They identified civilization with the continuance of their security. The *status quo* received a moral halo.

Whitehead realizes that sometimes the apparent form of government is deceptive. For example, in England during the first sixty years of the eighteenth century the government was ostensibly aristocratic. But the actual power did not belong to the traditional nobility. The group whose interests really were being furthered were the merchants of London and Bristol.

INTERNATIONAL RELATIONS

It has been shown that Whitehead does not content himself with pious generalities concerning the civilized approach to social problems. His specific suggestions with reference to internal problems confronting a social group have been outlined. His comments concerning international problems are also worthy of consideration. In 1939 he grappled directly with several of the main problems then confronting the Anglo-Saxon world. (This essay was entitled: "An Appeal to Sanity.") His remarks concerning these specific contemporary problems involve references to *principles* which, by implication, indicate the nature of civilized procedure in similar situations.

Isolation

In his discussion of international relations, Whitehead raises the question of whether or not a powerful nation is justified in practicing "isolation" when evil is present in the world. He is of the opinion that "each nation is a trustee for the fostering of certain types of civilization within areas for which it is directly responsible. Its supreme duty is there." [12] On the basis of this principle he suggests that a nation should remain isolated unless: (a) the evils interfere with its duty, or (b) the evils can be removed without preventing the nation from performing its own special duty. It is pointed out that the application of this point of view to the Munich crisis issues in the conclusion that Great

Britain acted wisely in refraining from war at that time. Britain's area of responsibility is "the Empire," not Europe. Further, he argues that a war to protect the frontiers of Czechoslovakia would have had little moral justification, and also little chance of success. Such an action would have little moral justification because while it would support Czech national aspirations, it would sanction the continued thwarting of the national aspirations of *some* Germans, Poles, and Hungarians. It would have had little chance of success because of lack of common frontiers.

Of course, there was the fundamental question (in the late 1930's): "Is Germany to be allowed to extend her direct power over the whole of Central and Western Europe?" Whitehead replies that Germany (or any other nation under similar conditions) should be forcibly prevented when three conditions are present: "(1) When she is violently interfering with the development of other states, without the justification of establishing any principle of social coordination, acknowledged as of prime importance; (2) When the consequences of an attempt at forcible prevention will not be worse than the consequences of acquiescence; (3) When such an attempt can secure its direct object." [13] He claims that in the case of Czechoslovakia these conditions were not met.

On December 24, 1940, the Boston *Globe* contained the following Letter to the Editor:

Many eminent people, including highly respected Harvard professors have published reasons why American activity should be restricted to defense within her own borders. We know how the Priest and the Levite explained to their friends their conduct during their famous walk from Jerusalem to Jericho. They were influenced by three reasons: (1) The assault happened "on the other side"; (2) They had an inherited distrust of "Samaria"; (3) After the incident had blown over, a profitable trade could be carried on with the thieves. These considerations justify the Priest and the Levite if we put aside the moral issues upon which the parable insists. In the present case the moral issue is the defense of freedom.

This letter was signed: *Alfred N. Whitehead.*

Communism

Whitehead's comments concerning Communism are singularly brief.[14] He suggests that the Russian Revolution was "horrible but probably beneficial." The ruling dynasty was "moronic." The aristocracy was brilliant, except it showed an almost complete lack of political skills. He remarks that while learned economists declare that the theory of Karl Marx's *Das Kapital* is not supported by the facts, yet its efficacy is at least symptomatic of the evils involved in the industrial revolution.

Whitehead is much more specific with reference to Russia as a factor in European power politics. In the context of the situation in Europe before the outbreak of World War II, he suggests that a war on behalf of Czechoslovakia would bring Russian troops into the heart of Central Europe. He asks, with obvious irony, whether the Russians would be likely to preserve "the nice little Czech State on the liberal lines approved by America." [15] He comments, further, that the presence of Russia in Central Europe would lead to a ghastly struggle and an uncertain future.

Incidentally, he states, with sickening accuracy, that if war broke out in Europe the signal would be given for the massacre of hundreds of thousands of Jews. The only mistake he made was that he underestimated the inhuman ferocity of those in power.

The "Jewish Question"

Whitehead's comments concerning the question of a Jewish "national home" are worthy of careful attention. He makes the thought-provoking suggestion that the Jews are not the only group to be unpopular because of their creative initiative. We are reminded that in the eighteenth century the Scotch performed for England services analogous to those rendered by the Jews today for all races west of India and Central Asia.

It is Whitehead's considered judgment that "the question at issue is not the happiness of a finite group. It is the fate of our civilization." [16] This somewhat sweeping generalization is supported by the argument that Jews tend to emphasize concepts and ideals, relevant to progress, which have been forgotten or overlooked by Gentile worshipers of the *status quo*. Having said all this, Whitehead is careful to point out that Jews are not the only ones productive of originality and progress.

What then is the solution for the Jewish problem? Whitehead recommends that there be a "settlement" of Jewish people in diverse regions, not just in Palestine. What of Palestine? He argues that a reading of history shows that Jews and Mahometans *can* live together with mutual benefit. In the Middle Ages these two groups united in the co-operative promotion of a flourishing civilization. From this source Aquinas received his knowledge of Aristotle, and Roger Bacon obtained some of the foundations of modern science. The commercial activities of Italian cities, in the Renaissance, were copied from the previous activities of Jews and Syrians. Voluntary co-operation is the only possible basis for a successful solution of the conflicting claims of Jews and Arabs in Palestine. Any solution imposed from outside must fail.

General Principles

The foregoing suggestions illustrate a basic principle: "Political solutions devoid of compromise are failures from the ideal of statesmanship." By various references to the British Empire Whitehead develops the point that it is possible to achieve widespread unification of effort without an appeal to force—for example, the peaceful solution of the problems confronting Britain and India.

In the course of this "Appeal to Sanity" Whitehead mentions several other general principles which are applicable not only to the world of 1939 but also the world of today. He claims that in the confused complexity of international relations "there are no clear issues." When a clear-cut solution is offered and guaranteed to be absolutely correct, one can be sure that he is dealing with an artificial oversimplification. At the best it is a useful suggestion to stimulate the imagination. Whitehead also adumbrates the principle that the "vague sanctity of international law" does not have the relevance which some of its devotees claim.

It is contended that "obligation, in European foreign policy, arises from the facts of the immediate situation and from duty to the future. Formal law can refer only to situations sufficiently stable." [17]

Whitehead suggests that nationalism and the more specific social "isms" (Liberalism, Capitalism, Communism) are in themselves neither completely good nor completely evil. It depends on the particular situation in which they exist. For example, the Czech state of 1939 included other racial groups. Its nationalism imposed restrictions on these minority groups. Whitehead contends that "there was nothing necessarily wrong in this policy. It might have succeeded, in another century, or in the absence of German, Magyar, and Polish states across the border." [18] These general principles are not the only ones used by Whitehead in his approach to international relations. There is the brilliant comment that other nations, just because they are different, should not be regarded as enemies, but rather as "godsends." "Men require of their neighbors something sufficiently akin to be understood, something sufficiently different to provoke attention, and something great enough to command admiration. We must not expect, however, all the virtues." [19]

This "Appeal to Sanity" is not an isolated phenomenon, suggesting that Whitehead is concerned with international relations only at periods of extreme stress. Those who are familiar with his wide-ranging interests realize that this problem always attracted his attention. For example, in February, 1925, he gave an address at Phillips Academy (Andover, Mass.) entitled, "The Importance of Friendly Relations Between England and the United States." He began by emphasizing the point that friendship does not mean "imitation." Rather, there should be a vigorous development of distinctive characteristics. However, there is a genuine kinship of spirit linking the two nations which is based on mutual devotion to common ideals. Chief among these beliefs is the conviction that people should control their own destiny under the direction of strong moral purpose. Here, then, is the familiar civilized emphasis on persuasion rather than force. The essentially co-operative nature of the British Empire is also noted. The address closes with a stirring appeal to

American youth to undertake the "adventure" of creating a better "international future"; yet to do so with tolerance for the mistakes of the past and appreciation of the foundations laid by past generations.

Writing in 1941, Whitehead faced the "Problem of Reconstruction." We find him reaffirming his basic convictions concerning the essential qualities of civilization and the increasing need for hastening their more adequate realization. With undiminished fervor he advocates a "reconstructed" world in which basic human needs are satisfied, needs beyond those of the mere animal. He reminds us that "order" is not enough. There must be social flexibility, so that there may be respect for individual differences. A willingness to work toward compromise in human relations is essential. With sane realism he re-emphasizes the point that freedom without opportunity is meaningless. There must be a high level of wisdom manifest among all citizens. The need for rigorous self-criticism and concern for higher values is greater than ever before. Again he stresses the point that there is no "simple solution," no one completely comprehensive "blueprint," which can be applied to the problems of every social group. The dizzy rate of social change is another inescapable fact which must be accorded a more serious consideration. As he remarked in his "Appeal to Sanity": "These warnings [and suggestions] are commonplace. Unfortunately they are required." [20]

Chapter 5 EDUCATION

INTRODUCTION

The type of education which aids in the achievement of civilized life is discussed with great care by Whitehead. He is, most emphatically, of the opinion that education should not be concerned *exclusively* with the development of abstract intellectual skills, and the acquisition of factual knowledge. All this is important, but it is not enough. Education is also the acquisition of the "art of the utilization of knowledge." [1] The pleasures of executing intellectual minuets may be appealing. But, the joys of the "lotus-eaters" are not synonymous with the fruits of education. Education should make it possible for a man to think *and act* in a "worthy" fashion. The man who is not fully appreciative of aesthetic, moral, and religious experience is not really educated. By appreciation Whitehead does not imply mere passive awareness. He means that these ideals should infuse all the details of thought, and action.

More specifically, education must provide the opportunity for a person to develop the potentialities that lie within him, in such a manner that he will deal with his environment in an effective and excellent fashion, guided always by the highest ideals of human envisagement. Education should evoke creative curiosity, imagination, balanced judgment, stability of character, and the ability to see general rules embedded in particular situations—plus the foresight to use this knowledge in dealing with "future" problems. The educated man will be able to distinguish between what is relatively certain and what is only probable. Because he recognizes the difference between what is little and what is great, he will act, without undue debate, before it is too late.

Such a life is characterized by "style"; that is to say, excellence in performance. Style, in Whitehead's sense, means a lack of waste and indecision. All phases of thought and action fit together in a harmonious fashion. The performance is brilliant, not in an obtrusive fashion. Rather it is restrained brilliance of a craftsman who knows what is to be done and does it well. Style demonstrates that excellence can be useful, that knowledge can be mated with action in the achievement of the good life. The truly educated man has the precise knowledge of the expert in some areas of human knowledge; but he retains the flexibility, versatility, and relaxed enjoyment of the amateur in his general approach to life. He is at home in the world. His world is vast, rich in achievement—with even greater values "beyond."

The preceding discussion makes meaningful an otherwise cryptic comment by Whitehead that "the essence of education is that it be religious." [2] This is an expression of his conviction that knowledge involves *responsibilities* and duties, that available knowledge should be used for the solving of human problems. The element of *reverence* should also be present. It must be recognized that the present is of vast importance. It carries the impact of the past and is the starting point for all that occurs in the future, be it good or ill. Thus, the "present is holy ground." Education, in coming to grips with *present* problems, therefore should involve the feeling of reverence that characterizes religion.

This sketch of *education as it should be* is admittedly highly idealized. However, it is not to be regarded as the idle dream of a nice old gentleman slumbering under the elms, safely sheltered behind a high red-brick wall. Whitehead was well aware of the sort of world in which he lived. He lost a son in World War I. He was immersed in the practical politics of the Labour party in England during the recession after the war. He felt the miseries of men all over the world. Despite his devotion to the "high" values of life, he was realistic concerning the need for effective dealing with brute destructive forces. He saw, as clearly as any man, that without trained intelligence, used in the struggle for survival, the supreme values of life could not be preserved. Blind heroism, brittle wit and charm, will not save a man or a nation. There must be a solid foundation of factual knowledge, and a high degree of skill in applying it to the problems of present-day existence. Certainly, the glorious achievements of the past will not guarantee a secure future. Unless a nation can plan, and produce "the bomb," and use it wisely, its future is dark indeed. It may have a great literature and scores of magnificent cathedrals, and in the past the sun may never have set on its flag—but, without trained intelligence, "the pit yawns." This is not to say that trained intelligence should be inoperative in fields other than science. The habits of thought which are effective in dealing with facts must also be used in dealing with values. However, the point remains: unless there is a foundation element of factual knowledge and technical skill, a fruitful fusing of fact and value is impossible.

GENERAL PRINCIPLES

The ideal education which Whitehead envisages is delineated in a number of general principles illustrated in the details of specific suggestions as to curricula and educational procedures.

There is a sense of profound urgency and deep concern in Whitehead's approach to education. "When one considers in its length and in its breadth the importance of this question of the education of a nation's young, the broken lives, the defeated hopes, the national failures, which result from the frivolous inertia with which it is treated, it is difficult to restrain within oneself a savage rage." [3] What then should be done?

In the first place it must be remembered that *the human mind is not analogous to a trunk* into which bits of "knowledge" can be piled without requiring any co-operation from the trunk, and without effecting the contents in any significant fashion, except that they are in the trunk. A much more accurate analogy is to regard the mind as a living organism, and what is learned as food necessary for continued life, health, and efficiency.

This, of course, involves a *denial of the "tool theory"* which regards the mind as an instrument that is first sharpened, by the educational process, and then used, later, in adult life. In a rather figurative sense, the mind is a "tool," i.e., it is used. To that extent the theory is a half truth. But the tool analogy is woefully wrong in its implication that the mind is a passive entity completely shaped by external stimuli and then, later, used as one would use a hammer. Actually, the mind is continuously active, in constant interaction with its environment. Further, the implication that knowledge is something to be used *later* is completely rejected by Whitehead. In his judgment, the focus of the mind, and its knowledge, should be the present. If knowledge is to be retained it must be "applied" at once.

This vital, *dynamic* approach to education, stressing the *usefulness of knowledge*, issues in a vigorous denunciation of the all too common educational system which forces meaningless, dead ideas on bitterly resentful and resisting students. Unless what a person is learning is interesting, and enjoyable, the process of self-development is seriously retarded; not nourishment but poison is being absorbed.

Many meaningless, or inert, ideas are such because they are rooted in a past which is no longer of interest to the student. Indeed, interest is derived from a recognition of the importance of the data under consideration. Above all, *what the person learns should be "his discovery"* as far as possible; not handed to him, but "found." In other words, knowledge should be apprehended as something fresh and vital. Consider, for example, the teaching of history. It has been, for the most part, a limp and deplorable procedure. As Whitehead remarks: "What purpose is effected by a catalogue of undistinguished kings and queens? Tom, Dick, or Harry, they are all dead. General resurrections are failures, and are better postponed." [4] This should not be interpreted to mean that the study of history is unimportant. The essential thing is to make historical facts meaningful and vital. If a "Harry" is seen, not as a weight on the memory, but as the reflection of an age from which much can be learned —then we are no longer dealing with an inert idea.

In brief, Whitehead contends that the *interests* and *needs* of the student should be the starting point in any educational program. This is not to say that a few shallow interests, or imagined needs, should be allowed to overbalance other, more fundamental interests and real needs which are involved in the full development of the individual.[5] Also, this does not mean that the educational process should be "fun and games," a carefree Indian summer of superficial pleasures. Whitehead is not suggesting that interest should be aroused by the *artificial* association of pleasure with some otherwise inherently disagreeble, or dull, subject matter. Rather, the enjoyment to which he refers must arise naturally.

There is hard work to be done. Facts, generalities, and techniques must be learned: reading, writing, arithmetic, the essential facts of history and geography—all this and much more. Such knowledge, even if initial interest is aroused, requires concentration and great exertion. Thus, obviously, Whitehead does not merit the criticism that he would make education too easy. He remarks, with characteristic humor, that "in education, as elsewhere, the broad primrose path leads to a nasty place."[6] It is true that this statement occurs in the context of a denunciation of the pedagogical method which is centered in a text to be memorized, for use in an external examination. However, this statement may be generalized to apply to any system of education which attempts a degree of simplification, and easiness, below the rigorous requirements of genuine self-development.

There must be discipline. Some tasks must be performed which are dull and routine. But at the beginning of the educational process, there should be a genuine desire to learn, on the part of the student. At the end of the process, there should be a sense of enjoyable achievement. The rigors of routine must be suffused with a sense of their value in the *total* program.

In this type of education, the teacher performs a difficult yet absolutely essential function. The teacher should arouse enthusiasm for valuable patterns of life by demonstrating the excellence of such patterns. Further, the teacher should exercise some control over the environment so that useful data may be available at suitable times. After all, there has been some human progress. Students should not be allowed to stumble along on the level of the cave man, when something better is available.

To repeat, in the last analysis, the student will accept discipline only if he sees its value in furthering his development, and is able to give it a personalized flavor—that is to say, experiences the *details* of the discipline in a personally selected fashion. Thus, discipline serves as the basis of a wider freedom. By self-imposed, or willingly accepted, discipline a man is freed from caprices of whim and from vagrant passion.

Whitehead's conclusion is that *education should be a mixture of discipline and freedom*. A person should be free to follow his genuine interests, and achieve deep enjoyments. But, he must willingly consider the requirements of the situation and the well-being of others, and make use of the techniques necessary to obtain the desired results.

Whitehead is sufficiently optimistic to believe that most students will be able to appreciate the worth of civilization, in all phases of human experience, and hence enjoy the high values which are available to man.

Whitehead's long life gave him ample opportunity to observe the absolute *asininity of dogmatism in knowledge*. He remarks, as has already been noted, that every basic generalization in mathematical physics he was taught at Cambridge during the years 1880-85, has since been abandoned; or, if at least the verbal formulation has been retained, the meaning has been changed. Not only is "knowledge content" continually being revised. There is also the inescapable fact of the limitation of human knowledge. As Whitehead, with somewhat extreme irony, says: even scholars and professors are, alike, ignoramuses. Tolerance, therefore, and the eager expectation of new knowledge are the appropriate attitudes for those who approach education in the proper fashion.

It should be obvious, from the foregoing, that Whitehead stresses the *necessity of firsthand knowledge* of facts, and values (both ideal and actual). One major defect, in much of educational procedure, is that books are allowed to come between the student and firsthand experience. The individual is confronted by unrelated scraps of secondhand "information." Whitehead bitterly remarks that the learned world is mediocre because it has never been "scared by the facts." He notes that, in the Garden of Eden, Adam and Eve saw the animals before they named them. Unfortunately, in the garden of North America, children usually know the names of animals they will never see. As a result of the bookishness of modern education, and our resultant immersion in words, we suffer from a serious malady— that of undue reliance on symbols. We neglect the things symbolized.

Basically, words are a series of squeaks. True, they can be made to serve as symbols, but they are often ambiguous in their reference. Further, words are designed to deal with frequently occurring, obvious objects. There simply is not an adequate vocabulary available for use with reference to subtle, infrequent, and complex factors in the environment or in the inner experience of men. The history of mathematics illustrates the fact that many basic ideas, in this field, cannot clearly be expressed. Indeed, it is a common experience in everyday life to grope unsuccessfully for a word to express what you have in mind. Intuition, immediate experience, exceeds our powers of symbolization. Thus, as system of education which *concentrates* on words, or other symbols, is doomed to myopic sterility.

Whitehead's emphasis on the value aspect of experience, and hence its importance in the educational procedure, has been noted. He points out that works of art, by revealing beauty, have great efficacy in impressing upon students the *importance of values in human experience.* Beauty, in art or in nature, reveals an excellence beyond the mere brute facts of animal existence. A work of art is a challenging example of human achievement. A sense of disciplined relaxation, and enjoyment, may also accrue to the beholder. For these reasons art, and the appreciation of the beauties of nature, should have a prominent place in any educational program.[7]

Whitehead is appalled at the lack of *organic interrelation* among the parts of the usual educational curriculum. He denounces those who seek to sunder the seamless robe of learning. Life should be a unity of various worth-while experiences. Education should make possible the attainment of this unity. It is not only inefficient, it is "soul murder" to perpetrate the usual system of instruction. Bits of mathematics, pellets of history, segments of literature, fragments of a language, are placed before uninterested students. They are then forced to pass uninspired examinations on this apparently meaningless, and irrelevant, material.

This series of chasms between uninteresting material can be replaced by something much more satisfactory. For example, in measuring the geographical extent of the community in which he lives, the student will learn not only mathematics but also surveying. Local history inevitably will come into focus, as landmarks are located. Considerable geographical information also will be absorbed. In the course of the project, an enlargement of psychological, and sociological, knowledge will take place. Thus, a comparatively simple project will enable a student to (begin to) understand his environment, and see the interrelations of the various complex factors therein.

One of the difficulties, which stands in the way of co-ordination, is the vast amount of factual knowledge and skills in the modern educational curriculum. Therefore, those who are directing the program must have the good sense to *concentrate only on what is really important.* It may even be necessary to delete some time-honored educational "ornaments" and monuments. This does not mean that excessive simplification is commendable. Life is complex. No adequate educational system can safely overlook that fact. Excessive concentration on one field of knowledge is disastrous, be it science, literature, or technology. It is, of course, essential to know *facts* and to acquire *skills.* But, without the guidance provided by awareness of *values,* a person wanders in the wilderness.

Thus, *specialization is necessary for efficiency, but maturity of judgment requires a broad background of general knowledge.* The dangers of restricted professional training are stated clearly by Whitehead. The result of such training is a great deal of knowledge about a few things, but woeful ignorance about many others. For example, our society has produced many men who are outstanding in science but have little knowledge, and less competence, in the fields of politics, art, and religion. Further, there is no adequate training for the task of co-ordinating the activities of these experts. Thus, to repeat an earlier point, there should be an aesthetic element in education—aesthetic in the sense that an awareness of the unity, and complexity, of data is attained. Things are seen in their interrelations, and their values are appreciated. In short, an adequate education requires a philosophic synthesis of the diverse elements of human experience.

Whitehead is anxious to emphasize the idea that there should not be an artificial dichotomy set up between general education, and specialized studies of some specific subject matter. In his opinion, the proper method is to deal with specific subjects by employing generality of outlook. Further, the best way to encourage generality of outlook is to arouse genuine interest in one subject. The good student will quickly realize that one subject leads to another, as in the case of the measuring of the boundaries of a community. Gradually, the general principles of human knowledge will emerge.

Whitehead gives much more than lip service to the ideal that *thought should be mated with bodily action.* After all, we are animals possessing bodies. We have a strong tendency to *do* things. Whitehead is inclined to believe that unless bodily activity is encouraged, brain lethargy results. He refers to the English aristocracy as a case in point. (In his opinion, fox hunting is not sufficient salvation!) He suggests, further, that scholars who spend all their time reading are not great thinkers. On the other hand, those who are faced with the necessity of expressing themselves, in speaking or writing, escape at least in part from the intellectual lassitude which accompanies bodily inactivity.

In this context, he stresses the great value of handicrafts, as an essential ingredient in education. It should be clear that manual dexterity, and skill in translating thoughts into the manipulation of the material environment, are very important in art, science, and technology. In short, we have many kinds of experience and interests. It is then artificial to disregard the skilled use of hands and feet. These activities are part of the unified development of the complete person. This emphasis on handicrafts should be maintained (with discretion) all through primary and secondary school, as one essential factor in the total pattern. Whitehead admits that when some students reach the university they may, legitimately, devote themselves almost en-

tirely to intellectual training. However, if a student is interested
in science, technology, or art, the "handicrafts" *relevant to these
fields* obviously should have an important place in the curriculum.

Despite his emphasis on usefulness and the need for immediate application of theories, Whitehead is well aware of the
dangers of haste in such matters. The theory must be understood
as thoroughly as possible before it is tested in the flux of experience. There is no point in putting a child to work applying
geometrical theory in laying out a ball park until he has mastered
the relevant principles of geometry. Thus, while there is danger
in delaying too long the use of theory in practical affairs, the opposite danger is just as great.

Our era is unique in the sense that *changes are so rapid we
cannot be sure that a set of ideas, and skills, can be provided for
the student which will "see him through"* his lifetime. Unless
this is recognized, the individual may be shackled by ideas and
patterns of thought and action. He will share the fate of the
dinosaur who also was caught unprepared for a rapidly changing environment. Thus, factual content, and skills, must be
taught; but at the same time the student must recognize their
transitory status in the scheme (and stream) of things. He
should be encouraged to develop flexibility and adaptability.
Habits of accurate observation; the power of recognizing generalizations, illustrated in a number of particular experiences,
which can be translated into predictions concerning the future;
a sense of the novelty of life: these—with an awareness, and appreciation, of the values life may bring—are the gifts which an
adequate education should provide.

If education is to meet the needs of individuals, it is obvious
that *no single, rigorous curriculum can be imposed on all.* There
are striking individual differences, both in ability and interest.
Adjustments must be made. Yet, as Whitehead goes on to argue,
it should be possible to outline a sufficiently comprehensive
system of education which will meet the *basic* human needs of
almost all students. Within this general program the details of
educational procedure, at any one school, must vary. This is so,
not only because of the nature of the students, but also because
of the characteristics of the teaching staff and the facilities pro-

vided by the school. Advantage should be taken of the presence of persons specially trained in some field, or the fact that the environment focuses attention on certain specific facts or problems.

Whitehead objects, very strenuously, to the prevalent system of common external examinations. He means examinations set by those who are not teachers of the students taking the examinations; for example, examinations written by all students in a large area or district. The objections offered by Whitehead are numerous. Such examinations tend to concentrate on minute facts which are memorized. In the process, the meaning of the facts is frequently lost. There is little or no opportunity for the student to show evidence of his initiative, soundness of judgment, or powers of generalization and foresight. True, these examinations "check up" on slackness. However, Whitehead believes that it is better to check the efficiency of the school. This would allow for greater possibility of individual development on the part of the student. As long as the school maintains a high standard of excellence, the details of the program could be varied to meet individual needs. The school certificate would be an adequate guarantee of the student's achievement. His teachers would, of course, examine his work. But it would be done far more directly, and thoroughly, than by a common external examination.

Having stressed the organic analogy in discussing the educational process, Whitehead points out that *educational growth is rhythmic in character*. It is not a continuous process, proceeding in a straight line, at the same pace. Effective education requires that this fact be recognized. That is to say, unless subject matter and methods of study are adjusted to the natural rhythm of human growth, the educational process will not facilitate human development.[8]

There are three main stages in the life of a person. First, there is the stage of *romance*. This is the period in which one experiences a vast range of data that excite interest. The full nature, and the complex relationships, of these data are not understood. The *joy of discovery* and the thrill of unexplored possibilities are the prominent elements found in this stage of human experience. Roughly speaking, it is the period from birth to the end of primary school education. Next there is the stage of *precision*. During this the student becomes aware of the *structure* of thought and of action. The grammatical aspect of language comes to the fore, and also the laws of science. Rules of behavior become important. A person's life, in all its phases, undergoes discipline. The data presented in the first stage (that of romance) are now organized, their meaning is clarified. Accuracy and efficiency, in thought and action, are being developed. This is the period of secondary school education. Finally, there is the stage of *generalization*. There is a rebirth of the enthusiasm which characterizes the stage of romance. The world is once again enjoyed in its rich complexity. But the rigorous training, provided by the stage of precision, results in a greater appreciation of the data provided by the environment. *General principles* are now a prominent feature of mental life. The bungling enthusiasms of youth are being replaced by the calm efficiency of maturity.

The practical applications of this analysis to the educational system are obvious. A considerable amount of drill and direction, in secondary education, is necessary because it is natural. But, it must presuppose a primary education which is characterized by "romance" rather than "precision." Those who go on to a university should not be submerged in the drill and routine of high school. As Whitehead says, the university student should stand up and look around, enjoying the world revealed by the techniques acquired during secondary education.

Within the *major* "three-stage rhythm" of development there are innumerable *minor* rhythms which must be considered. For example, a child, *during the period from birth to the end of primary education,* passes through stages of romance, precision, and generalization. His early consciousness reveals to him a vast, and highly interesting, world (romance). He develops some skills in language and action (precision). In due time he takes his place as a junior member of society, enthusiastically in search of new experiences, yet disciplined by the rigorousness of the period in which he laboriously learned to walk, talk, and act in a socially acceptable fashion (generalization). Thus, the first stage—romance—in the major (life-time) rhythm manifests a minor rhythm of three stages: romance, precision, and generalization. Further, Whitehead suggests that any *lesson*, at any stage in the educational process, should have a rhythmic character. There should be a stage of romance, in which interest and enthusiasm are aroused; next, a period of rigorous analysis and clarification (precision); finally, a full appreciation of the subject matter, a recognition of the fundamental principles illustrated in the specific subject under discussion (generalization).

Whitehead is very careful to point out that within any cycle, the distinction between stages is not absolute and clear cut. It is a difference in emphasis. Within any cycle, romance, precision, and generalization are present throughout.

It is necessary, for maximum efficiency, to obtain diversity of stages at any one time during the educational program. For example, in the period of secondary education, a student at the age of 15 will work to best advantage if he is at the stage of precision in language, but in the stage of romance as far as science is concerned. If the student is in the stage of precision in both language and science, there would be danger of interference, and lowering of efficiency. In general, the educational programs should be organized so that the student will be able to concentrate, in turn, on a variety of subjects. These should be integrated, in meaningful fashion, in such a way that the rigors of routine and drill are motivated by preliminary interest and enjoyment, and are seen to be steps toward greater values.

APPLICATIONS OF GENERAL PRINCIPLES IN SECONDARY SCHOOLS

Whitehead's discussion of these general principles is clarified by reference to more specific details, chiefly in the areas of secondary school and university education.

On the secondary school level, in particular, he discusses the nature of the *curriculum* which should be provided. It is composed of the three major elements: literary, scientific, and technological. All three elements should be present in the education of every student. There will, of course, be varying emphases depending on the interests and vocational needs of the individual students concerned.

Literary Education

The contribution of a literary education is that it acquaints the student with the best that has been thought, and imagined, in the realm of the higher values. A reading of literature does not only reveal ideals and introduce philosophical criticism and speculation. There is also the record of historical events—the greatness, littleness, and ordinariness, of men and women. Literature in general, history in particular, should be appreciated not only intellectually but also emotionally. The various individual facts, and values, should be apprehended as living elements in present experience. Unless the past, as recorded in historical documents, is a vital, effective factor in the present; unless present facts are seen in their context as part of the flux of history coming from the past, going onward into the future; then the present is mere shallow froth, and it loses its real meaning.

A genuine grasp of particular historical facts can be greatly facilitated by the presentation of models or pictures of buildings, clothing, household utensils, letters, and the like. Dramatic presentations are also effective methods for making historic knowledge specific, and vital.

The values of art, for education, have been mentioned previously. Here, again, attention must be called to Whitehead's contention that art can evoke vision, inspiration, insight, refreshment, discipline. For that reason, works of art should have a prominent place in the educational program of the secondary schools. He believes that dramas and films are particularly effective, paintings less so.

A study of the *Greek and Latin classics* has an honored place in Whitehead's scheme of secondary education, at least for a majority of students. He is convinced that a study of the *structure* of Latin will give a student valuable training in exact, logical thought. Further, the way the Romans expressed themselves, in the structure of their language, reveals much of their philosophy and history.

It may be objected that the best way to learn logic is to

study logic, rather than a language like Latin. Whitehead's reply is that at least until a student reaches the university, his approach to knowledge should be in terms of particulars. The logic studied should be the logics of something. Using an unfamiliar language avoids the difficulties which arise from the study of the structure of one's own language—the difficulties involved in boredom due to familiarity. Whitehead's general suggestion that a language reveals history, and philosophy, is worthy of note. Certainly English, for example, reveals the Norman invasion and the development of gadgets. The use of the first person singular, or lack of its use, is clearly indicative of the philosophy of life held by a person or a nation. Whitehead is prepared to admit that Latin is not a universally effective instrument for cultural development. Some very fine minds do much better when confronted by a butterfly, or a steam engine.

Language, of course, is embodied in a literature. In Whitehead's judgment, Roman literature is inferior to English literature. The trouble is that the Romans apparently regarded the "Forum as the foot stool of God." Roman literature sings the praises of Rome exclusively, and usually uncritically. Actually, much of Roman literature is lacking in depth, richness, and subtlety. In comparison with English, Latin literature is a poor second. Contrast the philosophical writings of Bacon, Hobbes, Locke, Berkeley, Hume, and even Mill, with those of—Cicero. Who else can Rome offer except Lucretius? When it comes to insight into the depths of human personality, Shakespeare and novelists like Dickens are head and shoulders above Terence and Plautus. What Roman author can equal the humor· of Dickens and Sheridan?

Yet, despite their inferiority as a literature, the Latin classics do provide valuable insight concerning the history, and geography, of Europe. The civilization of the distant past has come to us through Rome. Hence, the literature of Rome may be used, profitably, as a source of information about other races. It has a further value. Rome did things on a "grand scale." Roman aims, virtues, and vices were alike massive. Their "habitual vision of greatness" is one of the precious gifts of Rome to the modern world.

Whitehead remarks that when the possibility of using *"the classics in translation"* is introduced for discussion, classical scholars react as "decent" people do when confronted by a nasty sex problem. He suggests that it is realistic to recognize that most people are not able to master Greek and Latin to such an extent that they will be able to read even the minimum of Greek and Latin literature which is required for secondary school education. He portrays, with not very subtle irony, the laborious process by which the average student picks words out of a dictionary, and then loses the meaning of the sentence in a grammatical haze. He concludes, with considerable feeling: "You may take the noblest poetry in the world, and if you stumble through it at a snail's pace, it collapses from a work of art into a rubbish heap." [9] This is not to say that there should be absolutely no translation of the classics by students. Rather, what is attempted should be kept within reasonable limits, and undertaken only after a "scholar's translation" has given the student insight into the material to be read. Thus, Whitehead emphasizes the importance of "the classics in translation," but not as an escape from acquaintance with the original language. Rather, his purpose is to ensure that the acquaintance will be more effective. In any case, the emphasis on *both* original and translation, rather than a secondhand account—some digest prepared by a literary hack—is typical of Whitehead's general contention that ideas should have a firm foundation in the facts under consideration.

Whitehead indicates, in general, the type of Greek and Latin literature which should be read in translation: *Latin*—selections from Virgil, Lucretius, Cicero, Plutarch; *Greek*—selections from the *Odyssey*, Herodotus, some of the choruses of the great plays, Euclid.

Whitehead believes that by the time students finish secondary education they should have a good command of English, read simple French fluently, and have mastered elementary Latin. He admits that a minority of students should not be expected to reach these levels of attainment. Superior students should, in addition, have made a good start in Greek.

The Study of Natural Science

The study of the natural sciences provides an excellent opportunity to develop the art of thought. By this Whitehead means that a person will form the habit of "starting" and "ending" with firsthand experience. He will record data in clear and exact concepts. He will formulate general truths which have been discovered in particular observations. There will also be the working out of implications of these truths, which can then be applied and tested by reference to further particular data. Thus, science teaches the lesson that effective thought must be linked to observation. The value of an exploratory hypothesis in guiding observation should also be noted. It follows that scientific thinking is capable of disciplining the character of a man. The habits of thought developed in scientific work may color the whole texture of mental life and so exert a beneficial influence in other areas of mental life. However, Whitehead is quite prepared to admit that a man who thinks well in science *may* think poorly in the classics, and vice versa.

Turning to the details of the natural science curriculum, Whitehead suggests that probably no more than two subjects can be dealt with at the same time, in an efficient fashion—that is to say, supported by adequate laboratory work. Physics and chemistry seem the most suitable subjects for the majority of students. Incidentally, the interrelations of these two subjects should be made clearly evident. In addition to this "hard core" of scientific work, there should be a "soft"—i.e., non-laboratory —element in scientific education (at the secondary school level). There should be opportunity for "browsing": self-initiated study of some other fields of scientific knowledge, such as botany and astronomy. Further lectures could be provided to make up deficiencies in the program of study. Toward the end of the secondary school period, students might well spend very little time in the laboratory. They should concentrate on a lecture course dealing with the basic concepts, and laws, of science. Also, information should be provided concerning the applications of science, and the impact of these applications on the social, political, and industrial life of men.

Mathematics

Whatever the particular natural science subject matter may be, mathematics will have an essential place in the curriculum. In a somewhat extreme statement, Whitehead remarks: "To talk sense is to talk quantitatively." He means, of course, that everything has a mathematical aspect. This aspect cannot safely be disregarded. Even the flight of a bird, and the rhythm of poetry, can be stated mathematically. However, despite his enthusiasm for mathematics, Whitehead emphasizes that this is not the whole story.

The phases of mathematics which should be stressed are: relations of numbers, relations of quantities, relations of space.

One great value of mathematics is that it encourages the development of powers of abstract thinking, of generality, and thus frees the mind from bondage to particular data. It is characteristic of Whitehead's balanced approach to life that he remind us that, while abstract thinking has an essential place, it is equally important that generalizations be applied to particular facts for further verification. For example, in an educational program, the ideas of geometry should be applied to shop work, surveying, or map reading.

The value of geometry, in developing logical habits of thought, is strongly emphasized. Effective thought demands that one get hold of the most fundamental ideas, and then arrange all other ideas in relation to these—at the same time refusing to be distracted by irrelevant considerations. This is exactly what happens in geometry.

The phases of geometry to be studied in the secondary school curriculum must be carefully restricted. Students should be required to concentrate on congruence, similarity, trigonometry (regarded as the instrument by which the main geometrical ideas are made available for use). Periodicy should be studied. The value of trigonometry and algebraic functions, in providing precise statements of physical laws, should be emphasized and illustrated. Analytic geometry and, if possible, projective geometry should be included. Whitehead offers considerable detailed specification of contents within these areas of mathematical knowledge. In general, he concentrates on those which provide training in logical method, and the precise ideas which lie at the basis of scientific and philosophic investigation.

The interrelations of mathematics and other forms of knowledge are shown in the use of graphs (which express fundamental algebraic principles). These graphs reveal otherwise hidden relations between social phenomena; for example, industrial strife and attendance at the theater. Such a practical use of mathematics will not only demonstrate the unity of knowledge, and the usefulness of mathematics. It will also increase knowledge of mathematics as such, and social forces as such.

Technical Education

Technical education is important because it is the type which a considerable number of people chiefly need. Further, the nation requires a large number of skilled workers. Whitehead does not consider technical education as mere training for "factory hands." Rather, it should be regarded as a method of producing citizens who are skilled craftsmen, able to derive personal satisfaction from work which they find meaningful and worthwhile.

Technical education illustrates the essential educational principle that knowledge should be rooted in firsthand experience, and issue in practical results. It must not be forgotten that there is a basic intellectual factor in technical activity. Ideas are translated into manual skill. Manual skill frequently evokes ideas. Further, in successful technical activity, thought takes on the characteristics of foresight and is the foundation, and instrument, of achievement. For example, a person who is skillful in manipulating mechanical devices may produce unexpected, and surprising, results. This experience may stimulate him to try to understand how these results could occur. If this intellectual problem is solved, further technological development can be anticipated.

The acquisition of a narrow range of skills, in some special "trade," is not the goal of technical education. Personal and national needs require a high degree of flexibility in competence. No man should be shackled to one machine as the result of his technical education. He must be trained to adjust himself readily to a wide variety of particular situations.

This width of outlook, and proficiency, can be acquired most easily if technical education includes a study of the *natural science* most obviously related to the technical field in which the student is being trained. For example, geometry would be of value to carpenters and to workers in many arts. Biology would be of assistance to those majoring in agriculture. A *literary component* of technical education might well be the reading of history and geography, providing these have a bearing on the problems of ordinary social life. Books on recent developments in science would also be worth while. However, Whitehead does not intend to include popular tracts "inflated with gas on the wonders of science." [10] The purpose of including literature in the technical curriculum is to provide intellectual stimulus and enjoyment. It really does not matter what the students read as long as they enjoy literature (provided that it functions in the fashion outlined above). The enjoyment need not be exclusively the result of the stimulus derived from reading. There is also the enjoyment of relaxation, the escape from the immediate environment into the world of literature. Most certainly Whitehead does not regard technical education as a "poor relation," a second best in some rigid "aristocratic" academic hierarchy.

Summary: The Best Secondary School Curriculum

Whitehead contends that the best balance of intellect and character can be obtained only as the result of a *fusion* of literary, scientific, and technical training, designed to meet the needs of the individuals concerned. The preceding discussion of technical education has shown how the three elements can be interrelated, not just artificially piled together. In the program of technical training outlined above, the main stress is placed on the acquisition of manual and technical skills. But scientific and literary studies constitute essential elements in the total program, and facilitate the development of a desirable type of citizen.

A different emphasis, but the same basic elements, should be found in the so-called literary curriculum. For example, the

ideal literary curriculum is concerned chiefly with language, and
literature. But it ought to deal also with the *techniques* of verbal
expression and the *science* of the structure of language.

The ideal scientific curriculum is primarily concerned with
the accurate observation of natural phenomena, and the formulation of relevant laws. But *techniques* of observation and application are very important. No scientist can disregard the
literature of his subject, and his civilization.

Thus, in Whitehead's opinion, there are three roads to self-
development (on the secondary school level): a predominantly
literary education, a predominantly scientific education, a predominantly technical education. But in each there should be
elements of the other two. No one system will meet the needs
of all men. The academic garment should be tailored to fit the
wearer.

PRACTICAL APPLICATIONS IN
UNIVERSITY EDUCATION

Purpose

Whitehead believes that universities should be the chief
agencies encouraging the development of civilization in the
modern world. They must take the place of religious institutions
which, in the past, performed this function. He makes it clear
that he is here referring to a certain kind of university. He has
in mind the University of London, and American universities of
the same type. These are institutions of higher learning which
are designed to provide men and women of all classes, and interests, with opportunities to reach higher levels of self-development.

Whitehead is convinced that university education should
be concerned not only with facts and techniques but also with
values and powers of critical judgment. Another related function
of university education is training in ability to unify, and make
meaningful, the complexities of experience. Thus, Whitehead's
goal for university education is *primarily* the development of a

certain set of mental habits, and the ability to grasp a relatively few basic laws and principles which the student can learn to apply to any particular situation. In brief, the main purpose of the university is not to cram a large number of "facts" into the student's mind. Rather, habits of mind must be developed which will enable the student to act efficiently, when confronted with some specific problem. Further, he will become aware of the complexity of human experience and the limits of human knowledge. He will be developing a balanced maturity of judgment, which saves him from confusion in vital issues and removes him from the class on whom the Barnums of the world fatten their purses.

This is not to say that Whitehead underestimates the importance of facts, in the university stage of education. One important phase of university training consists in providing techniques for the skillful and effective discovery of facts, and the recording and presenting of these facts. What Whitehead is opposing is the *aimless, meaningless accumulation* of vast masses of factual knowledge. In short, he contends that at a university a person should acquire the ability to *use knowledge* in accordance with the selective and evaluative power of wisdom. Mere knowledge is not enough. Unless it is properly appreciated and used wisely, it may be a terrible curse.

In discussing factual knowledge, and the need to "approach" it in accordance with the dictates of wisdom, Whitehead occasionally makes somewhat misleading statements. For example: "Your learning is useless to you till you have lost your text-books, burnt your lecture notes, and forgotten the minutiae which you learned by heart for the examination. . . . The function of a university is to enable you to shed details in favor of principles." [11] These statements are balanced by remarks such as the following: "Of course, during this stage [University], precise knowledge will grow, and more actively than ever before, because the mind has experienced the power of definiteness, and responds to the acquisition of general truth, and of richness of illustration." [12] Thus, to repeat, the objection is not to the acquisition of facts as such, but rather to the slavish grubbing for facts, without enlightenment and generality of vision.

Clarity and Vagueness in Human Knowledge

The wise use of factual knowledge involves the recognition that *absolute* certainty, and clarity, of knowledge is impossible. For example, even in the so-called exact sciences of mathematics and logic, there is no agreement about the status of even the most familiar cardinal numbers. The same is the case with reference to apparently elementary concepts such as line and point. As for logic, "Logic is the chosen resort of clear-headed people, severally convinced of the complete adequacy of their doctrines. It is such a pity that they cannot agree with each other." [13] Widespread disagreements, and uncertainties, concerning the former citadels of certainty have aroused in many men a flippant, or sad, scepticism concerning all things. Not so in the case of Whitehead. He refuses to drown himself in a "sea of vacuity." He remarks, with sound common sense, that "the large practical effect of scepticism is gross acquiescence in what is immediate and obvious. Postponement, subtle interweaving, delicacies of adjustment, wide coordinations, moral restraint, the whole artistry of civilization, all presuppose understanding." [14]

The question naturally arises: How can there be understanding if absolute certainty is impossible? Referring again to mathematics, Whitehead notes that while we are very vague about the nature of numbers, we have relatively clear knowledge concerning their relationships. In other words, our knowledge of composites is much clearer than our knowledge of so-called basic elements. Thus, we are not restricted to mere vagueness in all areas of knowledge. The world is complex; nothing appears in absolute isolation. Therefore, we must be satisfied with a *mixture* of clarity and vagueness. Whitehead says "a baffling mixture." However, "baffling" does not mean "paralyzing." Rather, he is merely restating his previous contention that, since this is an organic universe, since human knowledge is limited, therefore we cannot have absolute clarity and certainty concerning any one segment of the universe. The infinity of interrelations is beyond our complete grasp.

He refers, with great approval, to Plato's approach to

knowledge. Plato "gave an unrivaled display of the human mind in action, with its ferment of vague obviousness, of hypothetical formulation, of renewed insight, of discovery of relevant detail of partial understanding, of final conclusion, with its disclosure of deeper problems as yet unsolved." [15] Unless universities emulate the example of Plato, they will fall into the preposterous egoism of the dogmatic pretense at absolute certainty, a shallow pseudo-knowledge without the saving grace of wisdom which recognizes the challenge of the "beyond."

Whitehead well recognizes the dangers involved in the fearless pursuit of information, and maturity of judgment. The torch of knowledge, in careless hands, may start a conflagration and destroy not only the structure of knowledge, but even the civilization on which it is based. But, the light of the torch may reveal further knowledge. So the risk must be taken— with care.

Universities and Imaginative Insight

Since the invention of printing, and hence the ready availability of books, a man does not need to attend a university to obtain advanced factual knowledge. Furthermore, extensive research activities take place outside universities. Whitehead contends that the *essential* characteristic of a university, as far as the provision of factual knowledge is concerned, is that facts are presented *imaginatively*, rich with meaning, relevant for use in solving human problems. Facts, when transmuted by the alchemy of the university, are no longer weights on the memory. They are sources of imaginative insight.

One of the great tragedies of human history is that men of imaginative vision have little practical experience or hard factual knowledge. On the other hand, those who have the factual knowledge, and practical experience, usually have little or no creative imagination or vision of the values of civilized life. It is one of the supremely important tasks of the university to weave together these two usually sundered ingredients, so that the deficiencies of the past may be overcome.

In this emphasis on the importance of fusing vision and experience, however, care must be taken that the vision be clearly formulated before immersion in the rough stream of adult experience takes place. The tender plant of imaginative vision must be healthy before it can be transplanted into the field of everyday life. Thus, the student should be given an opportunity to think and feel, undistracted by the demands of adult responsibility, until he reaches a stage when he can face the complexities of life without losing his ideals or vision of what the world "may be." The university student should have ample opportunity to "think rightly and wrongly . . . free to appreciate the variousness of the universe undisturbed by [the immediate pressures of] its perils." [16] Here is another instance of Whitehead's continuing emphasis on tolerance. A clash of doctrines, if some evidence is available to support them, should not be regarded as a calamity. Rather, as has been noted before, the clash can result in a step forward in human knowledge. The apparent conflict may be used as a source of suggestions.

Nevertheless, while stressing the importance of wide-ranging vision, the contemplation of a number of alternative possibilities, the student must not lose sight of the ultimate facts and values from which there can be no escape. One of the great dangers in university life (as in previous stages) is that all concerned may become so immersed in words that the underlying facts and values are almost disregarded. It is assumed that words are relatively clear and definite in meaning. This assumption frequently does not stand up under critical investigation. In any case, "experience does not occur in the clothing of verbal phrases. It involves clashes of emotion and unspoken revelations of the nature of things." [17] This reference to "revelation" need not cause alarm, or gratification. "Revelation" is being used here as a synonym for intuition—that is to say, *adequate* immediate experience. Whitehead is saying that we do have immediate experiences (concerning fundamental factors) which cannot be fitted satisfactorily into the narrow framework of our present system of words and concepts. Hence, he who is satisfied with words is dealing, at best, with the surface of the stream of life. Words, of course, are sometimes convenient symbols. But, they must not be regarded as identical with what they attempt to symbolize.

As one might expect, Whitehead suggests that a university should be both local and universal. It should strive to purvey and enhance "the wisdom of the ages." Yet it must function in a specific community. No university will serve its community here and now if its interests are focused on the long ago and far away. A university should be one of the chief agencies of social progress. Hence, the campus should be the meeting place of the scholars (men concerned with value ideals), discoverers (those who grasp important general ideas), and inventors (those who apply these general ideas to the details of particular action). Indeed, all men should be encouraged to be somewhat of a scholar, discoverer, and inventor.

University Staff

Obviously, if a university is to reach the level of excellence envisaged by Whitehead, it must be staffed by a certain type of professor. It is indeed difficult to find, and appoint, men who "wear their learning with imagination." [18] There are too many men who glory in pedantry, and pontifically expound ill-organized factual knowledge or unexamined prejudices. All too rare is the teacher who will appear before students in his proper guise: "as an ignorant man thinking, actively using his small store of knowledge." A great university requires great professors: men who approach knowledge with imagination and humility, and use what knowledge they have to further the self-development of all members of the community.

Certain characteristics are *usually* symptomatic of the most desirable type of professor: vigor, originality, genius, fruitful learning, dependability. The only practical difficulty is that what appears to be vigor may actually be only a loud voice. What looks like originality often turns out to be verbosity. The apparent genius sometimes is seen, on closer examination, to be mentally ill. On occasion, the dependable person is so stodgy that you can only depend on him to be that—stodgy. Whitehead, in the course of his university experience, discovered that the performance of a faculty does not depend on the characteristics of each member considered exclusively as an individual. The fact of mutual influence is important. It is necessary, therefore, to consider not only the man to be appointed but also the other members of the group to which he may be added.

Even when you find and appoint the right man, certain conditions must be present if he is to have a suitable environment. There should be leisure, freedom from irrational restraint on thought and action, freedom from financial worry, stimulating contacts with other keen minds in a variety of different fields of knowledge. There must also be the self-confidence which results from opportunities for achievement, and the recognition which logically follows. Research activities, which rise out of genuine human problems, provide a valuable background for the effective university teacher.

"Research"

If a man's research project is genuine intellectual adventure, he will be alive with living ideas, and his students will benefit from association with him. Conversely, he should avail himself of the opportunity to benefit from association with them. Young and keen minds provide both stimulation and penetrating criticism. Incidentally, there are two sources of mental stimulation: (a) the data of present experience; (b) traditional knowledge, formulated, and made respectable by time (the so-called orthodoxy of a subject). Even if these venerable theories are open to criticism, they can serve as a useful starting point. A person may be aroused to overcome their deficiencies. He may also make use of whatever insights of value are preserved in the ancestral lore.

One of the most common methods of determining the worth of a university professor is to count the number of printed words which are assigned to his name. This overlooks the basic fact that some of the best teachers publish little or nothing. Further, some published material is nonsense and should have been placed in the university incinerator, rather than flaunted on the pages of the university journal. In general, however, it is usually possible to gauge the value of a university faculty by noting the *quality* of work its members publish.

Success in any activity depends not only on insight but also on orderly procedure. Yet, a clear distinction must be made between order, as a basis of excellence, and order as destructive of novelty and vitality of experience. Education should, of course, encourage the development of skills. However, these skills should quickly drop into the unconscious. Thus they will be available instruments but will not distract attention from the main purposes of life. In this context, Whitehead makes an interesting remark concerning *scholarship:* "The . . . condition for high achievement is scholarship, in the enlarged sense including knowledge and acquired instinct controlling action." [19]

The Administration

In directing the activities of a university faculty, in order to attain a high level of performance, it is disastrous, says Whitehead (who once was a dean) to regard a faculty in the same fashion as the members of an industrial organization. The product of a university faculty—the encouragement, and aiding, of the self-development of human beings—is much more difficult to measure than the manufacture of shoes. Merely making sure that professors are at their desks or lecterns, and that students are "within range," is not enough. Indeed, Whitehead believes that the only safeguards for effective faculty action are the faculty members' own devotion to the responsibilities of university education, and the pressure of public opinion. He is prepared to admit that the pressure of public opinion frequently expresses itself slowly, and in distorted form. He suggests that some professors do a very thorough job of "soul murder" for years before the general public wakes up to what is going on.

The relation between faculty and administration should *not* be analyzed in terms of "justice" (as this term is usually understood). This is too gross a concept. It is not "appropriate" to say: "For 'so much' money I will give 'so many' lectures"; or "Since my expected raise in pay has not been forthcoming, I will raise a rumpus"; or "If you don't like this university you had better leave at once." A university is an agency in the process of achieving civilization. A common devotion to truth, beauty, and goodness should motivate *all* members of the university community. Relationships between parts of the university, e.g., administration and faculty, should not be conducted on a low plane of external, legalistic justice. A civilized man will keep his word, honor a contract written or implied. But he will do more than he has promised, if there is an opportunity to do so. He will be tolerant of the shortcomings of others. In brief, he will do justice (in the best sense of the term) not because he is forced to but because he wants to—as an ingredient in the good life of civilized existence. Thus, Whitehead is recommending that the affairs of a university should be conducted on a loftier plane than those of an embattled industry where labor and management eye each other suspiciously, sometimes with good cause.

The Business School

Whitehead discusses some of his ideals of university education in the special context of references to the business school of a university.

He notes, in passing, that a professional school is an excellent illustration of one of his basic contentions; namely that thought should have a practical bearing on the ordinary problems of life, guiding human affairs and receiving the stimulus of complex problem situations. He remarks that the divorce of the university from the market place is a relatively modern phenomenon. Greek and medieval universities had professional schools; or, at least, they provided professional training in science, law, medicine, education, and religion. The practical efficacy of Salerno, Pisa, Bologna, Cambridge, Paris, Edinburgh, Oxford, are well known. Whitehead suggests that if Aristotle were alive today he would be greatly interested in the Medical School, the Biology Department, and the School of Education. He would also "sit in" elsewhere. Certainly the Department of Political Science, and even the Department of Philosophy, might be honored by his presence. Plato too, it must be remembered, was interested in political activity in its most practical aspects. He made long and dangerous trips in order to participate, directly, in the affairs of state. He was well aware of the values of applied mathematics in military, and civilian, life.

Turning to the type of training which should be offered at

the Harvard Business School, or any business school for that matter, Whitehead contends that clothing facts with imaginative insight is an essential contribution to success in business. A man must project himself, imaginatively, into the total situation in which his business operates. Unless he thus understands his environment he will not be able to deal with it effectively.

Therefore, a course of study at a business school should make it possible for a person to stand, in imagination, with the men who "get out" the raw material, the men who transport it, the men who process it, the men who buy the finished product, the men who hold stock in the company, the men who are the company's chief competitors, and so on and on. Before he is through, the successful businessman must familiarize himself with history, geography, science, politics, religion—indeed most phases of human knowledge. Closely related to this is the ability to observe basic general laws immersed in a mass of specific facts; and, having recognized these laws, see how they can be applied in new problem situations. All this knowledge must be organized in terms of some value standard. The ability to perform this type of intellectual activity (the imaginative grasp of fact plus the efficiency of balanced judgment) with reference to commercial activities, is something which the university business school can help a student develop, as no other agent can. In short, Whitehead is arguing that the university should provide trained leaders for the field of business just as it has done, for centuries, in the fields of law, medicine, and religion.

This understanding of what is involved in business enterprise is invaluable to a young man during the first part of his business career. At the beginning he is likely to be assigned to some routine, apparently unimportant task. This is valuable discipline. Also he will learn many things which are not taught in business school. Yet, there is the danger that too much routine and apparently uninteresting work may sour a person, and lower efficiency. The broad perspective, provided by business school training, should help a young man to understand the place of the present "drudgery" in the total situation. It will then be at least endurable. It may become suffused with interest.

CONCLUSION

Whitehead does not make the foolish mistake of assuming that education ceases when one leaves the university, or terminates his formal education at an earlier stage. In view of the fact that no one learns everything in school, Whitehead suggests that a sensible person will continue his reading, even though there is no teacher or professor to "check up." He goes so far as to state: "Your real education comes in after life. I am not thinking of dull books. The best story books are some of your best teachers. A good novel or a good book of travel will let you know more of your world than many a treatise; only, for heaven's sake, think as you read. Try to imagine what it all means. Do not get a mere craving for print without thought. It is almost as bad as drink." [20] Ideally, the other phases of a person's education, scientific and technical, should be continued to the limits of his ability and the facilities available in his environment. After all, we go on growing as long as we live. Since it is the purpose of education to guide this growth as well as possible, the process of education should never cease.

It is obvious that Whitehead's system of education would aid in the attainment of a democratic society. Every opportunity is given the individual to develop his capacities to the full, in accordance with the highest value ideals. There is an emphasis on a proper balance between freedom and control. The recognition that human knowledge is limited, that new knowledge is continually being discovered, leads to an attitude of tolerance. Teachers are not masters but rather sources of inspiration and examples of excellence. They willingly share the results of their experience.

Plato envisaged a state ruled by a *few* "philosopher kings." Whitehead is in favor of a system in which the *many* "citizen rulers" will have a philosophical approach to life. His system of education is designed to assist all human beings to develop, as fully as possible, that depth and width of wisdom which is truly philosophic. Thus, he deplores the narrow specialization in knowledge which blinds even the best minds to wider perspectives, and provides no training for the essential task of co-ordinating highly specialized knowledge and action.

Whitehead has great respect for the democratic ideal of "equality." There must be equality of opportunity in education. With characteristic insight, however, he warns against equality of achievement obtained by letting the most inferior student "set the pace." Demanding the same educational performance from all is contrary to the basic principle of democracy: the fullest possible development of the individual. Individuals are different. They should not be compressed, arbitrarily, within the confines of one standard educational "strait jacket."

Modern education, in a democratic society, must recapture the old Roman stress on the "greatness of man." Education will not aid in the achieving of civilization unless it is recognized that human beings are capable of genuine devotion to truth, beauty, and goodness; capable of artistic activity, adventure, and that supreme achievement, peace.

Chapter 6 CRITICAL COMMENTS

INTRODUCTION

Critical Standard

This chapter is composed of a statement, and examination, of critical comments dealing with Whitehead's philosophy of civilization. The standard to be used is not one artificially imposed on his work from without. Whitehead proposes to provide a definition of civilization. His definition will be evaluated by determining whether or not it is an accurate statement of the essential qualities of the type of life which is termed civilized. He makes suggestions as to how the civilized type of life can be implemented and strengthened. The efficacy of these suggestions must be tested by reference to the observed nature of human beings and to the situation which confronts them. If Whitehead neglects relevant data his philosophy of civilization will be thereby either weakened or refuted. If there are no serious deficiencies, his philosophy of civilization will be, to that extent, verified.

No attempt has been made to evaluate Whitehead using some other philosophy of civilization as a standard. It seems wiser to refer directly, and without possible distortion, to the fundamental data in terms of which any philosophy of civilization must be evaluated.

Further, Whitehead's philosophy of civilization has not been subjected to a detailed and formal "contrast" with other philosophies of civilization, past or present. It was feared that such a procedure would introduce complexities and distract attention from the main project: an *outline* (and in this chapter, an evaluation) of Whitehead's philosophy of civilization. Yet, obviously, some comparison is involved, at least by implication—and in a few instances, directly. However, such comparisons are not in terms of a contrast of Whitehead with, e.g., Aquinas, Hegel, Marx, or Toynbee as such. Rather, Whitehead's position is compared with restricted or distorted views which may involve an overemphasis on religious, ideational, or economic factors.

It will be noticed that considerable space has been devoted to a discussion of Whitehead's philosophy of religion. That is so because this phase of his philosophy of civilization has attracted the most attention and aroused the most controversy. An attempt has been made to show the inadequacies of many of the criticisms of Whitehead which have been advanced by some religious leaders, orthodox (Roman Catholic and Protestant), and so-called "liberal" Protestants as well.

In addition to a series of specific evaluations, considerable emphasis has been placed in this chapter and in Chapter 7 on the fundamental fact that *Whitehead's philosophy of civilization has a firm metaphysical foundation.* That is to say, the basic concepts of his theory of reality are involved in his philosophy of civilization. The point is that since this metaphysical position is sound—i.e., validated as it seems to be by the data of the natural and social sciences and by fundamental moral, aesthetic, and religious insights—Whitehead's philosophy of civilization is vastly strengthened. More specifically, it can be shown that the concept of democracy held by the Western world is in accordance with the nature of the universe in general, and men in particular, as set forth by Whitehead's theory of actual entities. Therefore, the democratic way of life is not an artificial imposition. It is firmly grounded in the nature of man.

Whitehead's Method

It is very difficult, for people living in the twentieth century, to overcome a strong emotional revulsion to the term "intuition." Even the use of the synonymous terms "insight" and "direct apprehension" do not fare much better. There is the overwhelming suspicion that such an approach involves an appeal to something purely subjective and unwarranted. In so far as Whitehead bases his discussion ultimately on intuitions, he seems, to many contemporaries, to be building on nonexistent foundations.

It has been observed that by intuition, or insight, Whitehead does not mean something *purely* subjective, private, and un-verified. He is not withdrawing into the wilderness of irrational chaos. By intuition he means a direct grasp of *basic* factors in a situation. A direct grasp, an immediate awareness, of basic factors is regarded as fundamental in any branch of knowledge. Some rely on the direct and immediate awareness of sense data, some on the immediate awareness of tautologies. In short, natural science and the philosophies which lean on natural science use the same *general type* of method as the one em-ployed by Whitehead. The data "grasped" are open to public verification, if the observer is competent. The real difference between Whitehead and most other thinkers is that Whitehead uses his method of direct awareness to *focus on* (and take seri-ously) data much more profound and complex than the rela-tively clear-cut sense data and tautologies of the so-called scientifically minded. Whitehead intuits organic interrelations which are not obvious in clear sensory experience. In addition there are intuitions of moral, aesthetic, and spiritual data. Thus, the direct insights, the immediate awareness, of scientifically minded men are supplemented by the more profound and com-plex intuitions to which Whitehead calls special attention. Nevertheless, to repeat, Whitehead's intuitions are direct in-sights, immediate awareness, and they make one aware of data which have been experienced by numerous competent observers for centuries.

WHITEHEAD'S DEFINITION OF CIVILIZATION

Whitehead's definition of civilization (which emphasizes the qualities of truth, beauty, art, adventure, and peace) is based on a careful examination of those ways of life which are regarded as civilized. In so far as "civilization" has always been con-sidered an ideal, which at best has received only partial expres-sion, Whitehead has, quite properly, stressed the ideal aspects of civilization. Further, he has indicated the deviations from these ideals which have appeared in the so-called civilizations: Greek, Hellenistic, Roman, Hebrew, Renaissance, and Modern.

Thus, he has performed a real service in indicating the complex texture of civilization in its ideal aspects, and the serious deficiencies of all actual "civilizations."

It must be admitted, however, that because Whitehead provides a highly idealized definition of civilization, it is very difficult to decide whether a particular culture (or individual) has reached a sufficiently close approximation to the ideal qualities of civilization to merit the title "civilized." In other words, it is difficult to distinguish between "truly" and "so-called" civilized life. There is the further difficulty, noted at the beginning of this study, that Whitehead sometimes uses the term "civilization" as a synonym for "culture" (i.e., a characteristic pattern of behavior).

It may be objected that the ideal qualities, in terms of which Whitehead defines civilization, have been selected in a purely arbitrary fashion. Has he been guilty of concentrating on certain aspects of life commonly called civilized among middle-class Englishmen? Has he neglected other qualities equally or even more important? Does his definition reflect mere personal bias, and hence lose any claim to serious consideration? These questions can be settled only by reference to relevant data. What *are* the qualities which are most important in the way of life which is called civilized, by men at different times and at different places? Has Whitehead stated these qualities accurately?

(There is, of course, a much more fundamental question. Are the qualities called civilized really the essential ones? If "civilization" be a synonym for "the best possible type of life," then one must enquire if it is possible to envisage a way of life which exceeds, in excellence, the one portrayed by Whitehead. Here a person can rely only on an ultimate value judgment.)

Bearing in mind these crucial questions, it can be concluded that available evidence supports the definition of civilization offered by Whitehead.

In the course of his discussion Whitehead has corrected many mistaken notions concerning civilization. There is, for example, the widespread tendency to equate civilization with a superficial intellectual brilliance, or with technological development. Showing characteristic insight, he focuses attention on the basic values: truth, beauty, goodness, peace, the necessity of adventure in realms other than the obvious and physical. In brief, civilization is essentially an achievement, by individuals, of a quality of inner life characterized by a deep concern for the higher values. Yet, Whitehead does not overemphasize the place of beauty and artistic creation in civilized life. There must be a proper balance in devotion to the higher values. Further, he stresses the idea that a civilized person does not assume an attitude of lofty superiority, and withdraw from association with most of his fellow men. One of the characteristics of a civilized person is his tolerance and sympathy for individuals of all types.[1]

PHILOSOPHY OF HISTORY

Many Factors

In dealing with the factors which promote, and serve, the qualities of civilized life, Whitehead again does justice to the complexity of the subject matter. He refuses to succumb to the lure of a simple formula, erroneous in its particularity of emphasis. All relevant important factors are delineated: men as well as ideas, economic and technological factors as well as geographical ones, God as well as the brute irrational forces within and without man. In considerable detail, he shows why *all* these factors must be taken into consideration—for the simple reason that if any are omitted one's understanding is at the best partial, at the worst woefully erroneous. In discussing the impact of each factor, he corrects common misunderstandings concerning their efficacy. For example, he notes that great men cannot function unless the time is ripe; that great ideas need great men; that the environment, though very important, can be changed in many instances. His insight concerning the importance of technological developments is accurate and incisive. But here again, although (for example) he recognizes the efficacy of steam and electricity in making possible political democracy, he does not overlook the vast network of other conditions.

Whitehead's criticisms of the "Malthusian law" seem to embody a rather optimistic attitude concerning future food supplies. Moreover, there are no more "empty continents." No doubt technological developments will continue. But, recent investigations of population pressures, and the limited amount of available arable land, suggest strongly that the basic problem discussed by Malthus cannot be disposed of quite as easily as Whitehead's comments would seem to imply.

It must be admitted that Whitehead did not keep absolutely up to date in all specialized fields of knowledge. Thus it is possible to find flaws in exposition at some points. For example, he apparently does not appreciate the debt which ancient Greece owed to other civilizations even more ancient. This is obvious in his references to the Renaissance reliance on Greece. His lack of full appreciation of non-Greek sources of knowledge, including scientific knowledge, is revealed in his references to Persia, Mesopotamia, India, and China. Likewise he suggests that the commercial aristocracy of seventeenth-century England was not interested in the new scientific and philosophical ideas of the time. As a matter of fact these men were intensely interested in such ideas and encouraged their development.

RELIGION

God

Whitehead has been successful in his attempt to outline a theory of God which regards the divine being as one individual among other individuals, in "one world," the universe of nature. The basic concepts used in referring to other individuals (basic units of the universe) have been used in referring to God: i.e., individuality, process of creative interaction, permanence, value. Justification for the use of these concepts, with reference to God, has been provided.

In formulating his theory of God, Whitehead has given due weight to a number of recognized religious insights, particularly some of those expressed by Plato, the later Hebrew prophets and, pre-eminently, by Jesus of Nazareth. In this sense Whitehead's theory of God has a solid empirical basis. It is founded on the experience of competent human beings. He contends that if we wish to understand the nature and function of God we must concentrate on Jesus of Nazareth and men like him. These men not only penetrated further into the mysteries of the "divine"; they also clarified their insights by translating them into action. Thus, by depending on such sources of information Whitehead's view of God is not wishful thinking, blind faith, of mere emotional vaporizing. This theory is at worst a stimulating point of view, at best a profound achievement.

There are, of course, many objections to Whitehead's view of God. For example, there is the obvious one that Whitehead's "God" is not God at all. However, it may quite legitimately be remarked that the term *God* has many meanings, even in traditional Christianity. Further, Whitehead's view of God, to repeat, is based on religious insights to which traditional religion gives official sanction. It can plausibly be objected that Whitehead has disregarded many important phases of Christian doctrine. In reply it can be stated that these phases of Christian doctrine have been rejected because he can find no justification for them in the basic religious insights of the founder of Christianity. As has been noted, it is Whitehead's contention that when emphases on overwhelming power, inflexible, formalistic morality, and on abstract perfection in the divine nature occur, these emphases are unfortunate distortions that have tended to corrupt the high spirituality of the insights of Jesus of Nazareth. Thus Whitehead clarifies and justifies his position.

It is clear that many "devout Christians" would consider it shocking that Whitehead denies absolute perfection to God. They find it very difficult to think of God as immersed in the world of nature, growing even as other natural beings grow, limited in wisdom and power and even, in a sense, restricted in goodness. Such views are indeed different from those of much of traditional Christianity. Yet, are these theories of Whitehead as obnoxious and unjustified as they may seem?

It is true that Whitehead finds God in nature, and not outside nature. But, *this is not the "nature" of crass materialism.* Nor is it a nature fully describable in terms of physics, chemistry, and biology. It is a nature that includes the eternal ideals of truth, beauty, and goodness. It is a nature composed, in part, of men like Hosea, Isaiah, Jeremiah, Plato, and Jesus. Such a rich and complex "nature" removes it from the scope of the criticisms which are leveled against a much less complex view of nature. Of course, traditional Christianity is prepared to admit the immanence of God. However, critics may contend that Whitehead disregards the more fundamental transcendence of God. It is true that Whitehead does not consider God as a being, in part, outside the world; yet, in a sense, he regards God as transcendent. God transcends other individuals in the degree of his moral and spiritual achievements and in his function of organizing, and making available, possibilities for the use of other individuals. In short, Whitehead does not see any point in regarding God as dwelling in a realm apart, arbitrarily condescending to intervene in human affairs. Rather, he contends that the view of God as "divine companion" is more in accordance with the insights of the founder of Christianity.

A defense may also be offered for Whitehead's claim that God is limited in wisdom, power, and goodness. It justly may be remarked that in the traditional view there is a limitation on God's power, in the sense that man may freely choose evil and thus go contrary to the will of God. In a rather subtle sense traditional Christianity, *if it takes history seriously,* seems to imply a gap in God's wisdom and goodness because, as new events occur, increasingly God's knowledge is enlarged by the change from potential occurrence to actual occurrence.[2] Concrete facts are now present which previously were only in the realm of possibility. As God's providence works out in the world, goodness also changes from potential to actual. Thus, limitations are overcome. There is a further limitation of God's goodness in the sense that he experiences evil as well as good. That is to say, evil is experienced as real. There are tragic elements in God's life. However, God finally experiences "peace." This is the result of putting evil in its proper perspective, as a means to good.

The emphasis on change, so basic in Whitehead's philosophy, is not denied a place in traditional religious thought. Did

not God change, in a very real way, when Jesus began to walk
the hills of Galilee and the streets of Jerusalem? And, in so far
as the Holy Spirit continues to work in the world, God is involved in a process of development. Whitehead is convinced
that true greatness is found not in static perfection but in the
effective solving of problems as they arise. After all, did not
Jesus of Nazareth undergo a process of moral and spiritual
development, from birth to death on the cross. *If we take the
Gospels seriously,* we must note the fact that he was really
tempted, and that he overcame these temptations, including the
final one on the cross. His, then, was not a static perfection.
Rather, it was a process of excellence in performance in the face
of a variety of challenging stimuli.

The Whiteheadian theory that God depends on other individuals for part of his being, that God requires data from
others in order to be fully himself, sounds very strange to orthodox ears. Yet, there is a place in traditional thought for the
idea that God's work requires "human hands." In this sense,
God depends on man for God's own fulfillment.

While it has been argued here that the gaps between Whitehead's position and that of traditional Christian thought are not
as extreme as might appear at first sight, the fact remains, however, that there are very great differences in emphasis. At some
points there is complete disagreement as to fundamental points
of doctrine. The basic question then arises: Which approach
is more in accord with the relevant data? Whitehead has left
no doubt as to the foundations of his position. He contends
that, while he has made valid use of fundamental religious insights, traditional religion is, in part, guilty of unfortunate lack
of balance and corruption of basic religious insights. This has
occurred because of distortion by irrelevant theories produced
by social forces and by irrational human urges and emotions.
For example, there has been the naive tendency to think of
excellence in terms of mere brute force. Whitehead contends that
it is more enlightened, and mature, to emphasize moral and
spiritual achievement as the true excellence. Jesus did not use
overwhelming force as an "approved" instrument. It is true
that a scene in the Temple is portrayed in which Jesus "drove

out" the money-changers. Yet here the emphasis seems to be on "righteous indignation." The New Testament (Matt. 4:8-11) reports a "temptation" in which Jesus was confronted by the lure of political power based on brute force. He turned his back on this satanic temptation. Some theologians have not taken this message to heart.

Those who think of God in terms of justice, untinctured by mercy, talk like men frightened by an all-powerful lawgiver or an oriental despot. Those who speak of God in terms of absolute infinities, *completely* beyond human grasp, betray a hankering after the safety which comes from running away from the complex facts of human life, a weakness of spirit and a blindness of perception of the richness and promise of the world of nature. Thus, to the charge that his thought is not Christian, Whitehead is able to reply that in thinking of God primarily in terms of love, he is following the example of the first Christian.

There is the recurrent criticism that Whitehead's view of God is a metaphysical one, indulging in extreme abstraction and generality, and that hence it is not suitable for religious purposes. This criticism has, in part, been met in the course of the foregoing discussion. However, additional comment will clarify the matter.

He *has* formulated a theory of reality. Whitehead is, of course, a metaphysician. He attempts to discover the basic factors in the universe. One of these he finds to be God. However, it has been shown that in thinking of God *he does not stop at the generalities of metaphysical discussion.* Having argued that God functions in organizing the realm of possibility and making it available for the use of other individuals; having claimed that God, like every other individual, is involved in mutually beneficial creative interaction; having indicated the factors of permanence and value in God; having, in short, shown God's metaphysical status, Whitehead then proceeds to show that this being, in addition to his metaphysical aspects, has (*as revealed by basic religious insights*) certain other characteristics. These religious characteristics are not divorced from his metaphysical aspects. Indeed, they are grounded in the metaphysical characteristics. *God is one and the same being under discussion from the two interrelated points of view: metaphysical and religious.* This conclusion, however, concerning the suitability of Whitehead's God to perform religious functions, is denied by many of his critics.

It is argued, for example, that Whitehead's God is a poor, weak, helpless creature, in the clutches of a more ultimate—indeed *the* ultimate—reality named "creativity." This, however, is not actually Whitehead's position. Creativity is a characteristic manifest by all individuals, including God. Creativity is not an underlying ultimate reality. There is no creativity apart from the creative activities of individuals.

It has been objected that Whitehead's God has no concern for individuals. A careful reading of Whitehead's remarks will indicate that, while God provides patterns of possible action available for the use of all individuals, this does not mean that he is unconcerned with any one particular individual. Rather, as any individual arises, God is concerned that it reach its fullest possible degree of self-development and value experience. When the individual reaches the end of its career, God saves as much of value from the experience of this (any) individual *as can be saved.* God's *respect* for any individual is shown in his tenderness, love, and companionship. God does not force anything on any individual.

It has been argued that Whitehead's God is not concerned with *human* distinctions between good and evil. This is, obviously, incorrect since the distinction which we recognize is based on distinctions present in the mind of God. That is to say, the possibility "good" and the possibility "evil," as we envisage them, are also present in the mind of God. We, when we think accurately, make the distinction *because* God does. Actual goods and evils are present in God's experience in all their utter opposition. When God experiences our miseries he feels them as such. As Whitehead expresses it: God feels evil in the world with tragic intensity. Thus, in the experience of God, the reality of evil is not denied. However, God shows how evil, its reality fully recognized, can be overcome, transmuted, in the sense that it may be used as a means to good. This occurs in a similar fashion as when, in human experience, an automobile accident leads to the avoidance of accidents—good coming out of evil.

It should be clear that God does not obliterate the distinction between actual good and evil in an *aesthetic synthesis*. The word "aesthetic" is used frequently in a wide sense to mean value in general. Whitehead experiences value involving *patterned contrasts*. Such value is possible only because the individual distinctions of the elements are retained. In this sense his experience is aesthetic. This theory is incorrectly interpreted when it is thought to indicate an emphasis on beauty at the expense of disregarding moral goodness. Early in his discussion of God, Whitehead points out that the idea of power should be replaced by the idea of goodness.

It is erroneous to suggest, as some critics have, that God solves the problem of evil in his own experience, but leaves it unsolved in the arena of human affairs. (All is well with God, but man is left with the problem unsolved.) Whitehead's actual position is that God, having solved the problem of evil in his experience, thereby provides an example for our guidance. What has been achieved in the "heaven" of God's experience is made available for us in the "world" (of experience of ordinary individuals).

Whitehead's contrast between "heaven" and "the world" is not the contrast between two entirely separate realms. Rather, heaven is a term applied to God's experience. The world is a term applied to the experience of other individuals. God and other individuals are in the same universe. There are continuous interactions between these individuals, divine and human.

Another serious error is the claim that God uses our experiences for his own (narrowly selfish) satisfaction, disregarding our welfare. The fact of the matter is Whitehead regards God as a fellow sufferer, a great companion. His life may well be enriched by an achievement of ours. He, of course, is concerned with "the fulfilment of his own being." [3] But, the being who is "concerned" is not a selfish oriental despot but, rather, a being possessing characteristics manifest by Jesus of Nazareth.

The objection has been raised that God is really involved in evil, since the actual evil in the world is the expression of a possible evil envisaged by God, and made available for the use of other individuals. Thus, Whitehead seems to have fallen into the difficulty which he finds in the traditional view of God, namely, that God, as author of the play, is responsible for everything that happens—including evil. Whitehead's reply, *superficially* similar to the traditional one, is that individuals are free to choose the patterns of behavior which they will follow. However, the similarity is really superficial because Whitehead assigns far more genuine initiative to the individual than does the traditional view with its all-powerful God somehow granting man the ability to flout the will of the "all-powerful." In any case, Whitehead does not think of God in terms of overwhelming power, and hence does not become involved in the traditional difficulty.

It has been claimed that no man can *pray* to "Whitehead's God"—a mere "principle of concretion," a being with three confusing "natures": primordial, consequent, and superject. In all fairness it must be made clear that the technical terms employed by Christian theologians are just as confusing, to the uninitiated, as those used by Whitehead. The basic question is this: Is the being, to whom these terms apply, the sort of being to whom a man, in need, can pray? Thus we must face the question: Can God, as portrayed by Whitehead, *answer prayer?*

If prayer is communion between individuals, a great one and lesser ones; if prayer is a process in which the great helps the lesser; then, Whitehead's God is able to answer prayer. God confronts the receptive individual with ideal patterns of possible actions. God sets an example of how life's problems should be solved. Further, Whitehead contends that God's life flows back into the world. Thus, the impact of his personality is a factor in the lives of other individuals. It must be admitted that Whitehead contents himself with very vague generalities at this point. Yet this is an essential, though undeveloped, phase of his theory.

It should be obvious, from the preceding discussion, that while Whitehead criticizes concepts of God which attribute to him (a) overwhelming force, (b) a concern for unmerciful, formalistic morality, and (c) exclusive other-worldly metaphysical status—yet, he does not deny to God (a) an "attractive" power,

(b) a concern for genuine morality, or (c) a metaphysical status founded on modern knowledge.

Despite the fact that Whitehead discusses God in terms applicable to human individuals, that does not mean that all mystery, or greatness, is removed thereby. These humanly applicable terms are *the best we have* for use in referring to God. Whitehead does not claim that they are completely adequate. He contends that they are at least valid "as far as they go," since they are based on experience of the divine.[4] These terms report that God is a person, far more a person than the abstract, infinitely different God of some theologians. God, as envisaged by Whitehead, has power, wisdom, and goodness. But these qualities are such that he is in the close relationship of "companion," rather than the distant one of "supreme ruler." His qualities are far beyond the level of human excellence. However, the emphasis is on moral and spiritual achievement, rather than on the exertion of brute force and absolute control over all that happens. Since the divine excels the human, should this not be in areas where human performance is farthest removed from the animal and the inanimate level of nature? In any case, in his emphasis, Whitehead is simply taking seriously the teachings of Jesus of Nazareth, and avoiding the all too common practice of paying God degrading metaphysical compliments. While God is *beyond* man in all excellences of activity and attainment, yet he is *with* men in the midst of the complex affairs of life. God's "otherness" is not the type that results in the paralysis of human initiative, because of the assumption that God alone has initiative in the universe. Rather, God's superiority is a challenge and a "lure" to further human development and higher levels of value experience. God's otherness is not only a challenge. It involves the assistance of a "great companion."

It has been objected that you cannot explain the world of nature unless you refer to something outside it. Nature is not self-explanatory. Hence, there must be reliance on some supernatural factor. Whitehead's cogent reply is that if the supernatural factor is severed, in its essential characteristics, from nature, it can have *no* explanatory power. Basically, Whitehead's conception of nature is such that all beings, from "sticks and stones" to value ideals and God, are part of nature. *All* explanatory factors are found in nature, such as its richness and complexity. Therefore, it is not necessary to postulate an unknown, "wholly other," to account for nature. As was previously shown, this is not to say that Whitehead removes all mystery from religious matters, or from nature in general.

It has been argued that there must be creation by a creator-God, otherwise everything is unexplained. It can be replied, on Whitehead's behalf, that it is "as respectable as Aristotle" to deny the need for a first day of creation. It is true that many, including Aristotle, envisage a first cause as necessary. Yet, there seems no reason why there should not be a co-operating group of causal agents, God being chief among them but *not the only* cause. To repeat, the tendency to concentrate power and initiative in one being is an illustration of the mentality which cowers before an oriental despot. It is *not* in accordance with the fundamental insights of the founder of Christianity who, most certainly, did not do for people things which they were capable of doing themselves. In many areas of experience men have genuine creative powers.

It is customary to accuse Whitehead of involving himself in a hopeless morass of contradictions in his *summary* concerning God. God is stated to be *both:* finite and infinite, temporal and eternal, creator and created, and so on, and on. As the preceding exposition has indicated, these are not contradictions. As used by Whitehead, these terms are free from contradiction. They refer to different phases of God's nature. They indicate the complexity of this nature. There is no more contradiction here than there is to say: Mr. X is both conscious and unconscious (if your psychology permits this type of expression).

If it be objected that Whitehead's God is a mere postulate, based on (a) the metaphysical need for an agent to organize and make available a vast realm of possibilities and (b) a number of religious insights typified by Jesus of Nazareth—if it be argued that evidence for God is in this sense indirect, Whitehead would *not* be forced to agree. He points out that it is possible to have a direct experience of God, as the source of order. From it results the feelings of enrichment and inspiration which indicate the presence of the divine. As to the insights derived from the life of Jesus, Whitehead agrees in general with the traditional position that *in the life of Jesus of Nazareth the divine is revealed.* As to the claim that God should be thought of as still sharing his life with men, there is much to show that the impact of the divine is still a factor in the world. This is the report of many men whose judgment and veracity are accepted with reference to other data. Hence they are worthy of serious consideration when they claim to have experienced the "divine" presence. Such reports can not justifiably be disregarded unless there has been a serious attempt first to experience the data to which they refer.

Evaluation of Some Criticisms of Whitehead's General Position in Religion

Whitehead has been accused of taking a cold, overintellectualized approach to religion, of denying the importance of the emotional element. The inaccuracy of this criticism is obvious when it is recalled he contends that a genuine religion has a profound impact on a person. It effects a cleansing of the inner life. The doctrines of religion must be vividly and sincerely apprehended. Thus, a strong emotional factor is present. In discussing the relation of religion and philosophy he makes the same point. One function of religion is to provide emotional vitality for some of the great speculative theories formulated by philosophy. Religion thus is a source of emotional dynamic.

However, it will not do to shift the fire of criticism from the claim that Whitehead is too intellectual and coldly unemotional to the opposite contention that he overemphasizes emotion in his approach to religion. Whitehead strikes a sane balance between reason and emotion. Thus, he avoids the excesses of the extreme mystic, and the emotional whirlpools of some Christian existentialists. In Whitehead's opinion, dogma must be vivified by emotional infusion, an emotion guided and made fruitful by its marriage with reason.

Typical of an all too common, unjustified type of criticism is the claim that Whitehead wrongly accuses "communal religion" of being responsible for starting World War I, when actually the cause was misguided patriotism. A careful reading of White-head should have indicated that he is making the valid point that, on occasion, a misguided patriotism corrupts a communal type of religion and uses it for its selfish and nefarious purposes.

The same type of criticism is found in the suggestion that Whitehead is woefully inaccurate in suggesting that religion follows a rigid pattern of development: first ritual, then emotion, then belief, finally, rational religion. It is objected that these four factors are not found in isolation. A careful reading of White-head's statements indicates that he is well aware of that fact, and has not denied it.

Religion and Science

Whitehead's status in the field of science, and his obvious care to be accurate and just, make his discussion of the strengths and weaknesses of science very effective. He provides a valuable debunking of a prevalent modern idolatry, i.e., the uncritical worship of science. Yet, he avoids the equally common mistake of unwarranted denunciation of science in the interests of a semi, or totally, outdated type of religion. In the cases of both science and religion he has made a masterly effort to separate the wheat from the chaff and thus provide for "nourishment" and "fruitful growth."

The Bible

It has been objected that Whitehead's suggestion that the Revelation of St. John be deleted from the Bible, and replaced by Pericles' "funeral oration," is a gross act of secularization of Holy Writ. Revelation is a religious document, while the oration is not. Whitehead's point, of course, is that the moral, and even the spiritual, tone of the oration is much higher than that of Revelation. In any case, even if it be granted that the oration is a secular document, it is of recognized merit and should not be barred merely because of its reputed secularity. After all, there are other secular documents in the Bible; for example, *Ecclesiastes*.

Personal Immortality

The fact that apparently Whitehead does not accept the doctrine of personal immortality is, obviously, a ground for objection, in the opinion of many. Here he has made a clean break with Christianity in general, and in particular with the teachings of Jesus as set forth in the *New Testament*.

On Whitehead's behalf it might be argued that, in his view, what is of value in the lives of individuals is retained in God's experience. Further, the ideals which men strive to attain are realized in the life of God. It may be contended also that human life is a process involving continuous loss, in this sense, death. If then life is a continuous process of dying, why object to a final and complete obliteration of the self which temporarily dwells in a house of clay, subject to the vicissitudes of "the tooth of time"? Finally, it may be suggested that the desire to continue in existence, for an infinity of time, in the timeless realm of heaven—even if it be not a contradiction—is at least an obnoxious form of egoism parading in the guise of religious truth.

Yet, having said this, it must be admitted that it is difficult to escape the basic religious insight of Jesus that the human person is of great worth and should not be permitted to perish at the death of the body. It is true that the supposed details of this continued personal existence have been ineffectively, even grotesquely, stated in the past. But, the fact remains, the intuition of personal immortality seems to be one of the basic insights of the founder of Christianity. Here, at least, one might well reserve judgment, as Whitehead was prepared to do in *Religion in the Making*, rather than rule out the theory, as he apparently did in *Process and Reality*.

Other Deficiencies

It must be admitted that Whitehead *sometimes* is extreme in his criticisms of traditional religion. Necessary qualifications for sweeping generalizations are not always emphasized as vigorously as they should be. Sometimes the necessary qualifications are missing. The Hebrew emphasis on overwhelming power and on strict formalistic morality are at least supplemented by the moral and spiritual insight of the later prophets.[5] These two phases of Hebrew thought are not always placed in juxtaposition by Whitehead. The Psalms, for instance, are held up for ridicule because of their emphasis on barbaric power. He might well have balanced these passages by referring to those expressive of divine love and of moral and spiritual excellence. For example, emphasizing divine love, there is the famous Twenty-third Psalm which begins: "The Lord is my shepherd." Similar in tone are such lines as these: "God is our refuge and strength, a very present help in time of trouble" (Ps. 46); "He will cover thee with his feathers, and under his wings shalt thou trust" (Ps. 91); "He has not dealt with us after our sins, rewarded us according to our iniquities" (Ps. 103); "The Lord shall preserve thee from all evil; He shall preserve thy soul" (Ps. 121); "Oh give thanks unto the Lord for he is good: His mercy endureth forever" (Ps. 136). Among those emphasizing moral and spiritual excellence are the following: "Who shall dwell in thy holy hill? 'He that walketh uprightly, and worketh righteousness, and speaketh the truth in his heart' " (Ps. 15); "Behold, how good and pleasant it is for brethren to dwell together in unity" (Ps. 133); "Blessed is the man that walketh not in the counsel of the ungodly, nor standeth in the way of sinners, nor sitteth in the seat of the scornful" (Ps. 1).

Paul is blamed for much that is deplorable in Christian theology. It is true that he stressed "almightiness." Whitehead admits that Paul also refers to the divine being in terms of "love." Yet, in discussing Paul and later Christian theologians, he tends to concentrate on phases of their thought which stress divine completeness, perfection, compulsive power, divine "otherness." Whitehead, unfortunately, neglects other phases of their thought. For example, consider Paul from whose thought, of course, later theologians have drawn very heavily.[6] Paul claimed to have had direct experience of the presence of God and indeed, union with God, at his conversion and later. Paul, very frequently, did not refer to God in terms of overwhelming power or as a being enshrouded in theological mysteries. Rather, the term "father" seemed much more appropriate. God was regarded as a father who willingly made a supreme sacrifice for men like Paul. The legalistic approach to God, Paul tried and found wanting. (This, Whitehead notes "in passing.") After this occurred his conversion from Judaism to Christianity. He found, through his association with God, that morality consisted of inner devotion to noble purposes, rather than of external obedience to rigorous codes. In short, Paul portrays the glory of God, not in terms of compulsive physical power; instead he emphasizes self-sacrifice for spiritual goals.

Whitehead contends that the idea of God as "absolute despot" has undermined and corrupted the more tender and spiritual elements in traditional Christianity. "The doctrine of Grace has been degraded, and the doctrines of the Atonement are mostly crude." [7]

It is true that some statements of Christian doctrine have emphasized the divine despot; the stern moralist, just but without mercy; a metaphysical first principle. Yet, as has just been pointed out, within Christianity there is another strand of doctrine, another approach. The "sovereign lord," the "supreme being" has been interpreted in terms of "fatherhood" rather than of "imperial despotism," in terms of moral and spiritual excellence rather than of brute compulsive force and arbitrary control. In short, the idea of supreme being in one strand of Christian thought has not corrupted the "tender" moral and spiritual elements. On the contrary, due recognition of these higher elements has saved God from portrayal in terms of physical compulsion, superficial glory, and other shallow experiences.

Whitehead has done great service in emphasizing the defects of one strand of Christian thought. His concrete suggestions are challenging. They spring from a keen appreciation of the life and teachings of the founder of Christianity. Yet, he does not bring into clear focus one important phase of *traditional Christian* thought (as it developed after the death of Jesus), the one which is closer to his own point of view. It may be argued that the strand he criticizes is the major one in Christian thought. Nevertheless, he still might well have paid more attention to the other strand. In short, he might have tempered his criticisms of traditional Christianity *in general* by more reference to this other, less austere phase of doctrine.

SOCIAL PHILOSOPHY

Economic Reform

Whitehead's comments concerning social philosophy indicate his realistic appreciation of the importance of economic factors (among others) in influencing all phases of experience. His suggestions concerning improvements in the economic system are not particularly new or striking. They agree with enlightened "advanced" democratic thought. They are in accord with the suggestions of morale-building industrial consultants. However, it should be noted that the underlying purpose behind Whitehead's suggestions is more profound and comprehensive than in these other approaches. He recommends greater employer-employee co-operation, more opportunity for creative work, a greater recognition of the importance of beauty in industry, not merely to increase industrial efficiency or to implement some political theory. Rather, he recommends these changes so that there may be greater opportunities to develop the qualities of civilized life. In brief, he realizes that civilization cannot flourish in completely unsuitable surroundings.

Whitehead's sketch of the ideal "civilized businessman" may seem somewhat naive. This is true of any ideal when contrasted with decidedly un-ideal present actuality. However, Whitehead seems justified in contending that a civilized businessman is not only possible, but that in every generation some are in existence. In any case, if civilization is to be strengthened, an increasing number of the leaders of industry must be of this type. His suggestion that there should be a combination of mass production and individual craftsmanship in manufacturing seems inept. However, here again, Whitehead provides effective justification for his contention. He points out that, in at least some industries, the scheme is already in successful operation. Further, he argues with considerable effect that this sort of

reform is one price which must be paid for the result in question—an increased approximation to the ideals of civilized living.

In discussing the evils involved in industrial situations,
Whitehead seems to overlook the procedures of some labor
unions. He neglects to *stress* the need for wider perspectives,
greater appreciation of the higher values, a less selfish approach
to life, on the part of some leaders and members of powerful
labor unions.

His treatment of the problem of relating freedom and compulsion, in social life, is admittedly partial. It is based on the
assumption of membership in a professional group. The objection may legitimately be made that a large segment of the
population are not members of such a group. Yet, within the
narrow limits which he has set, his suggestions seem well
supported by actual enlightened present-day practice. The
behavior of professional groups is, of course, not always enlightened. Whitehead is familiar with the dangers which arise
when a self-satisfied institution settles down to a preferred place
in society. The result is the degradation that issues from
apathy. It is an enlightened and creative professional group
which Whitehead envisages as a fountainhead of freedom.

International Relations

In retrospect, Whitehead's justification of the Munich
Agreement seems to cast grave doubts on his wisdom in international affairs. However, he was no more wrong than many
other supposedly competent judges. More important, his conclusions, at least, were based on clearly stated premises and derived
from careful reasoning. His judgment was more sound with reference to the American approach to World War II. His comments
on the problem of a Jewish "national home" in Palestine, as in the
case of other discussions of international problems, are aptly
set in the context of a wide historical perspective. Up to the
present, his analysis seems unduly optimistic. There is little
strong evidence that Jews and Arabs are likely to live in fruitful
co-operation. However, he may, in time, be right. After all, time
does heal many very deep wounds.

The same general comments can be made concerning other

international troubles. It is true that the "thirteen North American colonies" now are associated with Great Britain by a different link from before. Yet, the fact remains that the earlier conflicts have been overcome. The same is true of the relations between India and Britain. Conflict has been replaced by co-operation. Whitehead does not imply that co-operation, among nations, based on rational persuasion would be completely free from friction. He is well aware of the prominence of blind emotion in human affairs. His point is that the evidence shows that rational persuasion *can* be efficacious. Peace can come after war. Certainly Whitehead has stated, with admirable clarity, the implications of civilization with reference to international relations.

However, his suggestion that each great nation is directly responsible for fostering civilization in a specific area of the world is not likely to arouse very favorable reactions from small nations in the areas involved.

In general, it is obvious that his definition of civilization provides a firm foundation for the democratic way of life, since civilization is said to involve respect for individuals and encourage tolerance and sympathy. Reforms in industry, due to increased co-operation in solving problems, the emphasis on rational persuasion rather than brute force, also embody the democratic approach.[8]

EDUCATION

General Principles

Whitehead's educational philosophy is rightly assigned an important place in his discussion of civilization. The ideals of civilization, obviously, cannot be implemented unless they are clearly understood and the proper techniques are provided. Whitehead sets forth very clearly the general principles which an informed educator must bear in mind. Further, he works out, in considerable detail, how these principles should be applied in the various stages of a person's development. In all this he shows an enlightened grasp of the facts of human behavior

and of the basic principles of human development. He recognizes the inescapable fact that the student is an organism in
necessary relationship with a very complex environment. His
comments concerning the specific subject matters to be taught
are based on a careful examination of what is relevant, with
due regard paid to individual differences. He is concerned with
the fullest possible development of all aspects of the human
being, not only intellectual and physical but also aesthetic,
moral, and spiritual.

More specifically, Whitehead's wisdom is shown in his recognition that the intellectual content of education must be made
vital—a stimulus to significant insight rather than a mere weight
on the memory. In other words, unless ideas are interesting and
enjoyable, little benefit will be derived from the educational
process. Yet, with characteristic "balance," he emphasizes the
essential reminder that hard work and discipline are necessary
ingredients if the student is to be effective, now and in the
future. He wisely reiterates the fact that the interests and enjoyments should not be those of a superficial, partial approach
to life's problems. He is referring to the more profound and
comprehensive interests and enjoyments present in the life of
a person who is living on a level considerably higher than a
superior type of animal. In debunking the traditional "mind
is an instrument" theory, he retains what is of value, namely,
that the mind must be used in solving human problems. However, the problems to be solved should be "present" ones. It is
most unfortunate to regard the mind as an instrument that is to
be prepared for use at some future date, but is meanwhile artificially withdrawn from the pressure of events of immediate
interest. The opposite error—namely, undue concentration on
handicrafts, manual dexterity, neat little building projects, for
the sake of keeping busy and developing social skills—is clearly
recognized. But, again, Whitehead provides the needed corrective. Unless ideas, when the need arises, can be expressed
through the medium of physical objects, the life of reason may
well suffer retardation. Further, if the social approach to manipulation of the physical environment is natural and significant,
then it should be encouraged.

Secondary School Education

The place of the Latin and Greek classics in modern education receives a stimulating reappraisal. The values of the experience of "working out" a translation are not denied. Rather, there is a realistic recognition of the needs and abilities of the majority of students. Running through all of Whitehead's comments is a very valuable emphasis on the necessity of firsthand experience and a warning against the siren lure of mere verbal proficiency. Words are useful as symbols, but excessive concentration on words frequently blinds one to the basic facts in the situation.

It has seemed to some critics that Whitehead does not take into consideration the inferior students who appear inevitably in the modern system of free, compulsory education. It does require a stretch of the imagination, and considerable optimism, to envisage some students (granted they may be a minority) measuring up to the minimum requirements of the common core of education proposed by Whitehead. Yet, it must be remembered that he had considerable experience with the educational problems of the city of London, on all levels. In this, as in other matters, it is at least possible that his apparently naive optimism is closer to reality than the so-called realism of his critics. In any case, it would appear that Whitehead is here discussing so-called normal individuals.

It may seem that Whitehead, in outlining his program of study for secondary school education, has made little or no provision for the social sciences. Economics, psychology, and sociology are not mentioned as subjects worthy of attention. In reply to this objection, it may be noted that Whitehead would expect students to become familiar with specific data, and principles, in these fields, as a result of their examination of literature and history. Literature brings into clear focus the facts of human behavior, and raises the question of interpretation of these facts.

University Education

Whitehead's own achievements as a civilized person, and his success as a teacher and supervisor of education, provide impressive support for his discussion of educational problems. Particularly noteworthy is his sketch of the ideal university, with its eager students encouraged by teachers who "wear their learning lightly" but have a deep love for their subject in particular and for all knowledge in so far as that is possible. There is also the administration, fully aware of the real nature of a university. With characteristic wit he delineates the difficulties confronting administrators when they try to find the right sort of man for a faculty position. This impressive mixture of idealism and realistic awareness of the practical difficulties involved in implementing these ideals, is one of the most valuable features of Whitehead's discussion of any topic.

WHITEHEAD'S CONCEPT OF THE PERSON

Since civilization is a way of life open to human beings, the ultimate question must be asked: Is Whitehead's view of the human person a sound one?

In so far as he stresses the essential interconnections of the bodily and mental aspects of human beings, he is "on firm ground." His emphasis on the creative power found in every individual is a necessary corrective of the all too common tendency to disregard the powers of the common man. His awareness of the importance of value in human affairs is another phase of Whitehead's analysis which is sound. The autonomy (i.e., the power of "self-creation" by the self-initiated selection and use of available data) which he finds in individuals seems justified in some instances; but with reference to many persons, he appears to be incorrect. It is very difficult, if not impossible, to escape being victimized by environmental pressures in some situations.

Thus, the question arises: "Does Whitehead place sufficient emphasis on human defects?" There can be no reasonable doubt that he is aware of the irrational, the evil, in the depths of human personality. However, it may seem that he is somewhat optimistic in these matters. Having sketched the deficiencies in human behavior (which have produced the obvious shortcomings in social, religious, and educational life), he offers his solutions with apparent confidence that improvement will be *relatively* easy. There are shadows of late-nineteenth-century optimism in Whitehead's thought. On his behalf, however, it may be said that this constitutes a useful corrective of our perhaps excessive and paralyzing twentieth-century gloom. After all, he does provide data to support his belief in the creative powers of human beings which enable them to rise above the level of lower animals and barbarians.

Notwithstanding these strong points, Whitehead's view of the human person seems incomplete, since he analyzes personality in terms of a series of "moments of experience." Thus, at any particular time a person (body and mind) is said to be composed of a large number of these individual moments of experience, some constituting the body, others constituting the mind. In the last analysis, according to Whitehead, there is nothing but this complex group of moments of experience.

It seems that there is more to be found than this. The "more" (not to be confused with James's "Divine More") is fairly obvious to one who carries out careful internal observation. However, Whitehead does not refer to it. This "more" is difficult to express verbally. It may perhaps be stated thus: there is an awareness of a *relatively enduring entity* (with the normal human life span), which *expresses itself* through its various moments of experience, and thereby develops itself. In short, it is contended that Whitehead does not do full justice to the depth and complexity of the human person.

This "restriction of view" does not undermine the validity of Whitehead's discussion of civilization in general—or of history, social relations, religion, or education in particular. Whitehead has delineated, with admirable clarity, *many* basic factors in human personality. His specific suggestions are firmly based on profound insights and broad experience. The objection here expressed is that he does not go far enough in his analysis of the vastly complex human self.

THE QUALITY OF WHITEHEAD'S
PHILOSOPHY OF CIVILIZATION

There are some critics of Whitehead who find a striking deterioration in the quality of his work when he moves from the fields of science, mathematics, and logic and begins to discuss various phases of civilization. He is accused of being common-place, incredibly naive in his comments on morals, politics, and education. As a moralist he is ridiculed as unjustifiably optimistic, even "time-serving"; as an educator, shallow and contradictory.

It must be admitted that some of Whitehead's remarks taken in isolation seem fair game for a critic in haste to pounce. It is easy to indulge in sweeping destructive criticisms of Whitehead if one is satisfied with a superficial examination of his work. However, a careful, thorough, and *reflective* examination of all that he has *written* (not undue concentration on random remarks attributed to him by his friends) on moral, political, and educational problems will indicate that Whitehead shows more insight than is recognized at first and that the contradictions are more apparent than real. True, Whitehead is optimistic. However he provides reasons for this optimism. It may well be that some of what Whitehead says is "common-place." Surely a philosopher should not be expected to say something new and startlingly profound about everything. Whitehead is attempting to deal with all available facts and values, familiar ones as well as relatively unfamiliar ones. If the term "common-place" refers to his forms of expression, here again one may remark that if a philosopher is to speak in an understandable fashion to men who are not equipped with technical jargon, he must use utterances which are common-place to some. Finally, although it is true that Whitehead's discussion of morals and politics is not as extensive as his treatments of logic, mathematics, science, education, and religion, nevertheless the basic principles are there even if some details are lacking. The ideals of civilization (and the related "conditions" necessary for the realization of these ideals) could be used to generate suggestions which might serve as rather specific guidance in the practical affairs of human life. Indeed, Whitehead himself has provided more "illustrations" than some of his critics are apparently aware.

In all phases of Whitehead's discussion of civilization (its definition in general, and his suggestions as to how these ideals may be implemented in special areas of human experience) there is emphasis on *linked pairs* of concepts which embody many fundamental insights. The neglect of these insights has vitiated many otherwise excellent projects in the realms of social relationships, religion, and education. For example, he stresses the mutually interrelated phenomena of change (novelty) *AND* endurance (routine); fact *AND* value; vagueness *AND* clarity; freedom *AND* compulsion; reason *AND* emotion. This exemplifies his general *organic* approach to any problem. All phases of the situation must be examined. A simple formula should be an object of immediate suspicion, because the universe is vast and complex, its elements in organic interrelation. Other recurrent themes, in all discussions of specialized topics, are: the dangers involved in overconfidence in the adequacy of language; the need for firsthand experience; the dangers implicit in neglecting the limits of human knowledge.

On the "debit side," it must be admitted that, in some instances, Whitehead is too general—and incomplete—in his discussion of a topic. Details which would clarify, or support, a point of view are missing. This is particularly true of his considerations of social philosophy. Also, his treatment of the Christian religion suffers from an overemphasis on one strand of its tradition.

In fairness to Whitehead, it must be emphasized that he was the first to stress the limitations of his conceptual scheme, the restricted scope of his observations, and the need for further investigation and thought.

One of the most impressive features of Whitehead's discussion of civilization is the metaphysical basis which he provides. His metaphysical position involves an emphasis on individuality, creative interaction, process, permanence, value, and God. These same basic concepts are also stressed in his discussion of the meaning of civilization, history, religion, society, and education.[9] For example, civilization is defined in terms of value ideals. The importance of the development of the individual, through creative interaction with his fellows, is given due weight in the discussion of history, religion, society, and education. The need for the recognition of the inescapability of change in all areas of experience is constantly to the fore. Equal stress is placed on enduring factors in these situations. The function of God is given a prominent place in the treatment of religion and history. One of the main characteristics of civilization—"peace"—implies a reference to God. Spiritual values are emphasized in Whitehead's discussion of education, society, and history. Thus, these key concepts—descriptive generalizations derived originally from a study of physical, biological, mathematical, and psychological data—are equally valid in dealing with civilization and its related topics. In brief, it should be noted that *Whitehead's philosophy of civilization is part of a total system.* The main concepts used in the philosophy of civilization are not artificial chimeras, arbitrarily constructed and unjustifiably superimposed on the "real facts" of physics, biology, mathematics, and psychology. Rather, to repeat, they are the same basic concepts. Hence, the validity of Whitehead's philosophy of civilization is enhanced, because of its identity with patterns of thought independently substantiated. In other words, the characteristics of civilized life are not contrary to the nature of things as revealed by the physical and social sciences.

However, it must be emphasized that Whitehead's philosophy of civilization in its entirety does not rise or fall with the metaphysical foundations which he has provided. *As it deals with the complex facts of human experience,* it is characterized by a balanced sanity and a wide-ranging wisdom, which is sadly lacking in many current philosophies of civilization. Even if the question of its metaphysical foundations is not taken into consideration, Whitehead's philosophy of civilization is still impressive.

The fact that Whitehead's philosophy of civilization *has*

a firm metaphysical basis serves to focus attention on his almost unique achievement. He is one of the few men in this age, or in any age, to have provided a *"complete" intellectual synthesis.* His basic concepts apply, legitimately, to all phases of human experience—the fields of natural science, social science, art, morality, and religion. Here is a foundation on which one can "see life steadily and see it whole." It is a unity of vision attained without the usual type of self-imposed myopia which obtains a pseudo-unity of system by refusing to consider large areas of relevant data.

Whitehead has taken into consideration *all the major factors* in the universe which are known to the human mind. There are some specific deficiencies of awareness, emphasis, and interpretation. But, to repeat, he does not disregard the major factors in a situation. He stands almost alone in his enlightened use of available data.

The phrase "available data" is crucial. Whitehead does not claim, for a moment, to have a complete grasp of "the ultimate mysteries of the universe." He is second to no man in his sense of "the vast beyond." Yet, always admitting human limitations, particularly his own, he has made impressive use of what is open to human observation and intelligence. Herein lies the greatness of Whitehead's philosophy. It does not make extravagant claims. It is the best that could be "worked out" by a great and wise man, living in the twentieth century, making magnificently effective use of all available human resources. It would be absurd to claim that Whitehead's philosophy of civilization is without a flaw. There are errors. There are some omissions at crucial points in the argument. However, these deficiencies should not blind a person to the magnitude of Whitehead's achievement.

Here is a simple, yet accurate, definition of that very elusive term: civilization. Here also is a comprehensive, enlightening, and sound analysis of the factors which influence human life. Finally, there are sane suggestions concerning the development, and retention, of the civilized way of life. Indeed, Whitehead's philosophy of civilization has come very close to meeting the challenge which Whitehead himself set forth in *Adventures of Ideas:* "Philosophy should now perform its final service. It should seek the insight, dim though it be, to escape the wide wreckage of a race of beings sensitive to values beyond those of mere animal enjoyment." [10]

Chapter 7   CIVILIZATION AND
METAPHYSICS

INTRODUCTION

It has been stated that a few *non-technical* terms are adequate to express, for the general reader, the essentials of Whitehead's theory of reality. These terms are: individuality, process, creative interaction, permanence, value, God. It must now be shown that these terms convey the same insights that Whitehead usually states in a very technical fashion. Further, when a minimum of technical terms have been introduced into the discussion, additional justification will be provided for the claim that the component elements of the universe, to which these terms refer, are such that the ideals of civilization may be regarded as based in the nature of things, and as capable of realization (granting that Whitehead has shown his view of the universe to be sound).

After extensive examination of mathematical, physical, and psychological data,[1] Whitehead reaches the conclusion that the universe is composed of individual centers of energy. These he terms "actual entities."[2]

WHITEHEAD'S METAPHYSICS

General Theory of Actual Entities

Each actual entity is an *individual* in *process* of *creative interaction* with other centers of energy. This process, by which an actual entity grows, is called concrescence. In this process of concrescence, an actual entity is confronted by data made available by other actual entities. These data are of two main sorts: (a) concrete, e.g., a particular sense datum, and (b) abstract, i.e., something grasped by reason—some generality which need not be expressed in particular form at any moment. (For example, the number two, rather than two apples.) Such abstract data are termed eternal objects. They are called eternal objects because Whitehead regards them as permanent factors in the universe. In the process of prehension (i.e., reaction to data), an actual entity takes into itself *some* of the data provided by other actual entities. This process of inclusion is termed positive prehension (or feeling). There are two types of positive prehension. When concrete data are positively prehended, it is called physical prehension. When abstract data (eternal objects) are positively prehended, this is termed conceptual prehension. Physical prehensions constitute the physical pole of an actual entity; conceptual prehensions, the mental pole. Not all data, of either type, are positively prehended. Some are rejected. This is negative prehension. The acceptance, or rejection, involves a favorable, or unfavorable, "attitude." This is termed subjective form. This complex process of reaction, and selection, manifests the subjective aim (purpose) of an actual entity. The actual entity's purpose, or aim, is an attempt to implement a self-selected pattern or ideal. Such patterns or ideals are, in Whitehead's opinion, eternal objects.

Value

Among these possible patterns of behavior are the *value* ideals—for example, truth, beauty, and goodness. When an actual entity illustrates one of these value ideals in its experience, then value is actualized in the world. In discussing *value*, Whitehead contends, further, that any actual entity, as such, is valuable (even if it does not manifest any of the major value ideals) because it is important. It cannot be disregarded. The universe would be different without it.

God

Among the interacting actual entities, each building itself up out of data made available by others, is the actual entity God. Whitehead claims that eternal objects are available as

possibilities, in organized fashion, to guide the development of
ordinary actual entities (i.e., those other than God), and for
their general use as data. This is so because God has organized
them and made them available. God has not created the eternal
objects; but, he envisages and organizes them in his so-called
"primordial nature."[3] Thus, eternal objects are made available
for the envisagement of all other actual entities, which then
benefit from God's experience. Any ordinary actual entity selects data provided by God *and* ordinary actual entities. In this
selective process, any actual entity is "causa sui" (autonomous).
Even God cannot force any type of data upon even the most
humble of developing actual entities.

In the process of concretion no actual entity, not even God,
can prehend, positively, the complete universe. Only God can
contemplate completely the infinite realm of eternal objects.
The life of an ordinary actual entity is very brief. When it
reaches its final stage (its "satisfaction"), it goes out of existence.
At that point, *and only then,* data from it are available for the
use of other actual entities (including God). The contents of
its experiences are available. But, the inner vitality of its life is
now terminated and cannot be absorbed, as datum, by any subsequent or present actual entity (not even God). Thus, and
within these limits, one actual entity may be "objectified" in
another. There is evil in the world because of the inescapability
of loss. Evil also arises because some actual entities have selected subjective aims which involve narrowly individualistic
competition.

In this changing universe (changing because ordinary actual
entities arise and pass away), God is a partial exception. God
continues in existence. He does not provide concrete data
through the medium of his demise. How it is possible for God
to provide concrete data (God's "superject nature") without
first going out of existence (as is the case with ordinary actual
entities) is not explained by Whitehead. In this aspect of his
being, God is quite different from ordinary actual entities. However, God does change, since he grows. His so-called "consequent nature" is continually taking in data from ordinary actual

entities as they terminate their careers. He absorbs not all data, but only what can be saved. In his life all data are put to their best possible use. An aesthetic harmony is achieved.[4]

Permanence

There are three elements of *permanence* in the universe: eternal objects, the continuing existence of God, and societies, i.e., groups of ordinary actual entities, in which the successive individual members, during their lifetimes, manifest the common, and repeated, pattern which characterizes the group.

Every object in the familiar world of inanimate objects, vegetables, lower animals, and human beings, is a complex society. The human body is composed of actual entities which are characterized by a restricted type of experience. There are vague pulsations of energy in the physical pole with so little activity in the mental pole that it can, for practical purposes, be disregarded. On the other hand, the actual entities composing the "mind" are much more complex in their experiences. A wide range of conceptual prehensions occur in the mental pole. The subjective aim is concerned with novelty, and richness, of experience. The concrete data of the physical pole reflect this aim.

Applications

Incidentally, the fact that any actual entity, including those constituting a human mind, is incapable of prehending everything in the universe (in view of the conditions under which data are made available) is the basis of Whitehead's repeated claim that there are very definite limits to human knowledge.

The details of mental life are explained in terms of the basic facts of "causal efficacy" (the impact of data coming from the past, dimly and vaguely felt), "presentational immediacy" (the clear-cut data of science, derived, by a process of abstraction, from causal efficacy), and the process of "symbolic reference" by which the data of presentational immediacy are referred to the sources indicated by causal efficacy. Propositions, consciousness, judgments—all very complex concepts which need not be explained here—are used to account for the complexities of mental life.[5]

The superficial nature of clear "experience in presentational immediacy" is the basis of Whitehead's repeated warning against undue reliance on what is clear. It is clear because it has neglected many of the essential data. On the other hand, while the vagueness of causal efficacy is annoying, yet this type of experience reveals much that is disregarded in presentational immediacy. Both types of experience have their value. Their weaknesses must be appreciated as well.

It is essential to realize that, in Whitehead's opinion, every quality found in a society has that quality only because some of the component actual entities also have that quality. In other words, in his later writings (*Process and Reality, Adventures of Ideas*) Whitehead does not admit the possibility that the "whole" may have emergent qualities not possessed by (at least some of) the parts.

The fact that the fundamental technical concepts involved in his metaphysical position are relevant to the more specialized discussion of civilization can be demonstrated. This serves to substantiate the point already made (pp. 171-72), stated in non-technical terminology, that Whitehead has provided a metaphysical basis for his approach to civilization. In so far as his metaphysics is sound, his discussion of civilization takes on added validity. Civilization is not an artificial chimera. It is grounded in the nature of things. Hence, it is not only valid but also possible of realization if the steps, outlined for the achievement of the ideals of civilization, are correctly delineated.

It will now be shown that not only is Whitehead's general discussion of the meaning of civilization in accordance with his metaphysical position, but that, also, the specific suggestions in the fields of history, religion, social philosophy, and education are likewise substantiated.

METAPHYSICAL BASIS FOR CIVILIZATION

The Nature of Civilization

The ideals of civilization—truth, beauty, adventure, peace —are eternal objects, part of the enduring structure of the universe, made available by God for the use of those actual entities which propose to use them and are capable of translating these potentialities into actuality.

In the following discussion it must be remembered that civilized human beings are composed (speaking technically) of complex societies of actual entities. Whitehead contends that the characteristics of any society are the characteristics of some (or all) of its component actual entities. Or, to express the same point in a different fashion: if actual entities are capable of manifesting certain types of behavior, it is possible for a society (of actual entities) to act in the same fashion. In the interest of simplicity of exposition, the following discussion of the metaphysical basis of civilization will concentrate on actual entities. However, to repeat, what may be said of them might equally well be said (though the expression would be more cumbersome) of complex societies of actual entities composing the bodies and minds of human beings.

It is possible to realize the ideal of adventure because the very nature of an actual entity is that it is self-creative. Each actual entity is a center of novelty—hence adventure. The vast realm of eternal objects, infinite in extent, provides the patterns of unlimited complexity. These patterns may be used to guide an actual entity to the most excellent types of adventure, as well as the most deplorable. In this very fact lies the possibility of conflict due to opposing adventures, the implementation of conflicting subjective aims. Adventure involves loss because, as an actual entity develops, some elimination of available data takes place. Further, in due course all actual entities (except God) die, and their inner life is gone forever, "worn out and satisfied."

Because of the essentially dynamic nature of actual entities, it is impossible to live in the past. The past can be used to provide content for the present, but the present uses the past in its own new fashion.

The harmony that is "peace" is possible of attainment because an actual entity, as such is a process of the harmonization of diverse elements. In the case of inferior actual entities, the harmonization is on a low level. The results are poor and feeble. But the excellent harmonization, revealed in the facing and overcoming of evil in victorious tragedy, indicates that peace can be experienced. It is achieved by God. With his help peace can be attained by man. That is to say, in God's consequent nature, data from the world of ordinary actual entities can be harmonized in accordance with his subjective aim. This aim involves selection and realization of the best possible pattern from the realm of eternal objects, as envisaged in his primordial nature. The harmonization is made available to the world of ordinary actual entities by the function of God's superject nature.

The ideal of "truth" can be realized in the world because the experience of an actual entity (of the type composing the mind of a human being) is sufficiently complex to hold before its inspection an eternal object, and to perceive correctly (truly) that this eternal object is expressed in the relevant actual entities in accordance with the claim made in the proposition under consideration.

However, there can be no final or complete system of true statements. In the first place, the universe is in a continual process of production of novel facts. Creativity is an ultimate category. Secondly, no actual entity, not even God, can at any moment positively prehend all data. Some data are still in the future. Further, there is some loss of data due to the demise of past actual entities and to the selective process involved in prehension. In short, all data cannot be prehended positively. Hence, knowledge is limited.

The eternal object "beauty" can be realized in the experience of an actual entity. The harmony which is basic to beauty is obtained in the contrast of strongly individualized elements. This is a pattern which sufficiently high-grade actual entities are obviously capable of realizing. Also, the creative initiative of some actual entities makes it possible for them to arrange data which will produce an "art object" capable of providing stimulus, refreshment, inspiration, and the other functions of an art object mentioned by Whitehead.

The status of "goodness" among the higher echelons of value ideals is seen from the fact that "good" is an eternal object mentioned by Whitehead in the same breath with beauty and truth.

Prerequisites

The essential nature of actual entities, these final real things of which the universe is made, underlines the importance of the individual. Actual entities *are individual* and autonomous centers of energy. Value is achieved only in the experience of individual actual entities. The creative process which characterizes the universe is the self-creative process of interacting, individual actual entities. Since an actual entity builds itself up, making use of available eternal objects and concrete data, its degree of attainment depends in part on the richness of data which are available. (The other basic factors are its own subjective form and aim.) Any excessive restrictions placed on the availability of data will thwart the life of the individual centers of value in the universe. Here, then, is an implied plea to respect the rights of individuals.

This need for *freedom*, if full development is to take place, does not justify license. Certain compulsions, or restrictions, are inescapable. There are only certain patterns of possibilities made available by God. It is true Whitehead says the realm of eternal objects is infinite. Yet, the fact remains that if a plan of action is once selected, and embarked on, the detailed *implications* of this course of action follow inevitably. Further, as has been noted, only certain types of concrete data are available. Also, in the interests of the highest type of self-development, narrowly selfish subjective aims and the resultant activities must be avoided. If an actual entity decides to engage in brutal conflict there is a resultant loss in fullness of development. For example, the excellent value "peace" will escape such an actual entity.

The civilized emphasis on *tolerance* is obviously based on the nature of things. Unless each individual is given an opportunity to develop values to the highest extent, in his own unique way, the maximum possible value will not be obtained. Each actual entity is unique. Each is a center of value. Only by co-operation can all rise to the highest possible levels of attainment. For this reason *persuasion* is the approved technique in social relations. Further, one basic characteristic of an actual

entity is that it selects what it sees fit. In that sense it is only
by persuasion that one actual entity will receive data from
another. An attempt to use force will only produce the attitude
(subjective form) of opposition. As Whitehead remarks, the
appeal to persuasion is in accordance with one of our most profound religious insights.

The *wisdom* Whitehead advocates is possible because there
exists the realm of eternal objects which establishes reason in
its province. That is to say, there are data for rational apprehension (conceptual prehension) in orderly relationships. Here
is the basis of those generalities which are required for effective
dealing with facts. Here also are the standards required for
sound criticism and intelligent action. The infinite realm of
eternal objects, spread before the "gaze" of an actual entity,
will make possible salvation from too narrow a view of the universe. But, in addition to the clarity of conceptual prehension,
there is also the vague emotional complexity of physical prehension. This serves as a reminder of the limits of reason and
the need for the comprehensive *wisdom* which uses reason,
supplements it by other types of experience and sources of information, and then tackles life's problems as effectively as
possible.

Actual entities are of such a nature that civilization is capable of being actualized. This, however, does not lead to the
conclusion that Whitehead is pretending that all actual entities
are civilized. Such is neither the case, nor his contention. He
is merely saying that some actual entities are capable of ap-
proximating, in varying degrees, the ideals of civilization.
Hence human beings, since they are composed of actual
entities, are capable of doing so.

Philosophy of History

In referring to *ideas* as factors which influence history,
Whitehead is concerned with eternal objects, or varying attempts to express the meaning of eternal objects. The "luring"
function of ideas is involved in his contention that an eternal
object appeals to a certain actual entity only if it is in accordance
with the purpose embodied in its subjective aim. The slowness

with which some great ideas become effective in the world is
due to the fact that no agency can force any actual entity to
accept any eternal object. Until an actual entity selects an
eternal object, on its own initiative, the eternal object cannot
be positively prehended, let alone actualized.

There are so-called "irrational" factors in the world (wind
and weather, steam, iron, electricity) because there are some
actual entities in which, for practical purposes, there is no aim
at novelty or at richness and complexity of experience. In such
a situation rationality, the contemplation and efficacy of eternal
objects, is at an unimportant minimum.

Great men are complex societies in which the component
"mind" societies are composed of actual entities whose subjective aim is such that the mental poles are very active in
apprehending complicated patterns of ideal possibilities not
envisaged by other actual entities. Such eternal objects then
are translated into action by the great men. In this fashion
they are brought to the attention of lesser men. These eternal objects become effective in their lives also (though to a lesser
extent), by a process of prehension between the component
actual entities. This, then, explains the influence of great "men
of ideas." Outstanding military leaders, on the other hand, are
composed of societies of actual entities which, in part, are concerned with exerting pressure of concrete data (often accompanied by vigorous conceptual activities) on other actual
entities. Such men set up an environment of a sort that the
actual entities composing other men are confronted by so many
data, coming with such force, that they decide to bow to the
impact of the actual entities composing the "men of power."
(It must be admitted that these references to great men—great
in intellectual and in military affairs—have been oversimplified
for purposes of brief exposition.)

Whitehead's stress on the necessity of considering *both*
rational persuasion and compulsive force obviously is based on
his claim that any actual entity has two poles. There are both
physical prehensions, receiving the compulsive impact of concrete data, and (rational) conceptual prehensions. Further,
while one kind of prehension will be predominant in one type

of actual entity, the other kind of prehension will be dominant
in a second main type of actual entity.

Whitehead's emphasis on *technology* reflects his theory that
eternal objects must be exemplified in the experience of some
particular actual entity, if they are to be completely effective.
In other words, a "good idea" is of little use unless it is translated
into action through the medium of an effective technique.

Institutions, which are so important in the process of history,
are in Whitehead's system vastly complex societies of actual
entities, embodying the strengths and weaknesses of their component elements.

Whitehead's technical discussion of symbolism involves a
clear recognition of the importance of an emotional factor in
effective symbolism. Any actual entity, in its aspect of subjective
form, embodies a strong emotional element. Symbols are, for
Whitehead, phases of the complex experience of some actual
entities. Brief reference already has been made (in discussing
the human mind) to his treatment of symbolism in terms of
causal efficacy, presentational immediacy, and symbolic reference.

The *economic interpretation of history* brings into focus the
activities of actual entities in which the physical pole (the
impact of concrete, tangible factors) is the more dominant
characteristic. The inadequacy of this approach is that there
are concrete data, available for physical prehension, more rich
and complex than the data of economics. These are neglected.
Further, there are also conceptual prehensions in any actual
entity. In at least some actual entities, the conceptual prehensions are predominant.

This same oversight vitiates the *evolutionary* theory. The
universe, most certainly, includes the impact of opposing forces.
But rational direction is also a factor in some cases. The subjective aim of some actual entities may have a relatively clear
grasp of an eternal object which embodies a value ideal or a
high-grade complex possibility of reason. The factor of conflict
is not the whole story. The experience of all actual entities involves some co-operation. Even the most "pugnacious" actual
entities require support from at least a few other actual entities.
Thus, Whitehead's theory of actual entities provides for more

co-operation than is recognized by the traditional evolutionary approach. Further, in stressing passive adaptation to the present environment, the evolutionary theory overlooks the essentially dynamic nature of actual entities, particularly the high degree of creativity attained by some of them.

In short, most philosophies of history overemphasize one factor in the complex life of actual entities: a restricted type of either physical prehension or conceptual prehension. An adequate philosophy of history must take into consideration both aspects of the ultimate elements in the universe and the varying degrees of emphasis and complexity in these basic factors. Incidentally, Whitehead's theory of reality—with its emphasis on the creative activity of actual entities, the inexhaustible realm of ideal possibilities, the vast complex of concrete data available —seems to tend toward an optimistic view of the future, rather than support the view, sometimes *apparently* expressed by Whitehead, that the "golden age" lies in the past.

Religion

If religion is characterized by concern for value, then Whitehead's actual entities support this emphasis. Each actual entity is a center of value. Further, and more important, the distinction between values, and the status of the highest values, is maintained in the realm of eternal objects. Whitehead's emphasis on solitariness is reflected in his theory that an actual entity is autonomous, in the use that it makes of available data. The inner life of an actual entity is the central core of reality. But, just as solitariness of religious experience issues in social effectiveness, so each actual entity is in essential interaction with other actual entities giving, and receiving, fundamental data. The inescapability of change in the life of each actual entity, even God, is involved in Whitehead's emphasis on the need for change in religious thought and action—in particular, the improvement of doctrines and creeds. The theory that God and the world (of ordinary actual entities) are both real, and are mutually requisite, reflects the basic contention that actual entities alone are real and are interdependent. God is regarded as an actual entity, one among many, because of the basic insight that God is genuinely immanent.

God's primordial nature makes eternal objects available for the use of ordinary actual entities. However, he does not force any actual entity to accept any eternal object. This is one metaphysical foundation of Whitehead's ascription to God of the qualities: tenderness, love, patience. The same attributes are also based on the functioning of his consequent nature. Having waited till the life of ordinary actual entities has terminated, he saves what otherwise would be lost; he saves what can be saved. In positively prehending the experiences of others, in showing how evil may be used for good despite tragedy, he is the fellow sufferer who understands. In so far as his superject nature (as well as his primordial nature) makes data available for other actual entities, God is the great companion.

Social Philosophy

The preceding discussions of the metaphysical basis of Whitehead's views concerning the value of the individual, tolerance, freedom, persuasion are relevant to his more specific treatment of these factors in civilized behavior in the industrial, social, and international contexts. Here again, with reference to his social philosophy, it is possible to indicate the metaphysical justifications for his emphasis on change and endurance, the proper use of the past, the need for compulsion as well as freedom, the value of symbolism in its use for communication and hence as a bond of unity. The same is true of the need for recognizing: the flux of rational and irrational factors in life, the areas of clarity and vagueness in experience. In discussing the political theory of the "social contract," Whitehead points out that it is impossible to disregard the importance of custom, as a foundation for society. Custom reflects the basic metaphysical fact of inheritance from the past. The notion of the establishment of a contract is an equally legitimate one (if kept in its proper perspective), since it refers to the metaphysical characteristic of spontaneity (novelty). Due regard for both factors is a condition for political wisdom.

It is important to note, in some detail (at the risk of repetition), that Whitehead's metaphysical position provides impressive support for the type of democracy advocated by the Western world.

There have been many definitions of democracy. Perhaps the most ferquently used are (a) "government of the people, by the people, for the people"; and (b) "liberty, equality, fraternity." In addition, however, democracy has been defined in terms of: (c) "justice"; (d) "majority rule"; (e) "minimum of government control." Further, democracy is described as that form of political organization where (f) inalienable rights are protected; (g) self-development is made possible; or (h) the "greatest happiness of the greatest number" is achieved.

At first sight, it would appear that democracy has no clearcut, or commonly accepted, meaning. However, a careful examination of these (apparently) diverse definitions reveals that they all fit into *one* rather complicated pattern. That is to say, we find that among them they provide a fairly complete outline of the complicated meaning of democracy.

A democratic society is one in which the "self-development" of all men and women is made possible because of "liberty, equality, and fraternity." In this fashion the "greatest happiness of the greatest number" is achieved. This pattern of life involves "self-government," either directly or through representatives who are servants of the people. There is some disagreement among leading exponents as to the extent of state control which is advisable, also as to the wisdom of accepting majority opinion. However, underlying all the discussion is the belief that any human being is at least of potential value, and should be given a chance to develop his powers so that he may contribute to the common good, in so far as he is able. (The concepts of right and justice are at least implied here.)

Turning now to Whitehead, the following statement indicates his general point of view. "The basis of democracy is the common fact of value-experience, as constituting the essential nature of each pulsation of actuality. Everything has some value for itself, for others, and for the whole." [6]

According to Whitehead, any actual entity enjoys a very

genuine "freedom." During the course of its self-development it follows its own self-selected pattern of development, and chooses the data of its component experiences. Not even God can force any actual entity to prehend data contrary to its own subjective aim.

Each actual entity is in creative interaction with other actual entities. Each actual entity makes use of data provided by others. These data are available only after the demise of other (ordinary) actual entities. In this sense, "self-sacrifice" is involved. If this self-sacrifice is carried out with a certain type of subjective aim and subjective form, the democratic ideal of "fraternity" may be manifest.

Actual entities illustrate the principle of "equality" (in at least some of its varied meanings). Each actual entity is equally free to select its own pattern of development, and use data made available by other actual entities. Each actual entity is equally available for favorable consideration by other actual entities.

"Justice," at least in the Platonic sense, is obviously involved in Whitehead's world view. The preceding discussion carries the implication that actual entities have basic "rights" (life and liberty) which cannot be denied. The right to "property" (perhaps the argument becomes subtle here) is supported by Whitehead's point that each actual entity requires a certain amount of data, in order to constitute itself.

The notion of "the sovereignty of the people" is illustrated in Whitehead's claim that each actual entity is ultimately the determiner of its own fate in the society of actual entities. The notion of "representative government," in which the officials are the servants of the people, finds metaphysical support in Whitehead. He points out that the actual entities which constitute the body are frequently under the direction of the high-grade actual entities which constitute the mind. However, the body actual entities are under no inescapable compulsion to accept the influence of the mind actual entities. This is the same situation as in an (ideal) democratic society in which citizens may reject the advice of their officials.

An examination of Whitehead's metaphysics reveals little or no support for the democratic ideal of "majority rule." This is because of his emphasis on the autonomy of the individual. The greatest happiness of the greatest number is not, for him, the supreme value. Self-realization seems to have primacy. It may be suggested, however, that after all, the highest form of democracy involves mutual co-operation, not a situation where a majority imposes its will on a minority. Further, there is no necessary opposition between self-realization and majority happiness.

Here, then, is a metaphysics which apparently provides support for most (if not all) of the basic ideals of Western democracy. This is a time when the intellectual environment, in which men live, exerts an increasingly important influence. The morale, and efficiency, of any man depend to a very considerable extent on the ideology (or lack of ideology) which he has at his disposal. The ultimate foundations on which an ideology is based are of great significance. An apparently impressive ideology is no stronger than its foundations. The democratic way of life is confronted by Communism, an ideology with a clearly stated metaphysical foundation. Whitehead has done great service to the cause of democracy, in that he has shown the ideals of Western democracy are in accordance with the nature of things, and are therefore not an artificial dream incapable of realization in the world in which we live. Since Whitehead's philosophy is more accurate than that of Communism's "materialism," the democratic ideology has a much better foundation than that available to Communism.

Incidentally, it becomes evident that civilization is possible only in a democratic society of the type discussed in the preceding sections. In the totalitarian system of Communism, *genuine respect* for the individual, for freedom, tolerance, and persuasion, and a *full appreciation* of truth, beauty, goodness, adventure, art, and peace are impossible.[7]

Education

Whitehead's contention that *education should include training in values as well as facts* reflects his characteristic stress on the value aspects of actual entities. His appreciation of the importance of the past is natural since the past provides essential data for present actual entities. Yet, only the present is vital. Therefore, education should not be "backward looking." Whitehead's claim that knowledge must be interesting is a corollary of the fact that no actual entity really will positively prehend data unless they are in accordance with its subjective aim. It is foolish, then, to try to force any datum on any actual entity or any group of actual entities. The teacher can be effective only as a source of data, combining the functions of lure and persuasive impact. But, to repeat, the lure and persuasion will be effective, ultimately, only if the actual entities involved decide to react positively.

The fact that effort is necessary, on the part of the student, follows naturally from the condition that an actual entity, in its process of self-development, must exert itself in the process of selecting, appropriating, organizing, and infusing the data with its own inner life. No external source can make an actual entity what it is, while it remains passive.

The preceding discussion of freedom and compulsion, clarity and vagueness, reason and emotion, symbolism, the limits of human knowledge, and the need to supplement knowledge with wisdom is relevant here but need not be repeated.

The emphasis on handicrafts, in all primary, secondary, and some university education, follows from Whitehead's recognition that physical activity is necessary since the subjective aims of some of the component actual entities of a human being are concerned with vague, massive pulsations of energy. Education should be concerned with the whole man.

There must be rhythm in education because there is a rhythmic process involved in the complex societies which compose a human being from birth to death. The component actual entities undergo a rhythmic process of development from initial data to final satisfaction.

A balanced, comprehensive curriculum is required because of the many important ingredients in the universe: facts (actual entities) and values (eternal objects—such as truth, beauty, goodness—as possible, and eternal objects as realized); complex rational factors (conceptual prehensions) and irrational, narrowly restricted factors (physical prehensions). These factors, and others, in varying degrees, issue in a wide variety of different experiences. None of these can be safely disregarded. All must be fitted into a harmonious pattern, if chaos is to be avoided and adequate self-development is to take place.

Whitehead thinks it is possible to have a fundamental common core in education because, despite the obvious differences in human needs and abilities, there are underlying similarities. All actual entities are confronted by the same realm of eternal objects, and by God. There are a number of relatively permanent societies constituting a stable environment (inanimate and, in varying degrees, animate societies). He contends that *what is important in these common factors* can be included in the common curriculum. Only on this foundation can the individual variations receive adequate development.

It is not surprising that Whitehead suggests a university should be both local and "universal." An actual entity is localized in a sense. But, its data come from everywhere, and its influence extends everywhere—unless artificial interference is introduced. The emphasis on the need for co-operation among the various components of the university is also in accordance with Whitehead's general position. The component actual entities are at their best when they function as co-operating individuals, developing themselves by this essential process of interaction and mutual support.

This technical chapter on "Civilization and Metaphysics" should be placed in proper perspective. One method for obtaining this result would be to recall the final paragraph of the *Preface* of this book.

"At a time when the applications of modern science seem to be dooming civilization to extinction, it is worth while to examine the attempt of a great twentieth-century mind—trained in science and steeped in the values of civilization—to develop a philosophy of civilization. Alfred North Whitehead (a) defines civilization, (b) states the conditions which make possible its existence, and (c) shows its worth. This 'philosophy of civilization' is one of the most important contributions made by Whitehead to the life of his age." [8]

NOTES

The following abbreviations of titles are here used to refer to works by Alfred North Whitehead:

A.E.   *The Aims of Education* (New York: The Macmillan Company, 1929)

A.I.   *Adventures of Ideas* (New York: The Macmillan Company, 1933)

F.R.   *The Function of Reason* (Princeton: Princeton University Press, 1929)

M.T.   *Modes of Thought* (New York: The Macmillan Company, 1938)

P.R.   *Process and Reality* (New York: The Macmillan Company, 1929)

R.M.   *Religion in the Making* (New York: The Macmillan Company, 1926)

S.M.W. *Science and the Modern World* (New York: The Macmillan Company, 1929 Edition)

Chapter 1

CIVILIZATION

1. In discussing civilization, Whitehead sometimes uses the term "culture" as a synonym for civilization. On other occasions culture has a more general meaning. It then refers to the characteristic activities of a social group. Some of these activities may exhibit the qualities of civilization. Some may not. In this sense there may be a civilized culture or an uncivilized culture. Generally speaking, the context will indicate whether the relation of culture and civilization is that of synonym, or genus and species.

2. As has been noted, Whitehead uses the term "beauty" in a wider sense than the familiar aesthetic one used in the preceding sentences. It is sometimes used in the Greek sense of fineness, excellence, or value in general.

3. This must be borne in mind while reading Whitehead's statement that an animal may show love and devotion but, since it lacks generality of understanding, it is deficient in civilization though a civilized being might be less in moral worth. This does not mean that civilization is non-moral. Rather there seems to be an overemphasis on one factor in civilization.

4. It is, of course, obvious from the preceding discussion that these defining characteristics of civilization do not occur in isolation one from the other. For example the type of adventure which constitutes civilization is adventure in the realms of truth, beauty, art, peace.

5. *A.I.*, p. 63.

6. *A.I.*, p. 105.

7. Whitehead, "An Appeal to Sanity," *The Atlantic Monthly*, Vol. CLXIII (1939), p. 320.

8. The phrase "facts *and* values" requires careful consideration. It is not intended to imply that facts, as dealt with by the natural and social sciences, are not valuable. Indeed, Whitehead contends that all facts are valuable, in the sense that they are important, cannot be overlooked. In short, the universe would be different if one fact were removed. However, in addition to this type of value, there are the value ideals such as: truth, beauty, and goodness. When these ideals are actualized, objects or persons (facts) acquire new qualities. They become truthful, beautiful, or good. In a sense, such value ideals, and their actualizations, are facts, i.e. data to be considered. In using the phrase "facts *and* values" an attempt is made to emphasize the importance of considering all types of data: (a) those which can be referred to in scientific terms and (b) those which can be referred to in such terms as truth, beauty, goodness. The preceding reference to values must be supplemented by the comment that there are not only the positive values such as truth, beauty, and goodness; there are also the opposing, negative values—falsehood, ugliness, and evil.

9. *A.I.*, p. 91.

Chapter 2

PHILOSOPHY OF HISTORY

1. *M.T.*, p. 87

2. Plato's technical discussion is in terms of "Ideas" (in his special usage of the term), physical elements, psyche, eros, harmony, mathematical relations, receptacle. See *A.I.*, pp. 188-93.

3. *F.R.*, p. 60.

4. *A.I.*, p. 59.

5. *The Philosophy of John Dewey*, ed. P. A. Schilpp, (Evanston: Northwestern University, 1941), p. 478. For Whitehead's comments on Dewey's philosophy, see Lucien Price, *The Dialogues of Alfred North Whitehead* (Boston: Little, Brown, 1954), pp. 176, 255, 338.

6. *A.I.*, p. 46.

7. *S.M.W.*, p. 295.

8. *A.I.*, p. 21.

9. *A.E.*, p. 111.

10. Whitehead, "Reconstruction," *The Atlantic Monthly*, Vol. CLXIX, p. 173.

11. *F.R.*, p. 4.

12. *S.M.W.*, p. 295.

13. *M.T.*, p. 89.

14. *M.T.*, p. 90.

15. Lucien Price, in *The Dialogues of Alfred North Whitehead*, refers to Whitehead's "fear for the future" which developed after the use of "the bomb." Yet, even this did not blot out Whitehead's enduring confidence in the creative processes present in the universe.

16. The preceding discussion must be borne in mind when examining

the earlier, highly generalized comments concerning "destruction" with which Whitehead concludes *Religion in the Making*. Here he states that the universe shows two aspects: physical wasting and spiritual progress. He envisages a distant day when the physical world, as we now know it, will be no more. But this is the result of *creative* development. Further, God and the eternal value ideals are not destroyed.

17. *A.I.*, pp. 108-109.

Chapter 3

RELIGION

1. *S.M.W.*, p. 275.
2. *R.M.*, p. 58.
3. *R.M.*, p. 58.
4. *R.M.*, p. 17.
5. *R.M.*, p. 60.
6. *R.M.*, p. 59.
7. In referring to God, Whitehead customarily refrains from capitalizing the personal pronoun "he." This is his procedure in the most comprehensive discussion of God, found in *Process and Reality*. (In the earlier books, *Religion in the Making* and *Science and the Modern World*, he tends to use the capital.) In this study, Whitehead's procedure in *Process and Reality* will be followed.
8. *R.M.*, pp. 37-38.
9. *R.M.*, p. 37.
10. *S.M.W.*, p. 275.
11. *A.I.*, p. 213.
12. *A.I.*, p. 214.
13. *R.M.*, p. 57.
14. See also pp. 77-81; *R.M.*, pp. 56-57, 72.
15. Whitehead draws a parallel between Paul and Socrates. He suggests that both were put to death by political leaders who feared the organizers of groups that did not fit into the established system of government. It was not that Paul's "doctrine" was regarded as a threat to the truth. Rather, Paul as a leader of men was regarded as dangerous and was dealt with in the usual fashion.
16. *P.R.*, p. 520.
17. *A.I.*, p. 182.
18. See p. 72.
19. *A.I.*, p. 27.
20. *A.I.*, p. 66.
21. *A.E.*, p. 62.
22. *A.I.*, p. 221.
23. *R.M.*, p. 146.
24. *S.M.W.*, pp. 269-70.
25. Whitehead is not criticizing all liberal theologians. He is denouncing only those who neglect the "essentials" stressed by Jesus of Nazareth.
26. *A.I.*, p. 208.
27. See also pp. 79-80.

28. *A.I.*, p. 41.

29. *P.R.*, p. 318.

30. Whitehead uses the terms *intuition, insight, direct apprehension* as synonymous. He is well aware of the dangers of an appeal to a purely private, highly emotionalized experience. He does not recommend such experiences. The institutions on which he bases his discussion of God are those shared by generations of reflective men. The data of these intuitions have been subjected to repeated verification.

This reference to intuition must be set in the context of Whitehead's general contention that there is no special religious sense. Intuition is *direct awareness of fundamental factors*. Intuition, in this sense of the term, is involved in all areas of accurate human knowledge, scientific as well as religious. Whitehead's remark that "religious truth must be developed from knowledge acquired when our ordinary senses and intellectual operations are at their highest pitch of discipline" (*R.M.*, p. 123) requires some explanation. The term "ordinary" is an attempt to emphasize the dangers of religious reliance on experiences in the realm of the *abnormal*. "Normal" would have been more appropriate to convey Whitehead's meaning. Religious insights are normal, and in this sense "ordinary."

31. In his *Dialogues of Alfred North Whitehead*, Lucien Price reports a conversation which took place November 19, 1941. In it Whitehead stated that "during the present world tumult" the Bible had "no longer much of anything in it for him." Mr. Price mentioned the Beatitudes, some of the sayings of Jesus, the saga of Elijah on Mount Carmel. Whitehead replied "as reported": "That is a great saga . . . but no more."

This conversation occurred when Whitehead admittedly was in a "curious overwrought state": "I have to try now one thing, now another." Such a conversation cannot be regarded as a denial of the view of God, and the approach to the problem of God, which Whitehead expressed in the books of his philosophical maturity. A man in his 81st year, weary and deeply disturbed by physical ills and the evils of a world at war, may be expected to utter *occasionally* remarks that are out of phase with views expressed in earlier, "better" days. Whitehead's views concerning religion can best be obtained from the statements provided in the books which he wrote between 1925 and 1933. In these books he expressed the results of a lifetime of calm, efficient reflection on the complexities of the universe.

The preceding comments should not be regarded as disparagement of Mr. Price's very valuable "picture" of Whitehead. The book provides many charming "word portraits" of Whitehead in "fine spirits" during much of the period covered in "The Dialogues." My comments are, rather, a reminder that these reports should be interpreted in the proper fashion.

32. *P.R.*, p. 520.

33. *R.M.*, p. 56.

34. See p. 69.

35. *P.R.*, p. 161.

36. *R.M.*, p. 105.

37. *P.R.*, p. 161.

38. *P.R.*, p. 526.
39. *S.M.W.*, p. 276.
40. *P.R.*, p. 521.
41. *P.R.*, p. 525 (emphasis added).
42. *P.R.*, p. 531.
43. See also p. 79.
44. *P.R.*, p. 521.
45. *P.R.*, p. 521.
46. *S.M.W.*, p. 249.

Chapter 4

SOCIAL PHILOSOPHY

1. *A.I.*, p. 79.
2. *A.E.*, p. 64.
3. Whitehead, "An Appeal to Sanity," *The Atlantic Monthly*, Vol. CLXIII (1939), p. 315.
4. *A.I.*, pp. 124-25.
5. A professional group is one which guides its activities by intellectual analysis, formulating theories derived from a careful observation of relevant data. A profession is concerned with some complex problem such as health, education, or the saving of souls. A *profession* can be distinguished from a *craft* since the craft is not founded primarily on careful theoretical analysis. Rather, it proceeds on the basis of custom, or trial and error. The professional man, however, if he is to be effective, must be competent in the practical aspects of his field. He will manipulate particular data in order to solve problems. Further, the craftsman engages in considerable intellectual activity as he meets the requirements of his craft. Thus, the distinction between a profession and a craft is not completely clear cut. It is a matter of emphasis.
6. *A.I.*, p. 78.
7. *A.I.*, p. 85.
8. *A.I.*, p. 354.
9. *A.I.*, p. 25.
10. *A.I.*, p. 24.
11. *A.I.*, p. 76.
12. "An Appeal to Sanity," p. 309.
13. *Ibid.*, p. 312.
14. Concerning Communism in America, there is the cryptic comment (written before 1933) that it is interesting to compare their place in society with that of the Christians in the early Roman Empire. Both were a "different" group, reputed to have dangerous political aspirations.
15. "An Appeal to Sanity," p. 314.
16. *Ibid.*, p. 315.
17. *Ibid.*, p. 310.
18. *Ibid.*, p. 311.
19. *S.M.W.*, p. 298.
20. "An Appeal to Sanity," p. 320.

Chapter 5
EDUCATION

1. *A.E.*, p. 6.
2. *A.E.*, p. 23.
3. *A.E.*, p. 22.
4. *A.E.*, p. 13.
5. See pp. 111-12.
6. *A.E.*, p. 7.
7. See pp. 124-26.
8. Incidentally, Whitehead debunks the common assumption that *education should proceed from the simple to the more complex.* It is obvious that one must begin with speech and writing. Yet, consider how very difficult speech is. It is the co-ordination of meaning with sound. Equally difficult is writing, the co-ordination of sounds and shapes. What could be more difficult than these gigantic tasks?
9. *A.E.*, p. 109.
10. *A.E.*, p. 88.
11. *A.E.*, p. 42.
12. *A.E.*, p. 59.
13. Whitehead, "Harvard: The Future," in *The Atlantic Monthly*, Vol. CLVIII (1936), p. 263.
14. *Ibid.*, p. 263.
15. *Ibid.*, p. 264.
16. *A.E.*, p. 140.
17. "Harvard: The Future," p. 265.
18. *A.E.*, p. 145.
19. *P.R.*, p. 514.
20. "Founder's Day Address" at Stanley Technical Trade School (London, Feb. 1, 1919).

Chapter 6
CRITICAL COMMENTS

1. An evaluation of Whitehead's discussion of "pre-requisites"—respect for the individual, freedom, tolerance, persuasion, and wisdom—will be found in Chapter 7, pp. 182-83, 187-90.
2. It must be admitted that some theologians would not accept this analysis.
3. *P.R.*, p. 161.
4. Whitehead, for example, admits that he uses "images" in referring to God. However, he contends that the images he uses are those "under which the operative growth of God's nature is best conceived" (*P.R.*, p. 525).

In general, he emphasizes a warning concerning all philosophical systems, including his own: "How shallow, puny, and imperfect are efforts to sound the depths in the nature of things" (*P.R.*, p. x). Nevertheless, such statements as these must be balanced against more optimistic remarks such as: "The nature of human limitations requires guarding. . . . Nor can I discern any reason . . . why any factor in the universe should not be manifest in some flash of human consciousness" ("Remarks," in *The Philosophical Review*, Vol. XLVI, p. 181).

5. See pp. 51-52.

6. See *The Abingdon Bible Commentary* (New York: Abingdon Press, 1929), pp. 931-43.

7. *A.I.*, p. 218.

8. For a more detailed discussion, see pp. 188-91.

9. For a discussion and validation of this claim involving the use of Whitehead's technical terminology, see Chapter 7: "Civilization and Metaphysics.

10. *A.I.*, p. 204.

Chapter 7

CIVILIZATION AND METAPHYSICS

1. It will be recalled that the contemporary physicist regards the universe as composed of centers of energy, in a process of interaction whereby each draws upon others and "gives out" in return. In this complex flux of energy, there are relatively permanent patterns. The endurance of a center of energy is brief, but its loss is another's gain. An examination of *mental life* reveals the same fundamental energy factor. There are also interaction and the factors of change and permanence. Here are found additional factors; namely, value experiences and the presence of the divine.

2. The following exposition of the meaning of Whitehead's technical terms is based on the treatment given in *Process and Reality*, Chapter 2 of Part I ("The Categoreal Scheme"). This provides a comprehensive survey which is supplemented by subsequent discussion. My exposition does not involve numerous footnote references to the Whitehead text. Such a procedure disturbs the continuity of treatment. It does not seem necessary for the purposes of this study. However, a detailed documentation of my exposition of the meaning of Whitehead's technical terms can be found in *Whitehead's Theory of Reality* (Boston: The Beacon Press, 1952).

3. Whitehead's "ontological principle" states that everything must ultimately be explained by reference to some actual entity. Much of what happens can be explained by reference to ordinary actual entities. They have subjective forms, subjective aims. They provide data of many sorts. But, the availability of eternal objects can be explained only by reference to God.

4. The last two pages of *Adventures of Ideas* are a very cryptic statement of the importance of a metaphysical basis for civilization. There is also a very compressed outline of the nature of this metaphysical basis. Careful examination indicates that he is here restating, in apparently "secular" language, his previous emphasis (*Process and Reality*) on the essential function of God. In *Adventures of Ideas* he refers to something "transcending" ordinary actual entities in order to account for adventure, zest, and peace. He also refers to the "unity of adventure" making *proper* use of a vast variety of individual elements, achieving the supreme harmony

of beauty and peace, despite tragedy. The term "final fact" is also applied to the achieved "unity of adventure." All these terms: "transcendence," "unity of adventure," "final fact" are alternate terms for God—as will be obvious from a careful examination of the "functions" which they perform.

5. See *Whitehead's Theory of Reality*, pp. 83-87.

6. *M.T.*, p. 151.

7. These values are impossible because of the dogmatic, restrictive use of force

8. It may be contended that this study has not really *shown the worth* of civilization (as defined by Whitehead). In reply, it is to be noted that on pages 171 to 174 it has been argued that, in so far as Whitehead's theory of reality is sound (that such is the case has been shown in my *Whitehead's Theory of Reality*), civilization is validated because it is supported by this theory of reality. In this sense its worth is shown.

It may be objected, further, that the question enclosed in brackets on page 146 is not adequately dealt with. This is the question as to whether Whitehead's definition of civilization covers the qualities which characterize the best possible type of life. It is obvious that Whitehead is of this opinion. However, a person who does not share the basic value intuitions, on which this judgment is based, would think otherwise. This book does not propose to be a general discussion of value theory. It is not its purpose to attempt a refutation of all positions alternative to that of Whitehead. It is sufficient, at this point, to indicate the somewhat specific meaning assigned to the phrase "show its worth."

BIBLIOGRAPHY

Listed here are: (a) Whitehead's major discussions of the philosophy of civilization, and (b) relevant critical comments. This bibliography does not provide a complete list of every comment made by Whitehead concerning civilization. Such a project would involve unnecessary duplication. Further, this bibliography does not refer to all "treatments" of Whitehead's philosophy of civilization. Here again repetition (and even irrelevance) would occur. However, the critical comments which have been mentioned are representative. The references are arranged according to the chapters in this book and, within each chapter, according to topic.

In addition to the books by Alfred North Whitehead listed on p. 193, the following books and articles by Whitehead are included in this bibliography:

Essays in Science and Philosophy (New York: The Philosophical Library, 1947)

"The Importance of Friendly Relations Between England and the United States," *The Phillips Bulletin,*" XIX, No. 3 (1925)

"Reconstruction," *The Atlantic Monthly,* CLXIX (1942)

Symbolism: Its Meaning and Effect (New York: The Macmillan Company, 1927)

(All page references to *Science and the Modern World* refer to the 1929 edition.)

Chapter 1 CIVILIZATION

Definition of Civilization:	*Adventures of Ideas,* 352-54, 11-31
	Modes of Thought, 4-5
Adventure:	*Adventures of Ideas,* 371, 353-54, 359-60
	Process and Reality, 514-15
	Science and the Modern World, 297-300
	Symbolism, 88
Peace:	*Adventures of Ideas,* 367-75
Art:	*Adventures of Ideas,* 348-50, 363-65
	Science and the Modern World, 286-300
Importance of the Individual:	*Adventures of Ideas,* 77-81
	Essays in Science and Philosophy, 64-66
Freedom:	*Adventures of Ideas,* 64-86
Tolerance:	*Adventures of Ideas,* 65-66
	Science and the Modern World, 267-69

Religion in the Making, 94-105, 149-60
Science and the Modern World, 249-50, 256-58, 275-76

Chapter 4 SOCIAL PHILOSOPHY

Economic Problems:

Adventures of Ideas, 83-86, 90-91, 112-26, 34-35, 87-88, 139-41
Aims of Education, 141-42, 66-70, 90-92, 111-13
Essays in Science and Philosophy, 153-69
Science and the Modern World, 279-82

Political Thought:

Adventures of Ideas, 38-48, 70-74, 79-81, 354
Science and the Modern World, 282-300

International Relations:

Essays in Science and Philosophy, 53-74
The Atlantic Monthly, CLXIX, 172-75
The Phillips Bulletin, XIX, No. 3

Chapter 5 EDUCATION

Principles and Applications in Secondary Schools:

Aims of Education, 1-40, 43-135
Essays in Science and Philosophy, 166-74, 189-99
Science and the Modern World, 282-89

University Education:

Adventures of Ideas, 110-26
Aims of Education, 40-43, 136-52
Essays in Science and Philosophy, 200-24
Modes of Thought, 233-38

Chapter 6 CRITICAL COMMENTS

Civilization

Goheen, J., "Whitehead's Theory of Value," in *The Philosophy of Alfred North Whitehead,* P. A. Schilpp, ed. Evanston, Ill., Northwestern University Press, 1941.
Hooper, S. E., "A Reasonable Theory of Morality" (Alexander and Whitehead), *Philosophy,* XXV (1950), 54-67.
Johnson, A. H., "'Truth, Beauty, and Goodness' in the Philosophy of

A. N. Whitehead," *Philosophy of Science*, XI (1944), 9-29.

Johnson, A. H., "Whitehead's Philosophy of Civilization," in *Whitehead and the Modern World*. Boston, The Beacon Press, 1950, 42-54.

Morgan, G., Jr., "Whitehead's Theory of Value," *International Journal of Ethics*, XLVII (1936-1937), 308-16.

Morris, B., "The Art-process and the Aesthetic Fact in Whitehead's Philosophy," in *The Philosophy of Alfred North Whitehead*, P. A. Schilpp, ed.

Schilpp, P. A., "Whitehead's Theory of Value," in *The Philosophy of Alfred North Whitehead*, P. A. Schilpp, ed.

Philosophy of History

Johnson, A. H., "Whitehead's Philosophy of History," *Journal of the History of Ideas*, VII (1946), 234-49.

Swabey, M. C., *The Judgment of History*. New York, Philosophical Library, 1954, 205-13.

Religion

Aubrey, E. E., *Present Theological Tendencies*. New York, Harper & Bros., 1936, Chap. 5.

Bixler, J. S., "Whitehead's Philosophy of Religion," in *The Philosophy of Alfred North Whitehead*, P. A. Schilpp, ed.

Braham, Ernest G., "The Place of God in A. N. Whitehead's Philosophy," *The London Quarterly and Holborn Review*, CLXIV (1939), 63-69.

Cesselin, Felix, *La Philosophie Organique de Whitehead*. Paris, Presses Universitaires de France, 1950, Chap. 6.

Ely, Stephen L., *The Religious Availability of Whitehead's God*. Madison, The University of Wisconsin Press, 1942.

Emmet, Dorothy M., *Whitehead's Philosophy of Organism*. London, Macmillan & Co. Ltd., 1932, Chaps. 5, 8, 9.

Foley, Leo A., *A Critique of the*

Philosophy of Being of Alfred North Whitehead. Washington, The Catholic University of America Press, 1946, Chaps. 5, 9.

Forsyth, T. M., "Creative Evolution in its Bearing on the Idea of God," *Philosophy,* XXV (1950), 203-08.

Fries, H. S., "The Functions of Whitehead's God," *The Monist,* XLVI (1936), 25-58.

Hartshorne, Charles, "Is Whitehead's God the God of Religion?" *Ethics,* LIII (1943), 219-27.

Hartshorne, Charles, *Reality as Social Process.* Glencoe, Ill., The Free Press, and Boston, The Beacon Press, 1953, Chaps. 7, 14.

Hartshorne, Charles, *The Divine Relativity.* New Haven, Yale University Press, 1948.

Hartshorne, Charles, "Whitehead's View of God," in *The Philosophy of Alfred North Whitehead,* P. A. Schilpp, ed.

Hooper, Sidney, "Whitehead's Philosophy: Eternal Objects and God," *Philosophy,* XVII (1942), 47-68.

Johnson, A. H., *Whitehead's Theory of Reality.* Boston, The Beacon Press, 1952, Chap. 4.

Lintz, Edward J., *The Unity of the Universe According to Alfred North Whitehead.* Baltimore, J. H. Furst, 1939.

Loomer, Bernard M., "Christian Faith and Process Philosophy," *The Journal of Religion,* XXIX (1949), 181-203.

Loomer, Bernard M., "Ely on Whitehead's God," *The Journal of Religion,* XXIV (1944), 162-79.

Loomer, Bernard M., "Neo-Naturalism and Neo-Orthodoxy," *The Journal of Religion,* XXVIII (1948), 70-91.

Lyman, Eugene W., *The Meaning and Truth of Religion.* London, Chas. Scribners' Sons, 1933, 272-83.

Martin, Oliver, "Whithead's Naturalism and God," *The Review of Re-*

ligion, III (1939), 149-60.

Moxley, D. J., "The Conception of God in the Philosophy of Whitehead," *Proceedings of the Aristotelian Society*, N.S. XXXIV (1934), 157-86.

Nedoncelle, M., *La Philosophie Religieuse en Grande Bretagne de 1850 a nos jours*. Paris, Bloud et Gay, 1933.

O'Brien, John A., "God in Whitehead's Philosophy," *The American Ecclesiastical Review*, CX, 444-50; CXI, 124-30.

Sheen, Fulton J., "Professor Whitehead and the Making of Religion," *The New Scholasticism*, I (1927), 147-62.

Slater, R. H. L., *God of the Living*. New York, Charles Scribners' Sons, 1939.

Taylor, A. E., "Dr. Whitehead's Philosophy of Religion," *Dublin Review*, CLXXX (1927), 17-41.

Temple, William, *Nature, Man and God*. London, Macmillan & Co., Ltd., 1935.

Thornton, Lionel S., *The Incarnate Lord*. London, Longmans, Green, 1928, 456-69.

Wieman, Henry N., and Meland, Bernard E., *American Philosophies of Religion*. Chicago, Willett, Clark, 1936, 229-42.

Wieman, Henry N., "Professor Whitehead's Concept of God," *Hibbert Journal*, XXV (1926-1927), 623-30.

Social Philosophy

Beer, S. H., *The City of Reason*. Cambridge, Mass., Harvard University Press, 1949.

Johnson, A. H., "The Social Philosophy of Alfred North Whitehead," *The Journal of Philosophy*, XL (1943), 261-71.

Johnson, A. H., "Whitehead and the Making of Tomorrow," *Philosophy and Phenomenological Research*, V (1945), 398-406.

Wells, H. K., "The Philosophy of

Education

A. N. Whitehead," *Science and Society*, XVI (1951-1952), 27-43.
Holmes, H. W., "Whitehead's Views on Education," *The Philosophy of Alfred North Whitehead*, P. A. Schilpp, ed.
Hutchins, R. M., "A Reply to Professor Whitehead," *The Atlantic Monthly*, CLVIII (1936), 582-88.
Johnson, A. H., "Whitehead's Discussion of Education," *Education*, LXVI (1946), 653-71.
Levi, A. W., "The Problem of Higher Education: Whitehead and Hutchins," *Harvard Educational Review*, VII (1937).

Chapter 7   CIVILIZATION AND METAPHYSICS

Whitehead's Metaphysics:

Adventures of Ideas, Chaps. 11-13
Modes of Thought, Chaps. 7, 8
Process and Reality, Part I; Part III, Chaps. 1-4
Cesselin, F., *La Philosophie Organique de Whitehead*. Paris, Presses Universitaires de France, 1950.
Das, R., *The Philosophy of Whitehead*. London, J. Clarke & Co. Ltd., 1938.
Emmet, D. M., *Whitehead's Philosophy of Organism*. London, Macmillan & Co., Ltd., 1932.
Hartshorne, C., "Whitehead's Metaphysics," in *Whitehead and the Modern World*. Boston, The Beacon Press, 1950, 25-41.
Hocking, W. E., "Whitehead on Mind and Nature," in *The Philosophy of Alfred North Whitehead*, P. A. Schilpp, ed.
Hooper, S. E., "Whitehead's Philosophy: Actual Entities," *Philosophy*, XVI (1941), 285-305.
Hooper, S. E., "Whitehead's Philosophy: The World as Process," *Philosophy*, XXIII (1948), 140-60.
Johnson, A. H., "The Intelligibility of Whitehead's Philosophy," *Phi-*

losophy of Science, X (1943), 47-55.

Johnson, A. H., "Whitehead's Theory of Actual Entities," Philosophy of Science, XII (1945), 237-95.

Johnson, A. H., Whitehead's Theory of Reality. Boston, The Beacon Press, 1952.

Lowe, V., "Alfred North Whitehead: Introduction," in Classic American Philosophers. New York, Appleton, Century, Crofts, 1951, 395-417.

Shahan, E. P., Whitehead's Theory of Experience. New York, King's Crown Press, 1950.

Wahl, J., "La Philosophie spéculative de Whitehead," Revue Philosophique, CXI (1931), 341-78; CXII (1931), 108-43.

Johnson, A. H., "The Social Philosophy of Alfred North Whitehead," The Journal of Philosophy, XL (1943), 261-71.

Johnson, A. H., "Whitehead's Philosophy of History," Journal of the History of Ideas, VII (1946), 234-49.

The Metaphysical Basis for Civilization

SUPPLEMENTARY BIBLIOGRAPHY

Whitehead's American Essays in Social Philosophy, A. H. Johnson, ed. New York, Harper and Brothers, 1959.

The Relevance of Whitehead, Ivor Leclerc, ed. New York, The Macmillan Co., 1961.

Buehrer, E. T., "Mysticism and A. N. Whitehead," in Mysticism and the Modern Mind, A. P. Stiernotte, ed. New York, The Liberal Arts Press, 1959, 60-70.

Geoghegan, W. D., Platonism in Recent Religious Thought. New York, Columbia University Press, 1958, Chapter 5.

INDEX of Terms and Topics

CATALOGUE OF DOVER BOOKS

Books Explaining Science and Mathematics

WHAT IS SCIENCE?, N. Campbell. The role of experiment and measurement, the function of mathematics, the nature of scientific laws, the difference between laws and theories, the limitations of science, and many similarly provocative topics are treated clearly and without technicalities by an eminent scientist. "Still an excellent introduction to scientific philosophy," H. Margenau in PHYSICS TODAY. "A first-rate primer . . . deserves a wide audience," SCIENTIFIC AMERICAN. 192pp. 5⅜ x 8.　　S43 Paperbound **$1.25**

THE NATURE OF PHYSICAL THEORY, P. W. Bridgman. A Nobel Laureate's clear, non-technical lectures on difficulties and paradoxes connected with frontier research on the physical sciences. Concerned with such central concepts as thought, logic, mathematics, relativity, probability, wave mechanics, etc. he analyzes the contributions of such men as Newton, Einstein, Bohr, Heisenberg, and many others. "Lucid and entertaining . . . recommended to anyone who wants to get some insight into current philosophies of science," THE NEW PHILOSOPHY. Index. xi + 138pp. 5⅜ x 8.　　S33 Paperbound **$1.25**

EXPERIMENT AND THEORY IN PHYSICS, Max Born. A Nobel Laureate examines the nature of experiment and theory in theoretical physics and analyzes the advances made by the great physicists of our day: Heisenberg, Einstein, Bohr, Planck, Dirac, and others. The actual process of creation is detailed step-by-step by one who participated. A fine examination of the scientific method at work. 44pp. 5⅜ x 8.　　S308 Paperbound **75¢**

THE PSYCHOLOGY OF INVENTION IN THE MATHEMATICAL FIELD, J. Hadamard. The reports of such men as Descartes, Pascal, Einstein, Poincaré, and others are considered in this investigation of the method of idea-creation in mathematics and other sciences and the thinking process in general. How do ideas originate? What is the role of the unconscious? What is Poincaré's forgetting hypothesis? are some of the fascinating questions treated. A penetrating analysis of Einstein's thought processes concludes the book. xiii + 145pp. 5⅜ x 8.　　T107 Paperbound **$1.25**

THE NATURE OF LIGHT AND COLOUR IN THE OPEN AIR, M. Minnaert. Why are shadows sometimes blue, sometimes green, or other colors depending on the light and surroundings? What causes mirages? Why do multiple suns and moons appear in the sky? Professor Minnaert explains these unusual phenomena and hundreds of others in simple, easy-to-understand terms based on optical laws and the properties of light and color. No mathematics is required but artists, scientists, students, and everyone fascinated by these "tricks" of nature will find thousands of useful and amazing pieces of information. Hundreds of observational experiments are suggested which require no special equipment. 200 illustrations; 42 photos. xvi + 362pp. 5⅜ x 8.　　T196 Paperbound **$2.00**

THE UNIVERSE OF LIGHT, W. Bragg. Sir William Bragg, Nobel Laureate and great modern physicist, is also well known for his powers of clear exposition. Here he analyzes all aspects of light for the layman: lenses, reflection, refraction, the optics of vision, x-rays, the photoelectric effect, etc. He tells you what causes the color of spectra, rainbows, and soap bubbles, how magic mirrors work, and much more. Dozens of simple experiments are described. Preface. Index. 199 line drawings and photographs, including 2 full-page color plates. x + 283pp. 5⅜ x 8.　　T538 Paperbound **$1.85**

SOAP-BUBBLES: THEIR COLOURS AND THE FORCES THAT MOULD THEM, C. V. Boys. For continuing popularity and validity as scientific primer, few books can match this volume of easily-followed experiments, explanations. Lucid exposition of complexities of liquid films, surface tension and related phenomena, bubbles' reaction to heat, motion, music, magnetic fields. Experiments with capillary attraction, soap bubbles on frames, composite bubbles, liquid cylinders and jets, bubbles other than soap, etc. Wonderful introduction to scientific method, natural laws that have many ramifications in areas of modern physics. Only complete edition in print. New Introduction by S. Z. Lewin, New York University. 83 illustrations; 1 full-page color plate. xii + 190pp. 5⅜ x 8½.　　T542 Paperbound **95¢**

CATALOGUE OF DOVER BOOKS

THE STORY OF X-RAYS FROM RONTGEN TO ISOTOPES, A. R. Bleich, M.D. This book, by a member of the American College of Radiology, gives the scientific explanation of x-rays, their applications in medicine, industry and art, and their danger (and that of atmospheric radiation) to the individual and the species. You learn how radiation therapy is applied against cancer, how x-rays diagnose heart disease and other ailments, how they are used to examine mummies for information on diseases of early societies, and industrial materials for hidden weaknesses. 54 illustrations show x-rays of flowers, bones, stomach, gears with flaws, etc. 1st publication. Index. xix + 186pp. 5⅜ x 8.   T622 Paperbound **$1.50**

SPINNING TOPS AND GYROSCOPIC MOTION, John Perry. A classic elementary text of the dynamics of rotation — the behavior and use of rotating bodies such as gyroscopes and tops. In simple, everyday English you are shown how quasi-rigidity is induced in discs of paper, smoke rings, chains, etc., by rapid motions; why a gyrostat falls and why a top rises; precession; how the earth's motion affects climate; and many other phenomena. Appendix on practical use of gyroscopes. 62 figures. 128pp. 5⅜ x 8.   T416 Paperbound **$1.25**

SNOW CRYSTALS, W. A. Bentley, M. J. Humphreys. For almost 50 years W. A. Bentley photographed snow flakes in his laboratory in Jericho, Vermont; in 1931 the American Meteorological Society gathered together the best of his work, some 2400 photographs of snow flakes, plus a few ice flowers, windowpane frosts, dew, frozen rain, and other ice formations. Pictures were selected for beauty and scientific value. A very valuable work to anyone in meteorology, cryology; most interesting to layman; extremely useful for artist who wants beautiful, crystalline designs. All copyright free. Unabridged reprint of 1931 edition. 2453 illustrations. 227pp. 8 x 10½.   T287 Paperbound **$3.00**

A DOVER SCIENCE SAMPLER, edited by George Barkin. A collection of brief, non-technical passages from 44 Dover Books Explaining Science for the enjoyment of the science-minded browser. Includes work of Bertrand Russell, Poincaré, Laplace, Max Born, Galileo, Newton; material on physics, mathematics, metallurgy, anatomy, astronomy, chemistry, etc. You will be fascinated by Martin Gardner's analysis of the sincere pseudo-scientist, Moritz's account of Newton's absentmindedness, Bernard's examples of human vivisection, etc. Illustrations from the Diderot Pictorial Encyclopedia and De Re Metallica. 64 pages.   **FREE**

THE STORY OF ATOMIC THEORY AND ATOMIC ENERGY, J. G. Feinberg. A broader approach to subject of nuclear energy and its cultural implications than any other similar source. Very readable, informal, completely non-technical text. Begins with first atomic theory, 600 B.C. and carries you through the work of Mendelejeff, Röntgen, Madame Curie, to Einstein's equation and the A-bomb. New chapter goes through thermonuclear fission, binding energy, other events up to 1959. Radioactive decay and radiation hazards, future benefits, work of Bohr, moderns, hundreds more topics. "Deserves special mention . . . not only authoritative but thoroughly popular in the best sense of the word," Saturday Review. Formerly, "The Atom Story." Expanded with new chapter. Three appendixes. Index. 34 illustrations. vii + 243pp. 5⅜ x 8.   T625 Paperbound **$1.60**

THE STRANGE STORY OF THE QUANTUM, AN ACCOUNT FOR THE GENERAL READER OF THE GROWTH OF IDEAS UNDERLYING OUR PRESENT ATOMIC KNOWLEDGE, B. Hoffmann. Presents lucidly and expertly, with barest amount of mathematics, the problems and theories which led to modern quantum physics. Dr. Hoffmann begins with the closing years of the 19th century, when certain trifling discrepancies were noticed, and with illuminating analogies and examples takes you through the brilliant concepts of Planck, Einstein, Pauli, Broglie, Bohr, Schroedinger, Heisenberg, Dirac, Sommerfeld, Feynman, etc. This edition includes a new, long postscript carrying the story through 1958. "Of the books attempting an account of the history and contents of our modern atomic physics which have come to my attention, this is the best," H. Margenau, Yale University, in "American Journal of Physics." 32 tables and line illustrations. Index. 275pp. 5⅜ x 8.   T518 Paperbound **$1.50**

SPACE AND TIME, E. Borel. Written by a versatile mathematician of world renown with his customary lucidity and precision, this introduction to relativity for the layman presents scores of examples, analogies, and illustrations that open up new ways of thinking about space and time. It covers abstract geometry and geographical maps, continuity and topology, the propagation of light, the special theory of relativity, the general theory of relativity, theoretical researches, and much more. Mathematical notes. 2 Indexes. 4 Appendices. 15 figures. xvi + 243pp. 5⅜ x 8.   T592 Paperbound **$1.75**

FROM EUCLID TO EDDINGTON: A STUDY OF THE CONCEPTIONS OF THE EXTERNAL WORLD, Sir Edmund Whittaker. A foremost British scientist traces the development of theories of natural philosophy from the western rediscovery of Euclid to Eddington, Einstein, Dirac, etc. The inadequacy of classical physics is contrasted with present day attempts to understand the physical world through relativity, non-Euclidean geometry, space curvature, wave mechanics, etc. 5 major divisions of examination: Space; Time and Movement; the Concepts of Classical Physics; the Concepts of Quantum Mechanics; the Eddington Universe. 212pp. 5⅜ x 8.   T491 Paperbound **$1.35**

Nature, Biology,

NATURE RECREATION: Group Guidance for the Out-of-doors, William Gould Vinal. Intended for both the uninitiated nature instructor and the education student on the college level, this complete "how-to" program surveys the entire area of nature education for the young. Philosophy of nature recreation; requirements, responsibilities, important information for group leaders; nature games; suggested group projects; conducting meetings and getting discussions started; etc. Scores of immediately applicable teaching aids, plus completely updated sources of information, pamphlets, field guides, recordings, etc. Bibliography. 74 photographs. + 310pp. 5⅜ x 8½. **T1015 Paperbound $1.75**

HOW TO KNOW THE WILD FLOWERS, Mrs. William Starr Dana. Classic nature book that has introduced thousands to wonders of American wild flowers. Color-season principle of organization is easy to use, even by those with no botanical training, and the genial, refreshing discussions of history, folklore, uses of over 1,000 native and escape flowers, foliage plants are informative as well as fun to read. Over 170 full-page plates, collected from several editions, may be colored in to make permanent records of finds. Revised to conform with 1950 edition of Gray's Manual of Botany. xlii + 438pp. 5⅜ x 8½. **T332 Paperbound $2.00**

HOW TO KNOW THE FERNS, F. T. Parsons. Ferns, among our most lovely native plants, are all too little known. This classic of nature lore will enable the layman to identify almost any American fern he may come across. After an introduction on the structure and life of ferns, the 57 most important ferns are fully pictured and described (arranged upon a simple identification key). Index of Latin and English names. 61 illustrations and 42 full-page plates. xiv + 215pp. 5⅜ x 8. **T740 Paperbound $1.35**

MANUAL OF THE TREES OF NORTH AMERICA, Charles Sprague Sargent. Still unsurpassed as most comprehensive, reliable study of North American tree characteristics, precise locations and distribution. By dean of American dendrologists. Every tree native to U.S., Canada, Alaska, 185 genera, 717 species, described in detail—leaves, flowers, fruit, winterbuds, bark, wood, growth habits etc. plus discussion of varieties and local variants, immaturity variations. Over 100 keys, including unusual 11-page analytical key to genera, aid in identification. 783 clear illustrations of flowers, fruit, leaves. An unmatched permanent reference work for all nature lovers. Second enlarged (1926) edition. Synopsis of families. Analytical key to genera. Glossary of technical terms. Index. 783 illustrations, 1 map. Two volumes. Total of 982pp. 5⅜ x 8. **T277 Vol. I Paperbound $2.25**
T278 Vol. II Paperbound $2.25
The set $4.50

TREES OF THE EASTERN AND CENTRAL UNITED STATES AND CANADA, W. M. Harlow. A revised edition of a standard middle-level guide to native trees and important escapes. More than 140 trees are described in detail, and illustrated with more than 600 drawings and photographs. Supplementary keys will enable the careful reader to identify almost any tree he might encounter. xiii + 288pp. 5⅜ x 8. **T395 Paperbound $1.35**

GUIDE TO SOUTHERN TREES, Ellwood S. Harrar and J. George Harrar. All the essential information about trees indigenous to the South, in an extremely handy format. Introductory essay on methods of tree classification and study, nomenclature, chief divisions of Southern trees, etc. Approximately 100 keys and synopses allow for swift, accurate identification of trees. Numerous excellent illustrations, non-technical text make this a useful book for teachers of biology or natural science, nature lovers, amateur naturalists. Revised 1962 edition. Index. Bibliography. Glossary of technical terms. 920 illustrations; 201 full-page plates. ix + 709pp. 4⅝ x 6⅜. **T945 Paperbound $2.35**

FRUIT KEY AND TWIG KEY TO TREES AND SHRUBS, W. M. Harlow. Bound together in one volume for the first time, these handy and accurate keys to fruit and twig identification are the only guides of their sort with photographs (up to 3 times natural size). "Fruit Key": Key to over 120 different deciduous and evergreen fruits. 139 photographs and 11 line drawings. Synoptic summary of fruit types. Bibliography. 2 Indexes (common and scientific names). "Twig Key": Key to over 160 different twigs and buds. 173 photographs. Glossary of technical terms. Bibliography. 2 Indexes (common and scientific names). Two volumes bound as one. Total of xvii + 126pp. 5⅝ x 8⅜. **T511 Paperbound $1.25**

INSECT LIFE AND INSECT NATURAL HISTORY, S. W. Frost. A work emphasizing habits, social life, and ecological relations of insects, rather than more academic aspects of classification and morphology. Prof. Frost's enthusiasm and knowledge are everywhere evident as he discusses insect associations and specialized habits like leaf-rolling, leaf-mining, and case-making, the gall insects, the boring insects, aquatic insects, etc. He examines all sorts of matters not usually covered in general works, such as: insects as human food, insect music and musicians, insect response to electric and radio waves, use of insects in art and literature. The admirably executed purpose of this book, which covers the middle ground between elementary treatment and scholarly monographs, is to excite the reader to observe for himself. Over 700 illustrations. Extensive bibliography. x + 524pp. 5⅜ x 8. **T517 Paperbound $2.50**

CATALOGUE OF DOVER BOOKS

COMMON SPIDERS OF THE UNITED STATES, J. H. Emerton. Here is a nature hobby you can pursue right in your own cellar! Only non-technical, but thorough, reliable guide to spiders for the layman. Over 200 spiders from all parts of the country, arranged by scientific classification, are identified by shape and color, number of eyes, habitat and range, habits, etc. Full text, 501 line drawings and photographs, and valuable introduction explain webs, poisons, threads, capturing and preserving spiders, etc. Index. New synoptic key by S. W. Frost. xxiv + 225pp. 5⅜ x 8.   T223 Paperbound **$1.45**

THE LIFE STORY OF THE FISH: HIS MANNERS AND MORALS, Brian Curtis. A comprehensive, non-technical survey of just about everything worth knowing about fish. Written for the aquarist, the angler, and the layman with an inquisitive mind, the text covers such topics as evolution, external covering and protective coloration, physics and physiology of vision, maintenance of equilibrium, function of the lateral line canal for auditory and temperature senses, nervous system, function of the air bladder, reproductive system and methods—courtship, mating, spawning, care of young—and many more. Also sections on game fish, the problems of conservation and a fascinating chapter on fish curiosities. "Clear, simple language . . . excellent judgment in choice of subjects . . . delightful sense of humor," New York Times. Revised (1949) edition. Index. Bibliography of 72 items. 6 full-page photographic plates. xii + 284pp. 5⅜ x 8.   T929 Paperbound **$1.65**

BATS, Glover Morrill Allen. The most comprehensive study of bats as a life-form by the world's foremost authority. A thorough summary of just about everything known about this fascinating and mysterious flying mammal, including its unique location sense, hibernation and cycles, its habitats and distribution, its wing structure and flying habits, and its relationship to man in the long history of folklore and superstition. Written on a middle-level, the book can be profitably studied by a trained zoologist and thoroughly enjoyed by the layman. "An absorbing text with excellent illustrations. Bats should have more friends and fewer thoughtless detractors as a result of the publication of this volume," William Beebe, Books. Extensive bibliography. 57 photographs and illustrations. x + 368pp. 5⅜ x 8½.
T984 Paperbound **$2.00**

BIRDS AND THEIR ATTRIBUTES, Glover Morrill Allen. A fine general introduction to birds as living organisms, especially valuable because of emphasis on structure, physiology, habits, behavior. Discusses relationship of bird to man, early attempts at scientific ornithology, feathers and coloration, skeletal structure including bills, legs and feet, wings. Also food habits, evolution and present distribution, feeding and nest-building, still unsolved questions of migrations and location sense, many more similar topics. Final chapter on classification, nomenclature. A good popular-level summary for the biologist; a first-rate introduction for the layman. Reprint of 1925 edition. References and index. 51 illustrations. viii + 338pp. 5⅜ x 8½.   T957 Paperbound **$1.85**

LIFE HISTORIES OF NORTH AMERICAN BIRDS, Arthur Cleveland Bent. Bent's monumental series of books on North American birds, prepared and published under auspices of Smithsonian Institute, is the definitive coverage of the subject, the most-used single source of information. Now the entire set is to be made available by Dover in inexpensive editions. This encyclopedic collection of detailed, specific observations utilizes reports of hundreds of contemporary observers, writings of such naturalists as Audubon, Burroughs, William Brewster, as well as author's own extensive investigations. Contains literally everything known about life history of each bird considered: nesting, eggs, plumage, distribution and migration, voice, enemies, courtship, etc. These not over-technical works are musts for ornithologists, conservationists, amateur naturalists, anyone seriously interested in American birds.

BIRDS OF PREY. More than 100 subspecies of hawks, falcons, eagles, buzzards, condors and owls, from the common barn owl to the extinct caracara of Guadaloupe Island. 400 photographs. Two volume set. Index for each volume. Bibliographies of 403, 520 items. 197 full-page plates. Total of 907pp. 5⅜ x 8½.   Vol. I   T931 Paperbound **$2.50**
Vol. II T932 Paperbound **$2.50**

WILD FOWL. Ducks, geese, swans, and tree ducks—73 different subspecies. Two volume set. Index for each volume. Bibliographies of 124, 144 items. 106 full-page plates. Total of 685pp. 5⅜ x 8½.   Vol. I   T285 Paperbound **$2.50**
Vol. II T286 Paperbound **$2.50**

SHORE BIRDS. 81 varieties (sandpipers, woodcocks, plovers, snipes, phalaropes, curlews, oyster catchers, etc.). More than 200 photographs of eggs, nesting sites, adult and young of important species. Two volume set. Index for each volume. Bibliographies of 261, 188 items. 121 full-page plates. Total of 860pp. 5⅜ x 8½.   Vol. I   T933 Paperbound **$2.35**
Vol. II T934 Paperbound **$2.35**

THE LIFE OF PASTEUR, R. Vallery-Radot. 13th edition of this definitive biography, cited in Encyclopaedia Britannica. Authoritative, scholarly, well-documented with contemporary quotes, observations; gives complete picture of Pasteur's personal life; especially thorough presentation of scientific activities with silkworms, fermentation, hydrophobia, inoculation, etc. Introduction by Sir William Osler. Index. 505pp. 5⅜ x 8.   T632 Paperbound **$2.00**

Puzzles, Mathematical Recreations

SYMBOLIC LOGIC and THE GAME OF LOGIC, Lewis Carroll. "Symbolic Logic" is not concerned with modern symbolic logic, but is instead a collection of over 380 problems posed with charm and imagination, using the syllogism, and a fascinating diagrammatic method of drawing conclusions. In "The Game of Logic" Carroll's whimsical imagination devises a logical game played with 2 diagrams and counters (included) to manipulate hundreds of tricky syllogisms. The final section, "Hit or Miss" is a lagniappe of 101 additional puzzles in the delightful Carroll manner. Until this reprint edition, both of these books were rarities costing up to $15 each. Symbolic Logic: Index. xxxi + 199pp. The Game of Logic: 96pp. 2 vols. bound as one. 5⅜ x 8.   T492 Paperbound **$1.75**

PILLOW PROBLEMS and A TANGLED TALE, Lewis Carroll. One of the rarest of all Carroll's works, "Pillow Problems" contains 72 original math puzzles, all typically ingenious. Particularly fascinating are Carroll's answers which remain exactly as he thought them out, reflecting his actual mental process. The problems in "A Tangled Tale" are in story form, originally appearing as a monthly magazine serial. Carroll not only gives the solutions, but uses answers sent in by readers to discuss wrong approaches and misleading paths, and grades them for insight. Both of these books were rarities until this edition, "Pillow Problems" costing up to $25, and "A Tangled Tale" $15. Pillow Problems: Preface and Introduction by Lewis Carroll. xx + 109pp. A Tangled Tale: 6 illustrations. 152pp. Two vols. bound as one. 5⅜ x 8.   T493 Paperbound **$1.50**

AMUSEMENTS IN MATHEMATICS, Henry Ernest Dudeney. The foremost British originator of mathematical puzzles is always intriguing, witty, and paradoxical in this classic, one of the largest collections of mathematical amusements. More than 430 puzzles, problems, and paradoxes. Mazes and games, problems on number manipulation, unicursal and other route problems, puzzles on measuring, weighing, packing, age, kinship, chessboards, joiners', crossing river, plane figure dissection, and many others. Solutions. More than 450 illustrations. vii +. 258pp. 5⅜ x 8.   T473 Paperbound **$1.25**

THE CANTERBURY PUZZLES, Henry Dudeney. Chaucer's pilgrims set one another problems in story form. Also Adventures of the Puzzle Club, the Strange Escape of the King's Jester, the Monks of Riddlewell, the Squire's Christmas Puzzle Party, and others. All puzzles are original, based on dissecting plane figures, arithmetic, algebra, elementary calculus and other branches of mathematics, and purely logical ingenuity. "The limit of ingenuity and intricacy," The Observer. Over 110 puzzles. Full Solutions. 150 illustrations. vii + 225pp. 5⅜ x 8.   T474 Paperbound **$1.25**

MATHEMATICAL EXCURSIONS, H. A. Merrill. Even if you hardly remember your high school math, you'll enjoy the 90 stimulating problems contained in this book and you will come to understand a great many mathematical principles with surprisingly little effort. Many useful shortcuts and diversions not generally known are included: division by inspection, Russian peasant multiplication, memory systems for pi, building odd and even magic squares, square roots by geometry, dyadic systems, and many more. Solutions to difficult problems. 50 illustrations. 145pp. 5⅜ x 8.   T350 Paperbound **$1.00**

MAGIC SQUARES AND CUBES, W. S. Andrews. Only book-length treatment in English, a thorough non-technical description and analysis. Here are nasik, overlapping, pandiagonal, serrated squares; magic circles, cubes, spheres, rhombuses. Try your hand at 4-dimensional magical figures! Much unusual folklore and tradition included. High school algebra is sufficient. 754 diagrams and illustrations. viii + 419pp. 5⅜ x 8.   T658 Paperbound **$1.85**

CALIBAN'S PROBLEM BOOK: MATHEMATICAL, INFERENTIAL AND CRYPTOGRAPHIC PUZZLES, H. Phillips (Caliban), S. T. Shovelton, G. S. Marshall. 105 ingenious problems by the greatest living creator of puzzles based on logic and inference. Rigorous, modern, piquant; reflecting their author's unusual personality, these intermediate and advanced puzzles all involve the ability to reason clearly through complex situations; some call for mathematical knowledge, ranging from algebra to number theory. Solutions. xi + 180pp. 5⅜ x 8.   T736 Paperbound **$1.25**

MATHEMATICAL PUZZLES FOR BEGINNERS AND ENTHUSIASTS, G. Mott-Smith. 188 mathematical puzzles based on algebra, dissection of plane figures, permutations, and probability, that will test and improve your powers of inference and interpretation. The Odic Force, The Spider's Cousin, Ellipse Drawing, theory and strategy of card and board games like tit-tat-toe, go moku, salvo, and many others. 100 pages of detailed mathematical explanations. Appendix of primes, square roots, etc. 135 illustrations. 2nd revised edition. 248pp. 5⅜ x 8.   T198 Paperbound **$1.00**

MATHEMAGIC, MAGIC PUZZLES, AND GAMES WITH NUMBERS, R. V. Heath. More than 60 new puzzles and stunts based on the properties of numbers. Easy techniques for multiplying large numbers mentally, revealing hidden numbers magically, finding the date of any day in any year, and dozens more. Over 30 pages devoted to magic squares, triangles, cubes, circles, etc. Edited by J. S. Meyer. 76 illustrations. 128pp. 5⅜ x 8.   T110 Paperbound **$1.00**

CATALOGUE OF DOVER BOOKS

THE BOOK OF MODERN PUZZLES, G. L. Kaufman. A completely new series of puzzles as fascinating as crossword and deduction puzzles but based upon different principles and techniques. Simple 2-minute teasers, word labyrinths, design and pattern puzzles, logic and observation puzzles — over 150 braincrackers. Answers to all problems. 116 illustrations. 192pp. 5⅜ x 8.
T143 Paperbound **$1.00**

NEW WORD PUZZLES, G. L. Kaufman. 100 ENTIRELY NEW puzzles based on words and their combinations that will delight crossword puzzle, Scrabble and Jotto fans. Chess words, based on the moves of the chess king; design-onyms, symmetrical designs made of synonyms; rhymed double-crostics; syllable sentences; addle letter anagrams; alphagrams; linkograms; and many others all brand new. Full solutions. Space to work problems. 196 figures. vi + 122pp. 5⅜ x 8.
T344 Paperbound **$1.00**

MAZES AND LABYRINTHS: A BOOK OF PUZZLES, W. Shepherd. Mazes, formerly associated with mystery and ritual, are still among the most intriguing of intellectual puzzles. This is a novel and different collection of 50 amusements that embody the principle of the maze: mazes in the classical tradition; 3-dimensional, ribbon, and Möbius-strip mazes; hidden messages; spatial arrangements; etc.—almost all built on amusing story situations. 84 illustrations. Essay on maze psychology. Solutions. xv + 122pp. 5⅜ x 8.
T731 Paperbound **$1.00**

MAGIC TRICKS & CARD TRICKS, W. Jonson. Two books bound as one. 52 tricks with cards, 37 tricks with coins, bills, eggs, smoke, ribbons, slates, etc. Details on presentation, misdirection, and routining will help you master such famous tricks as the Changing Card, Card in the Pocket, Four Aces, Coin Through the Hand, Bill in the Egg, Afghan Bands, and over 75 others. If you follow the lucid exposition and key diagrams carefully, you will finish these two books with an astonishing mastery of magic. 106 figures. 224pp. 5⅜ x 8. T909 Paperbound **$1.00**

PANORAMA OF MAGIC, Milbourne Christopher. A profusely illustrated history of stage magic, a unique selection of prints and engravings from the author's private collection of magic memorabilia, the largest of its kind. Apparatus, stage settings and costumes; ingenious ads distributed by the performers and satiric broadsides passed around in the streets ridiculing pompous showmen; programs; decorative souvenirs. The lively text, by one of America's foremost professional magicians, is full of anecdotes about almost legendary wizards: Dede, the Egyptian; Philadelphia, the wonder-worker; Robert-Houdin, "the father of modern magic;" Harry Houdini; scores more. Altogether a pleasure package for anyone interested in magic, stage setting and design, ethnology, psychology, or simply in unusual people. A Dover original. 295 illustrations; 8 in full color. Index. viii + 216pp. 8⅜ x 11¼.
T774 Paperbound **$2.25**

HOUDINI ON MAGIC, Harry Houdini. One of the greatest magicians of modern times explains his most prized secrets. How locks are picked, with illustrated picks and skeleton keys; how a girl is sawed into twins; how to walk through a brick wall — Houdini's explanations of 44 stage tricks with many diagrams. Also included is a fascinating discussion of great magicians of the past and the story of his fight against fraudulent mediums and spiritualists. Edited by W.B. Gibson and M.N. Young. Bibliography. 155 figures, photos. xv + 280pp. 5⅜ x 8.
T384 Paperbound **$1.35**

MATHEMATICS, MAGIC AND MYSTERY, Martin Gardner. Why do card tricks work? How do magicians perform astonishing mathematical feats? How is stage mind-reading possible? This is the first book length study explaining the application of probability, set theory, theory of numbers, topology, etc., to achieve many startling tricks. Non-technical, accurate, detailed! 115 sections discuss tricks with cards, dice, coins, knots, geometrical vanishing illusions, how a Curry square "demonstrates" that the sum of the parts may be greater than the whole, and dozens of others. No sleight of hand necessary! 135 illustrations. xii + 174pp. 5⅜ x 8.
T335 Paperbound **$1.00**

EASY-TO-DO ENTERTAINMENTS AND DIVERSIONS WITH COINS, CARDS, STRING, PAPER AND MATCHES, R. M. Abraham. Over 300 tricks, games and puzzles will provide young readers with absorbing fun. Sections on card games; paper-folding; tricks with coins, matches and pieces of string; games for the agile; toy-making from common household objects; mathematical recreations; and 50 miscellaneous pastimes. Anyone in charge of groups of youngsters, including hard-pressed parents, and in need of suggestions on how to keep children sensibly amused and quietly content will find this book indispensable. Clear, simple text, copious number of delightful line drawings and illustrative diagrams. Originally titled "Winter Nights Entertainments." Introduction by Lord Baden Powell. 329 illustrations. v + 186pp. 5⅜ x 8½.
T921 Paperbound **$1.00**

STRING FIGURES AND HOW TO MAKE THEM, Caroline Furness Jayne. 107 string figures plus variations selected from the best primitive and modern examples developed by Navajo, Apache, pygmies of Africa, Eskimo, in Europe, Australia, China, etc. The most readily understandable, easy-to-follow book in English on perennially popular recreation. Crystal-clear exposition; step-by-step diagrams. Everyone from kindergarten children to adults looking for unusual diversion will be endlessly amused. Index. Bibliography. Introduction by A. C. Haddon. 17 full-page plates. 960 illustrations. xxiii + 401pp. 5⅜ x 8½.
T152 Paperbound **$2.00**

Entertainments, Humor

ODDITIES AND CURIOSITIES OF WORDS AND LITERATURE, C. Bombaugh, edited by M. Gardner. The largest collection of idiosyncratic prose and poetry techniques in English, a legendary work in the curious and amusing bypaths of literary recreations and the play technique in literature—so important in modern works. Contains alphabetic poetry, acrostics, palindromes, scissors verse, centos, emblematic poetry, famous literary puns, hoaxes, notorious slips of the press, hilarious mistranslations, and much more. Revised and enlarged with modern material by Martin Gardner. 368pp. 5⅜ x 8. T759 Paperbound $1.75

A NONSENSE ANTHOLOGY, collected by Carolyn Wells. 245 of the best nonsense verses ever written, including nonsense puns, absurd arguments, mock epics and sagas, nonsense ballads, odes, "sick" verses, dog-Latin verses, French nonsense verses, songs. By Edward Lear, Lewis Carroll, Gelett Burgess, W. S. Gilbert, Hilaire Belloc, Peter Newell, Oliver Herford, etc., 83 writers in all plus over four score anonymous nonsense verses. A special section of limericks, plus famous nonsense such as Carroll's "Jabberwocky" and Lear's "The Jumblies" and much excellent verse virtually impossible to locate elsewhere. For 50 years considered the best anthology available. Index of first lines specially prepared for this edition. Introduction by Carolyn Wells. 3 indexes: Title, Author, First lines. xxxiii + 279pp. T499 Paperbound $1.35

THE BAD CHILD'S BOOK OF BEASTS, MORE BEASTS FOR WORSE CHILDREN, and A MORAL ALPHABET, H. Belloc. Hardly an anthology of humorous verse has appeared in the last 50 years without at least a couple of these famous nonsense verses. But one must see the entire volumes—with all the delightful original illustrations by Sir Basil Blackwood—to appreciate fully Belloc's charming and witty verses that play so subacidly on the platitudes of life and morals that beset his day—and ours. A great humor classic. Three books in one. Total of 157pp. 5⅜ x 8. T749 Paperbound $1.00

THE DEVIL'S DICTIONARY, Ambrose Bierce. Sardonic and irreverent barbs puncturing the pomposities and absurdities of American politics, business, religion, literature, and arts, by the country's greatest satirist in the classic tradition. Epigrammatic as Shaw, piercing as Swift, American as Mark Twain, Will Rogers, and Fred Allen, Bierce will always remain the favorite of a small coterie of enthusiasts, and of writers and speakers whom he supplies with "some of the most gorgeous witticisms of the English language" (H. L. Mencken). Over 1000 entries in alphabetical order. 144pp. 5⅜ x 8. T487 Paperbound $1.00

THE PURPLE COW AND OTHER NONSENSE, Gelett Burgess. The best of Burgess's early nonsense, selected from the first edition of the "Burgess Nonsense Book." Contains many of his most unusual and truly awe-inspiring pieces: 36 nonsense quatrains, the Poems of Patagonia, Alphabet of Famous Goops, and the other hilarious (and rare) adult nonsense that place him in the forefront of American humorists. All pieces are accompanied by the original Burgess illustrations. 123 illustrations. xiii + 113pp. 5⅜ x 8. T772 Paperbound $1.00

MY PIOUS FRIENDS AND DRUNKEN COMPANIONS and MORE PIOUS FRIENDS AND DRUNKEN COMPANIONS, Frank Shay. Folksingers, amateur and professional, and everyone who loves singing: here, available for the first time in 30 years, is this valued collection of 132 ballads, blues, vaudeville numbers, drinking songs, sea chanties, comedy songs. Songs of pre-Beatnik Bohemia; songs from all over America, England, France, Australia; the great songs of the Naughty Nineties and early twentieth-century America. Over a third with music. Woodcuts by John Held, Jr. convey perfectly the brash insouciance of an era of rollicking unabashed song. 12 illustrations by John Held, Jr. Two indexes (Titles and First lines and Choruses). Introductions by the author. Two volumes bound as one. Total of xvi + 235pp. 5⅜ x 8½. T946 Paperbound $1.25

HOW TO TELL THE BIRDS FROM THE FLOWERS, R. W. Wood. How not to confuse a carrot with a parrot, a grape with an ape, a puffin with nuffin. Delightful drawings, clever puns, absurd little poems point out far-fetched resemblances in nature. The author was a leading physicist. Introduction by Margaret Wood White. 106 illus. 60pp. 5⅜ x 8. T523 Paperbound 75¢

PECK'S BAD BOY AND HIS PA, George W. Peck. The complete edition, containing both volumes, of one of the most widely read American humor books. The endless ingenious pranks played by bad boy "Hennery" on his pa and the grocery man, the outraged pomposity of Pa, the perpetual ridiculing of middle class institutions, are as entertaining today as they were in 1883. No pale sophistications or subtleties, but rather humor vigorous, raw, earthy, imaginative, and, as folk humor often is, sadistic. This peculiarly fascinating book is also valuable to historians and students of American culture as a portrait of an age. 100 original illustrations by True Williams. Introduction by E. F. Bleiler. 347pp. 5⅜ x 8. T497 Paperbound $1.50

CATALOGUE OF DOVER BOOKS

THE HUMOROUS VERSE OF LEWIS CARROLL. Almost every poem Carroll ever wrote, the largest collection ever published, including much never published elsewhere: 150 parodies, burlesques, riddles, ballads, acrostics, etc., with 130 original illustrations by Tenniel, Carroll, and others. "Addicts will be grateful . . . there is nothing for the faithful to do but sit down and fall to the banquet," N. Y. Times. Index to first lines. xiv + 446pp. 5⅜ x 8.
T654 Paperbound **$2.00**

DIVERSIONS AND DIGRESSIONS OF LEWIS CARROLL. A major new treasure for Carroll fans! Rare privately published humor, fantasy, puzzles, and games by Carroll at his whimsical best, with a new vein of frank satire. Includes many new mathematical amusements and recreations, among them the fragmentary Part III of "Curiosa Mathematica." Contains "The Rectory Umbrella," "The New Belfry," "The Vision of the Three T's," and much more. New 32-page supplement of rare photographs taken by Carroll. x + 375pp. 5⅜ x 8.
T732 Paperbound **$2.00**

THE COMPLETE NONSENSE OF EDWARD LEAR. This is the only complete edition of this master of gentle madness available at a popular price. A BOOK OF NONSENSE, NONSENSE SONGS, MORE NONSENSE SONGS AND STORIES in their entirety with all the old favorites that have delighted children and adults for years. The Dong With A Luminous Nose, The Jumblies, The Owl and the Pussycat, and hundreds of other bits of wonderful nonsense. 214 limericks, 3 sets of Nonsense Botany, 5 Nonsense Alphabets, 546 drawings by Lear himself, and much more. 320pp. 5⅜ x 8.
T167 Paperbound **$1.00**

THE MELANCHOLY LUTE, The Humorous Verse of Franklin P. Adams ("FPA"). The author's own selection of light verse, drawn from thirty years of FPA's column, "The Conning Tower," syndicated all over the English-speaking world. Witty, perceptive, literate, these ninety-six poems range from parodies of other poets, Millay, Longfellow, Edgar Guest, Kipling, Masefield, etc., and free and hilarious translations of Horace and other Latin poets, to satiric comments on fabled American institutions—the New York Subways, preposterous ads, suburbanites, sensational journalism, etc. They reveal with vigor and clarity the humor, integrity and restraint of a wise and gentle American satirist. Introduction by Robert Hutchinson. vi + 122pp. 5⅜ x 8½.
T108 Paperbound **$1.00**

SINGULAR TRAVELS, CAMPAIGNS, AND ADVENTURES OF BARON MUNCHAUSEN, R. E. Raspe, with 90 illustrations by Gustave Doré. The first edition in over 150 years to reestablish the deeds of the Prince of Liars exactly as Raspe first recorded them in 1785—the genuine Baron Munchausen, one of the most popular personalities in English literature. Included also are the best of the many sequels, written by other hands. Introduction on Raspe by J. Carswell. Bibliography of early editions. xliv + 192pp. 5⅜ x 8.
T698 Paperbound **$1.00**

THE WIT AND HUMOR OF OSCAR WILDE, ed. by Alvin Redman. Wilde at his most brilliant, in 1000 epigrams exposing weaknesses and hypocrisies of "civilized" society. Divided into 49 categories—sin, wealth, women, America, etc.—to aid writers, speakers. Includes excerpts from his trials, books, plays, criticism. Formerly "The Epigrams of Oscar Wilde." Introduction by Vyvyan Holland, Wilde's only living son. Introductory essay by editor. 260pp. 5⅜ x 8.
T602 Paperbound **$1.00**

MAX AND MORITZ, Wilhelm Busch. Busch is one of the great humorists of all time, as well as the father of the modern comic strip. This volume, translated by H. A. Klein and other hands, contains the perennial favorite "Max and Moritz" (translated by C. T. Brooks), Plisch and Plum, Das Rabennest, Eispeter, and seven other whimsical, sardonic, jovial, diabolical cartoon and verse stories. Lively English translations parallel the original German. This work has delighted millions since it first appeared in the 19th century, and is guaranteed to please almost anyone. Edited by H. A. Klein, with an afterword. x + 205pp. 5⅝ x 8½.
T181 Paperbound **$1.15**

HYPOCRITICAL HELENA, Wilhelm Busch. A companion volume to "Max and Moritz," with the title piece (Die Fromme Helena) and 10 other highly amusing cartoon and verse stories, all newly translated by H. A. Klein and M. C. Klein: Adventure on New Year's Eve (Abenteuer in der Neujahrsnacht), Hangover on the Morning after New Year's Eve (Der Katzenjammer am Neujahrsmorgen), etc. English and German in parallel columns. Hours of pleasure, also a fine language aid. x + 205pp. 5⅝ x 8½.
T184 Paperbound **$1.00**

THE BEAR THAT WASN'T, Frank Tashlin. What does it mean? Is it simply delightful wry humor, or a charming story of a bear who wakes up in the midst of a factory, or a satire on Big Business, or an existential cartoon-story of the human condition, or a symbolization of the struggle between conformity and the individual? New York Herald Tribune said of the first edition: ". . . a fable for grownups that will be fun for children. Sit down with the book and get your own bearings." Long an underground favorite with readers of all ages and opinions. v + 51pp. Illustrated. 5⅜ x 8½.
T939 Paperbound **75¢**

RUTHLESS RHYMES FOR HEARTLESS HOMES and MORE RUTHLESS RHYMES FOR HEARTLESS HOMES, Harry Graham ("Col. D. Streamer"). Two volumes of Little Willy and 48 other poetic disasters. A bright, new reprint of oft-quoted, never forgotten, devastating humor by a precursor of today's "sick" joke school. For connoisseurs of wicked, wacky humor and all who delight in the comedy of manners. Original drawings are a perfect complement. 61 illustrations. Index. vi + 69pp. Two vols. bound as one. 5⅜ x 8½.
T930 Paperbound **75¢**

Say It language phrase books

These handy phrase books (128 to 196 pages each) make grammatical drills unnecessary for an elementary knowledge of a spoken foreign language. Covering most matters of travel and everyday life each volume contains:

Over 1000 phrases and sentences in immediately useful forms — foreign language plus English.

Modern usage designed for Americans. Specific phrases like, "Give me small change," and "Please call a taxi."

Simplified phonetic transcription you will be able to read at sight.

The only completely indexed phrase books on the market.

Covers scores of important situations: — Greetings, restaurants, sightseeing, useful expressions, etc.

These books are prepared by native linguists who are professors at Columbia, N.Y.U., Fordham and other great universities. Use them independently or with any other book or record course. They provide a supplementary living element that most other courses lack. Individual volumes in:

Russian 75¢	Italian 75¢	Spanish 75¢	German 75¢
Hebrew 75¢	Danish 75¢	Japanese 75¢	Swedish 75¢
Dutch 75¢	Esperanto 75¢	Modern Greek 75¢	Portuguese 75¢
Norwegian 75¢	Polish 75¢	French 75¢	Yiddish 75¢
Turkish 75¢		English for German-speaking people 75¢	
English for Italian-speaking people 75¢		English for Spanish-speaking people 75¢	

Large clear type. 128-196 pages each. 3½ x 5¼. Sturdy paper binding.

Listen and Learn language records

LISTEN & LEARN is the only language record course designed especially to meet your travel and everyday needs. It is available in separate sets for FRENCH, SPANISH, GERMAN, JAPANESE, RUSSIAN, MODERN GREEK, PORTUGUESE, ITALIAN and HEBREW, and each set contains three 33⅓ rpm long-playing records—1½ hours of recorded speech by eminent native speakers who are professors at Columbia, New York University, Queens College.

Check the following special features found only in LISTEN & LEARN:

● **Dual-language recording.** 812 **selected phrases and sentences,** over 3200 **words,** spoken first in English, then in their foreign language equivalents. A suitable pause follows each foreign phrase, allowing you time to repeat the expression. You learn by unconscious assimilation.

● 128 to 206-page manual contains everything on the records, plus a simple phonetic pronunciation guide.

● **Indexed for convenience. The only set on the market** that is completely indexed. No more puzzling over where to find the phrase you need. Just look in the rear of the manual.

● **Practical.** No time wasted on material you can find in any grammar. LISTEN & LEARN covers central core material with phrase approach. Ideal for the person with limited learning time.

● **Living, modern expressions,** not found in other courses. Hygienic products, modern equipment, shopping—expressions used every day, like "nylon" and "air-conditioned."

● **Limited objective.** Everything you learn, no matter where you stop, is immediately useful. You have to finish other courses, wade through grammar and vocabulary drill, before they help you.

● **High-fidelity recording.** LISTEN & LEARN records equal in clarity and surface-silence any record on the market costing up to $6.

"Excellent . . . the spoken records . . . impress me as being among the very best on the market," **Prof. Mario Pei,** Dept. of Romance Languages, Columbia University. "Inexpensive and well-done . . . it would make an ideal present," CHICAGO SUNDAY TRIBUNE. "More genuinely helpful than anything of its kind which I have previously encountered," **Sidney Clark,** well-known author of "ALL THE BEST" travel books.

UNCONDITIONAL GUARANTEE. Try LISTEN & LEARN, then return it within 10 days for full refund if you are not satisfied.

Each set contains three twelve-inch 33⅓ records, manual, and album.

SPANISH	the set $5.95	GERMAN	the set $5.95
FRENCH	the set $5.95	ITALIAN	the set $5.95
RUSSIAN	the set $5.95	JAPANESE	the set $6.95
PORTUGUESE	the set $5.95	MODERN GREEK	the set $5.95
MODERN HEBREW	the set $5.95		

Americana

THE EYES OF DISCOVERY, J. Bakeless. A vivid reconstruction of how unspoiled America appeared to the first white men. Authentic and enlightening accounts of Hudson's landing in New York, Coronado's trek through the Southwest; scores of explorers, settlers, trappers, soldiers. America's pristine flora, fauna, and Indians in every region and state in fresh and unusual new aspects. "A fascinating view of what the land was like before the first highway went through," Time. 68 contemporary illustrations, 39 newly added in this edition. Index. Bibliography. x + 500pp. 5⅜ x 8.   T761 Paperbound **$2.25**

AUDUBON AND HIS JOURNALS, J. J. Audubon. A collection of fascinating accounts of Europe and America in the early 1800's through Audubon's own eyes. Includes the Missouri River Journals —an eventful trip through America's untouched heartland, the Labrador Journals, the European Journals, the famous "Episodes", and other rare Audubon material, including the descriptive chapters from the original letterpress edition of the "Ornithological Studies", omitted in all later editions. Indispensable for ornithologists, naturalists, and all lovers of Americana and adventure. 70-page biography by Audubon's granddaughter. 38 illustrations. Index. Total of 1106pp. 5⅜ x 8.   T675 Vol I Paperbound **$2.25**
T676 Vol II Paperbound **$2.25**
The set **$4.50**

TRAVELS OF WILLIAM BARTRAM, edited by Mark Van Doren. The first inexpensive illustrated edition of one of the 18th century's most delightful books is an excellent source of first-hand material on American geography, anthropology, and natural history. Many descriptions of early Indian tribes are our only source of information on them prior to the infiltration of the white man. "The mind of a scientist with the soul of a poet," John Livingston Lowes. 13 original illustrations and maps. Edited with an introduction by Mark Van Doren. 448pp. 5⅜ x 8.
T13 Paperbound **$2.00**

GARRETS AND PRETENDERS: A HISTORY OF BOHEMIANISM IN AMERICA, A. Parry. The colorful and fantastic history of American Bohemianism from Poe to Kerouac. This is the only complete record of hoboes, cranks, starving poets, and suicides. Here are Pfaff, Whitman, Crane, Bierce, Pound, and many others. New chapters by the author and by H. T. Moore bring this thorough and well-documented history down to the Beatniks. "An excellent account," N. Y. Times. Scores of cartoons, drawings, and caricatures. Bibliography. Index. xxviii + 421pp. 5⅝ x 8⅜.   T708 Paperbound **$1.95**

THE EXPLORATION OF THE COLORADO RIVER AND ITS CANYONS, J. W. Powell. The thrilling first-hand account of the expedition that filled in the last white space on the map of the United States. Rapids, famine, hostile Indians, and mutiny are among the perils encountered as the unknown Colorado Valley reveals its secrets. This is the only uncut version of Major Powell's classic of exploration that has been printed in the last 60 years. Includes later reflections and subsequent expedition. 250 illustrations, new map. 400pp. 5⅝ x 8⅜.
T94 Paperbound **$2.25**

THE JOURNAL OF HENRY D. THOREAU, Edited by Bradford Torrey and Francis H. Allen. Henry Thoreau is not only one of the most important figures in American literature and social thought; his voluminous journals (from which his books emerged as selections and crystallizations) constitute both the longest, most sensitive record of personal internal development and a most penetrating description of a historical moment in American culture. This present set, which was first issued in fourteen volumes, contains Thoreau's entire journals from 1837 to 1862, with the exception of the lost years which were found only recently. We are reissuing it, complete and unabridged, with a new introduction by Walter Harding, Secretary of the Thoreau Society. Fourteen volumes reissued in two volumes. Foreword by Henry Seidel Canby. Total of 1888pp. 8⅜ x 12¼.   T312-3 Two volume set, Clothbound **$20.00**

GAMES AND SONGS OF AMERICAN CHILDREN, collected by William Wells Newell. A remarkable collection of 190 games with songs that accompany many of them; cross references to show similarities, differences among them; variations; musical notation for 38 songs. Textual discussions show relations with folk-drama and other aspects of folk tradition. Grouped into categories for ready comparative study: Love-games, histories, playing at work, human life, bird and beast, mythology, guessing-games, etc. New introduction covers relations of songs and dances to timeless heritage of folklore, biographical sketch of Newell, other pertinent data. A good source of inspiration for those in charge of groups of children and a valuable reference for anthropologists, sociologists, psychiatrists. Introduction by Carl Withers. New indexes of first lines, games. 5⅜ x 8½. xii + 242pp.   T354 Paperbound **$1.75**

Art, History of Art, Antiques, Graphic Arts, Handcrafts

ART STUDENTS' ANATOMY, E. J. Farris. Outstanding art anatomy that uses chiefly living objects for its illustrations. 71 photos of undraped men, women, children are accompanied by carefully labeled matching sketches to illustrate the skeletal system, articulations and movements, bony landmarks, the muscular system, skin, fasciae, fat, etc. 9 x-ray photos show movement of joints. Undraped models are shown in such actions as serving in tennis, drawing a bow in archery, playing football, dancing, preparing to spring and to dive. Also discussed and illustrated are proportions, age and sex differences, the anatomy of the smile, etc. 8 plates by the great early 18th century anatomic illustrator Siegfried Albinus are also included. Glossary. 158 figures, 7 in color. x + 159pp. 5⅝ x 8⅜. T744 Paperbound **$1.50**

AN ATLAS OF ANATOMY FOR ARTISTS, F Schider. A new 3rd edition of this standard text enlarged by 52 new illustrations of hands, anatomical studies by Cloquet, and expressive life studies of the body by Barcsay. 189 clear, detailed plates offer you precise information of impeccable accuracy. 29 plates show all aspects of the skeleton, with closeups of special areas, while 54 full-page plates, mostly in two colors, give human musculature as seen from four different points of view, with cutaways for important portions of the body. 14 full-page plates provide photographs of hand forms, eyelids, female breasts, and indicate the location of muscles upon models. 59 additional plates show how great artists of the past utilized human anatomy. They reproduce sketches and finished work by such artists as Michelangelo, Leonardo da Vinci, Goya, and 15 others. This is a lifetime reference work which will be one of the most important books in any artist's library. "The standard reference tool," AMERICAN LIBRARY ASSOCIATION. "Excellent," AMERICAN ARTIST. Third enlarged edition. 189 plates, 647 illustrations. xxvi + 192pp. 7⅞ x 10⅝. T241 Clothbound **$6.00**

AN ATLAS OF ANIMAL ANATOMY FOR ARTISTS, W. Ellenberger, H. Baum, H. Dittrich. The largest, richest animal anatomy for artists available in English. 99 detailed anatomical plates of such animals as the horse, dog, cat, lion, deer, seal, kangaroo, flying squirrel, cow, bull, goat, monkey, hare, and bat. Surface features are clearly indicated, while progressive beneath-the-skin pictures show musculature, tendons, and bone structure. Rest and action are exhibited in terms of musculature and skeletal structure and detailed cross-sections are given for heads and important features. The animals chosen are representative of specific families so that a study of these anatomies will provide knowledge of hundreds of related species. "Highly recommended as one of the very few books on the subject worthy of being used as an authoritative guide," DESIGN. "Gives a fundamental knowledge," AMERICAN ARTIST. Second revised, enlarged edition with new plates from Cuvier, Stubbs, etc. 288 illustrations. 153pp. 11⅜ x 9. T82 Clothbound **$6.00**

THE HUMAN FIGURE IN MOTION, Eadweard Muybridge. The largest selection in print of Muybridge's famous high-speed action photos of the human figure in motion. 4789 photographs illustrate 162 different actions: men, women, children—mostly undraped—are shown walking, running, carrying various objects, sitting, lying down, climbing, throwing, arising, and performing over 150 other actions. Some actions are shown in as many as 150 photographs each. All in all there are more than 500 action strips in this enormous volume, series shots taken at shutter speeds of as high as 1/6000th of a second! These are not posed shots, but true stopped motion. They show bone and muscle in situations that the human eye is not fast enough to capture. Earlier, smaller editions of these prints have brought $40 and more on the out-of-print market. "A must for artists," ART IN FOCUS. "An unparalleled dictionary of action for all artists," AMERICAN ARTIST. 390 full-page plates, with 4789 photographs. Printed on heavy glossy stock. Reinforced binding with headbands. xxi + 390pp. 7⅞ x 10⅝. T204 Clothbound **$10.00**

ANIMALS IN MOTION, Eadweard Muybridge. This is the largest collection of animal action photos in print. 34 different animals (horses, mules, oxen, goats, camels, pigs, cats, guanacos, lions, gnus, deer, monkeys, eagles—and 21 others) in 132 characteristic actions. The horse alone is shown in more than 40 different actions. All 3919 photographs are taken in series at speeds up to 1/6000th of a second. The secrets of leg motion, spinal patterns, head movements, strains and contortions shown nowhere else are captured. You will see exactly how a lion sets his foot down; how an elephant's knees are like a human's—and how they differ; the position of a kangaroo's legs in mid-leap; how an ostrich's head bobs; details of the flight of birds—and thousands of facets of motion only the fastest cameras can catch. Photographed from domestic animals and animals in the Philadelphia zoo, it contains neither semiposed artificial shots nor distorted telephoto shots taken under adverse conditions. Artists, biologists, decorators, cartoonists, will find this book indispensable for understanding animals in motion. "A really marvelous series of plates," NATURE (London). "The dry plate's most spectacular early use was by Eadweard Muybridge," LIFE. 3919 photographs; 380 full pages of plates. 440pp. Printed on heavy glossy paper. Deluxe binding with headbands. 7⅞ x 10⅝. T203 Clothbound **$10.00**

THE AUTOBIOGRAPHY OF AN IDEA, Louis Sullivan. The pioneer architect whom Frank Lloyd Wright called "the master" reveals an acute sensitivity to social forces and values in this passionately honest account. He records the crystallization of his opinions and theories, the growth of his organic theory of architecture that still influences American designers and architects, contemporary ideas, etc. This volume contains the first appearance of 34 full-page plates of his finest architecture. Unabridged reissue of 1924 edition. New introduction by R. M. Line. Index. xiv + 335pp. 5⅜ x 8. **T281 Paperbound $2.00**

THE DRAWINGS OF HEINRICH KLEY. The first uncut republication of both of Kley's devastating sketchbooks, which first appeared in pre-World War I Germany. One of the greatest cartoonists and social satirists of modern times, his exuberant and iconoclastic fantasy and his extraordinary technique place him in the great tradition of Bosch, Breughel, and Goya, while his subject matter has all the immediacy and tension of our century. 200 drawings. viii + 128pp. 7¾ x 10¾. **T24 Paperbound $1.85**

MORE DRAWINGS BY HEINRICH KLEY. All the sketches from Leut' Und Viecher (1912) and Sammel-Album (1923) not included in the previous Dover edition of Drawings. More of the bizarre, mercilessly iconoclastic sketches that shocked and amused on their original publication. Nothing was too sacred, no one too eminent for satirization by this imaginative, individual and accomplished master cartoonist. A total of 158 illustrations. lv + 104pp. 7¾ x 10¾. **T41 Paperbound $1.85**

PINE FURNITURE OF EARLY NEW ENGLAND, R. H. Kettell. A rich understanding of one of America's most original folk arts that collectors of antiques, interior decorators, craftsmen, woodworkers, and everyone interested in American history and art will find fascinating and immensely useful. 413 illustrations of more than 300 chairs, benches, racks, beds, cupboards, mirrors, shelves, tables, and other furniture will show all the simple beauty and character of early New England furniture. 55 detailed drawings carefully analyze outstanding pieces. "With its rich store of illustrations, this book emphasizes the individuality and varied design of early American pine furniture. It should be welcomed," ANTIQUES. 413 illustrations and 55 working drawings. 475. 8 x 10¾. **T145 Clothbound $10.00**

THE HUMAN FIGURE, J. H. Vanderpoel. Every important artistic element of the human figure is pointed out in minutely detailed word descriptions in this classic text and illustrated as well in 430 pencil and charcoal drawings. Thus the text of this book directs your attention to all the characteristic features and subtle differences of the male and female (adults, children, and aged persons), as though a master artist were telling you what to look for at each stage. 2nd edition, revised and enlarged by George Bridgman. Foreword. 430 illustrations. 143pp. 6⅛ x 9¼. **T432 Paperbound $1.50**

LETTERING AND ALPHABETS, J. A. Cavanagh. This unabridged reissue of LETTERING offers a full discussion, analysis, illustration of 89 basic hand lettering styles — styles derived from Caslons, Bodonis, Garamonds, Gothic, Black Letter, Oriental, and many others. Upper and lower cases, numerals and common signs pictured. Hundreds of technical hints on make-up, construction, artistic validity, strokes, pens, brushes, white areas, etc. May be reproduced without permission! 89 complete alphabets; 72 lettered specimens. 121pp. 9⅜ x 8. **T53 Paperbound $1.35**

STICKS AND STONES, Lewis Mumford. A survey of the forces that have conditioned American architecture and altered its forms. The author discusses the medieval tradition in early New England villages; the Renaissance influence which developed with the rise of the merchant class; the classical influence of Jefferson's time; the "Mechanicsvilles" of Poe's generation; the Brown Decades; the philosophy of the Imperial facade; and finally the modern machine age. "A truly remarkable book," SAT. REV. OF LITERATURE. 2nd revised edition. 21 illustrations. xvii + 228pp. 5⅜ x 8. **T202 Paperbound $1.75**

THE STANDARD BOOK OF QUILT MAKING AND COLLECTING, Marguerite Ickis. A complete easy-to-follow guide with all the information you need to make beautiful, useful quilts. How to plan, design, cut, sew, appliqué, avoid sewing problems, use rag bag, make borders, tuft, every other aspect. Over 100 traditional quilts shown, including over 40 full-size patterns. At-home hobby for fun, profit. Index. 483 illus. 1 color plate. 287pp. 6¾ x 9½. **T582 Paperbound $2.00**

THE BOOK OF SIGNS, Rudolf Koch. Formerly $20 to $25 on the out-of-print market, now only $1.00 in this unabridged new edition! 493 symbols from ancient manuscripts, medieval cathedrals, coins, catacombs, pottery, etc. Crosses, monograms of Roman emperors, astrological, chemical, botanical, runes, housemarks, and 7 other categories. Invaluable for handicraft workers, illustrators, scholars, etc., this material may be reproduced without permission. 493 illustrations by Fritz Kredel. 104pp. 6½ x 9¼. **T162 Paperbound $1.00**

PRIMITIVE ART, Franz Boas. This authoritative and exhaustive work by a great American anthropologist covers the entire gamut of primitive art. Pottery, leatherwork, metal work, stone work, wood, basketry, are treated in detail. Theories of primitive art, historical depth in art history, technical virtuosity, unconscious levels of patterning, symbolism, styles, literature, music, dance, etc. A must book for the interested layman, the anthropologist, artist, handicrafter (hundreds of unusual motifs), and the historian. Over 900 illustrations (50 ceramic vessels, 12 totem poles, etc.). 376pp. 5⅜ x 8. **T25 Paperbound $2.25**

Fiction

FLATLAND, E. A. Abbott. A science-fiction classic of life in a 2-dimensional world that is also a first-rate introduction to such aspects of modern science as relativity and hyperspace. Political, moral, satirical, and humorous overtones have made FLATLAND fascinating reading for thousands. 7th edition. New introduction by Banesh Hoffmann. 16 illustrations. 128pp. 5⅜ x 8.   T1 Paperbound **$1.00**

THE WONDERFUL WIZARD OF OZ, L. F. Baum. Only edition in print with all the original W. W. Denslow illustrations in full color—as much a part of "The Wizard" as Tenniel's drawings are of "Alice in Wonderland." "The Wizard" is still America's best-loved fairy tale, in which, as the author expresses it, "The wonderment and joy are retained and the heartaches and nightmares left out." Now today's young readers can enjoy every word and wonderful picture of the original book. New introduction by Martin Gardner. A Baum bibliography. 23 full-page color plates. viii + 268pp. 5⅜ x 8.   T691 Paperbound **$1.50**

THE MARVELOUS LAND OF OZ, L. F. Baum. This is the equally enchanting sequel to the "Wizard," continuing the adventures of the Scarecrow and the Tin Woodman. The hero this time is a little boy named Tip, and all the delightful Oz magic is still present. This is the Oz book with the Animated Saw-Horse, the Woggle-Bug, and Jack Pumpkinhead. All the original John R. Neill illustrations, 10 in full color. 287 pp. 5⅜ x 8.   T692 Paperbound **$1.50**

28 SCIENCE FICTION STORIES OF H. G. WELLS. Two full unabridged novels, MEN LIKE GODS and STAR BEGOTTEN, plus 26 short stories by the master science-fiction writer of all time! Stories of space, time, invention, exploration, future adventure—an indispensable part of the library of everyone interested in science and adventure. PARTIAL CONTENTS: Men Like Gods, The Country of the Blind, In the Abyss, The Crystal Egg, The Man Who Could Work Miracles, A Story of the Days to Come, The Valley of Spiders, and 21 more! 928pp. 5⅜ x 8.
T265 Clothbound **$4.50**

THREE MARTIAN NOVELS, Edgar Rice Burroughs. Contains: Thuvia, Maid of Mars; The Chessmen of Mars; and The Master Mind of Mars. High adventure set in an imaginative and intricate conception of the Red Planet. Mars is peopled with an intelligent, heroic human race which lives in densely populated cities and with fierce barbarians who inhabit dead sea bottoms. Other exciting creatures abound amidst an inventive framework of Martian history and geography. Complete unabridged reprintings of the first edition. 16 illustrations by J. Allen St. John. vi + 499pp. 5⅜ x 8½.   T39 Paperbound **$1.85**

SEVEN SCIENCE FICTION NOVELS, H. G. Wells. Full unabridged texts of 7 science-fiction novels of the master. Ranging from biology, physics, chemistry, astronomy to sociology and other studies, Mr. Wells extrapolates whole worlds of strange and intriguing character. "One will have to go far to match this for entertainment, excitement, and sheer pleasure . . .," NEW YORK TIMES. Contents: The Time Machine, The Island of Dr. Moreau, First Men in the Moon, The Invisible Man, The War of the Worlds, The Food of the Gods, In the Days of the Comet. 1015pp. 5⅜ x 8.   T264 Clothbound **$4.50**

THE LAND THAT TIME FORGOT and THE MOON MAID, Edgar Rice Burroughs. In the opinion of many, Burroughs' best work. The first concerns a strange island where evolution is individual rather than phylogenetic. Speechless anthropoids develop into intelligent human beings within a single generation. The second projects the reader far into the future and describes the first voyage to the Moon (in the year 2025), the conquest of the Earth by the Moon, and years of violence and adventure as the enslaved Earthmen try to regain possession of their planet. "An imaginative tour de force that keeps the reader keyed up and expectant," NEW YORK TIMES. Complete, unabridged text of the original two novels (three parts in each). 5 illustrations by J. Allen St. John. vi + 552pp. 5⅜ x 8½.
T1020 Clothbound **$3.75**
T358 Paperbound **$2.00**

3 ADVENTURE NOVELS by H. Rider Haggard. Complete texts of "She," "King Solomon's Mines," "Allan Quatermain." Qualities of discovery; desire for immortality; search for primitive, for what is unadorned by civilization, have kept these novels of African adventure exciting, alive to readers from R. L. Stevenson to George Orwell. 636pp. 5⅜ x 8.
T584 Paperbound **$2.00**

A PRINCESS OF MARS and A FIGHTING MAN OF MARS: TWO MARTIAN NOVELS BY EDGAR RICE BURROUGHS. "Princess of Mars" is the very first of the great Martian novels written by Burroughs, and it is probably the best of them all; it set the pattern for all of his later fantasy novels and contains a thrilling cast of strange peoples and creatures and the formula of Olympian heroism amidst ever-fluctuating fortunes which Burroughs carries off so successfully. "Fighting Man" returns to the same scenes and cities—many years later. A mad scientist, a degenerate dictator, and an indomitable defender of the right clash—with the fate of the Red Planet at stake! Complete, unabridged reprinting of original editions. Illustrations by F. E. Schoonover and Hugh Hutton. v + 356pp. 5⅜ x 8½.
T1140 Paperbound **$1.75**

Music

A GENERAL HISTORY OF MUSIC, Charles Burney. A detailed coverage of music from the Greeks up to 1789, with full information on all types of music: sacred and secular, vocal and instrumental, operatic and symphonic. Theory, notation, forms, instruments, innovators, composers, performers, typical and important works, and much more in an easy, entertaining style. Burney covered much of Europe and spoke with hundreds of authorities and composers so that this work is more than a compilation of records . . . it is a living work of careful and first-hand scholarship. Its account of thoroughbass (18th century) Italian music is probably still the best introduction on the subject. A recent NEW YORK TIMES review said, "Surprisingly few of Burney's statements have been invalidated by modern research . . . still of great value." Edited and corrected by Frank Mercer. 35 figures. Indices. 1915pp. 5⅜ x 8. 2 volumes.
T36 The Set, Clothbound **$12.50**

A DICTIONARY OF HYMNOLOGY, John Julian. This exhaustive and scholarly work has become known as an invaluable source of hundreds of thousands of important and often difficult to obtain facts on the history and use of hymns in the western world. Everyone interested in hymns will be fascinated by the accounts of famous hymns and hymn writers and amazed by the amount of practical information he will find. More than 30,000 entries on individual hymns, giving authorship, date and circumstances of composition, publication, textual variations, translations, denominational and ritual usage, etc. Biographies of more than 9,000 hymn writers, and essays on important topics such as Christmas carols and children's hymns, and much other unusual and valuable information. A 200 page double-columned index of first lines — the largest in print. Total of 1786 pages in two reinforced clothbound volumes. 6¼ x 9¼.
The set, T333 Clothbound **$17.50**

MUSIC IN MEDIEVAL BRITAIN, F. Ll. Harrison. The most thorough, up-to-date, and accurate treatment of the subject ever published, beautifully illustrated. Complete account of institutions and choirs; carols, masses, and motets; liturgy and plainsong; and polyphonic music from the Norman Conquest to the Reformation. Discusses the various schools of music and their reciprocal influences; the origin and development of new ritual forms; development and use of instruments; and new evidence on many problems of the period. Reproductions of scores, over 200 excerpts from medieval melodies. Rules of harmony and dissonance; influence of Continental styles; great composers (Dunstable, Cornysh, Fairfax, etc.); and much more. Register and index of more than 400 musicians. Index of titles. General Index. 225-item bibliography. 6 Appendices. xix + 491pp. 5⅝ x 8¾.
T705 Clothbound **$10.00**

THE MUSIC OF SPAIN, Gilbert Chase. Only book in English to give concise, comprehensive account of Iberian music; new Chapter covers music since 1941. Victoria, Albéniz, Cabezón, Pedrell, Turina, hundreds of other composers; popular and folk music; the Gypsies; the guitar; dance, theatre, opera, with only extensive discussion in English of the Zarzuela; virtuosi such as Casals; much more. "Distinguished . . . readable," Saturday Review. 400-item bibliography. Index. 27 photos. 383pp. 5⅜ x 8.
T549 Paperbound **$2.25**

ON STUDYING SINGING, Sergius Kagen. An intelligent method of voice-training, which leads you around pitfalls that waste your time, money, and effort. Exposes rigid, mechanical systems, baseless theories, deleterious exercises. "Logical, clear, convincing . . . dead right," Virgil Thomson, N.Y. Herald Tribune. "I recommend this volume highly," Maggie Teyte, Saturday Review. 119pp. 5⅜ x 8.
T622 Paperbound **$1.35**

Prices subject to change without notice.

Dover publishes books on art, music, philosophy, literature, languages, history, social sciences, psychology, handcrafts, orientalia, puzzles and entertainments, chess, pets and gardens, books explaining science, intermediate and higher mathematics, mathematical physics, engineering, biological sciences, earth sciences, classics of science, etc. Write to:

Dept. catrr.
Dover Publications, Inc.
180 Varick Street, N.Y. 14, N.Y.